The Lonely Entrepreneur

Michael Dermer

For information about this title or to order other books and/
or electronic media, contact the publisher:

TLE Enterprises, LLC
110 E 25th St, New York, NY 10010

www.lonelyentrepreneur.com
webmaster@lonelyentrepreneur.com

ISBNs:
Hard Cover: 978-0-9976239-9-4
Soft Cover: 978-0-9976239-8-7
eBook: 978-0-9976239-7-0

Printed in the United States of America

To Dad, for teaching me manners, chivalry, dedication, hard work, respect, sacrifice, what it means to be a man and for sharing your life's wisdom. Part of you is in everything I do. It is a blessing to be your son.

To Mom, for teaching me everything else. And perhaps more importantly for living a life of unconditional love and showing me what the strength of a woman can mean to so many lives and most importantly your family. It is a blessing to be your son.

To Dan, for reminding me I wish I were more like you every day.

To Alyse, for your sacrifice for family above all else when getting caught between the Dermers would have made other women hide.

To Brendan and Reyna, for the smiles that gave me energy every day when I needed it most.

Contents

Introduction

THE COLD SHOWER

Building my company was one of the most rewarding, challenging and humbling experiences of my life. I am proud to be part of that dysfunctional class of individuals called "entrepreneurs" who show the grit and strength of character to pursue their vision, and take on all challenges along the way. No one knows what it is like unless you have been there. There is no personal life and business life. It is your life. It is your soul. It is your oxygen. It is your spirit. Guilty as charged and proud of it.

But would I want to relive the experience of creating my first company—IncentOne? Not exactly. After all, sitting in the shower under freezing water for five minutes seemed easier than building IncentOne at times. Don't get me wrong, we did fine but we could have done better. You can too.

As for the shower:

> *I did it for the first time by mistake. The cold shower. No not that kind. I was religious about daily workouts when I was building my company. My workouts were always hyper-intense and often my escape. It's hard to worry about your technology vendor when you are sweating your ass off. I had just finished a workout and was taking a shower. I turned the water to only cold by mistake. It shocked me.*

> *A thought crossed my mind. This is what it felt like running my company after the financial crisis of 2008. I tried something. I wanted to see how much I could take. If I could stand in the freezing water without flinching, then nothing that came across my desk would seem tough. From that day on, I did it every day and every day I added some time under the freezing water. By January 2009, I was standing under the water for five minutes. I promised myself I would do*

1

that every day until we got the company back on its feet. Try it sometime. Like the rest of us crazy entrepreneurs, when I got it up to five minutes, I thought "can I spare that five minutes?"

At the end of each shower, I would turn the water from cold to warm. Wow did that feel good. Welcome to the life of an entrepreneur.

Why do we do it? Being an entrepreneur can be a deeply rewarding experience. We revel in the triumph, big or small, that comes after hours of practice, years of struggle and devotion to a craft. If you have experienced the feeling of hitting a baseball cleanly, you know there is nothing like it. It feels as if you didn't even hit a ball. Your body feels drugged. It's the satisfaction that comes from fighting for your dream. It's the ballerina who spends countless hours on the plié, relevé, and sauté until her feet bleed and then nails her routine in a ballet performance in front of a packed house. It's the golfer who goes to the driving range, hits thousands of balls, and then bribes the owner to let him keep hitting balls until 2 a.m. He plays round after round and struggles with his game. Then comes the shot. The clean drive. The wedge to within ten feet.

The same is true for the entrepreneur. There are few feelings like building something from nothing. All the hard work seems worthwhile when our vision comes to life. Most of us will never forget our first logo, office and investment. Our first customer. The first day we made a profit. When we served that first piece of pizza. When someone wore our jewelry. The first press we got—it might have been a mention in the *St. Lance Gazette* with a circulation of 1,000, but it still felt great. Once we become the entrepreneur, there is a transformation that subsumes all that we do. It doesn't matter whether you are designing jewelry, building a new app, starting a catering business, opening a restaurant, or creating a healthcare company. You might be an innovator in the new sharing economy with a business on Uber, Etsy, Airbnb, or TaskRabbit. Whatever you're doing—if you're an entrepreneur—it is an obsession.

If you've never been an entrepreneur, here's what you might not understand: being an entrepreneur is not just a job. It is an identity. Entrepreneurism is like oxygen. It's not optional. Once you have an idea, you need it to breathe. Once you have that vision, it's a drug that seethes through your blood every day. We say things to ourselves like, "What was I doing with my life before I came across this?" It may seem melodramatic, but not to those with a vision. There is nothing like it. And once you've experienced it, there's no going back.

Sounds pretty good, right? But entrepreneurship is not for the faint of heart. You're heading into uncharted territory, probably without a map, or the right tools and enough supplies. There will be many days as an entrepreneur when you question what you are doing. Days when you don't know what you are doing. Days when you know what you are doing but are not sure why. Days when you are not proud of yourself. Days when success seems so near. And days when success seems out of reach. Life would be fine, or at least manageable, if you were simply making a business decision. But it is much more than that. As entrepreneurs, we take this stuff personally. We question our purpose, our character, our will, our motivations, our capabilities, and our ability to bring our visions to life. The happiest day can also be the loneliest one. This is the nature of the beast. It's a complex animal all of us entrepreneurs have to face.

My guess is that if you've picked up this book, you are experiencing at least one of the following feelings: You're carrying the world on your shoulders. You don't have the money or resources you need. You feel like no one understands what you are going through. Your relationships are strained. Your friends, family and co-workers think you are crazy, stupid or selfish. You find yourself in a crowded room but feel alone. You are exhausted but you can't sleep. You are hungry but you can't eat. You are home but feel lost. Standing in the shower under freezing cold water for five minutes seems easier than running your venture. Sound familiar? I've been there. It's one thing to create solutions to business problems. It's quite another to create them when you feel the world is on your shoulders. When that happens, we feel like we are sprinting through cement even when we have talent and great business ideas.

All of the conflicting feelings that come with the territory are at the heart of the big question facing all of us: will we make it? How we cope with "the struggle" has as much, if not more, impact on our fate as the business decisions we make. Though I didn't know it at the time, **The Lonely Entrepreneur** was born in the middle of my own struggle—actually—in the middle a struggle that can only be described as the "perfect storm."

After a decade of blood, sweat and tears, we closed our first big outside investment on October 15, 2008—nearly ten years to the day from when we opened the doors. We should have been celebrating our recent successes and a big new investment. The financial crisis of 2008 was already brewing and hit us like an enormous, crushing wave. Among other catastrophes, it bankrupted our biggest clients and severed relationships that had taken years to build. Our business? A decade of work virtually gone in ten days. We were on the brink of disaster. I didn't know if the business was going to survive, but for it to have a chance, I knew it would take two years of twenty-hour days to dig ourselves out. Imagine that—two years to save what it took ten years to build—and there was no guarantee we'd make it.

Weathering the storm, as you'll see, was a serious fight—one I almost lost. The stakes were high: I wasn't just fighting to save the business. I was fighting to save my employees, my clients, my investors, my family, my deteriorating relationship with my brother, and myself—though I would have gladly sacrificed myself if it would have saved everyone else.

I needed solutions immediately, desperately. Yet in the eye of this perfect storm, I realized quickly that the normal solutions were not going to work. It was no longer a decision to take "this road" or "that road"—there weren't any roads left. The roads and bridges had been annihilated by the financial crisis. All familiar routes were gone. There was no shortage of tools—business plans, financing strategies, advisors and the like. But in the eye of this storm, these familiar strategies failed. The solution was not another business plan or spreadsheet. What I needed most was not a "tool" but rather something more fundamental.

I was leaving the gym one morning after the typical 5 a.m. start to my twenty-hour day, and it hit me. If traditional solutions were not going to work, I needed to look at everything in a different way. **What I needed was a change in perspective.** Maybe two plus two didn't need to equal four! Change the way you see things and the things you see will change.

As I applied this to our perfect storm, I discovered, repeatedly, that the difference between thriving in this struggle—and barely surviving it—always depended upon my perspective.

I realized that in the midst of the struggle, it is our "perspective" on the business and personal issues we face that determines success or failure. With the wrong perspective, even the simplest of tasks seem impossible. But with the right perspective, solutions come to life for even the toughest of challenges. Same resources. Same obstacles. Different results.

I also discovered, through my own mistakes, that the struggle itself creates a number of damaging perspectives. Our perspectives are influenced by what I call the "Four Ps" of being the entrepreneur—Pressure, Passion, Pleasure and Pain—which you will become intimately familiar with in Section 1. When we are under the influence of the Four Ps, we develop perspectives that stifle the advancement of our business. While it is natural to develop these perspectives, they blind us, obscure solutions and undermine our success.

Entrepreneurs not only develop these perspectives, but also fail to recognize when they are exhibiting them and take corrective action. Just try this—tell an entrepreneur to prioritize, to take a day off or to sleep more. Try telling an entrepreneur that they can't do everything. Try telling an entrepreneur that they should listen to the seasoned executive that has never known what it's like to miss payroll. You'll definitely get a dirty look, or if you're standing too close, something worse.

In the thick of things, we become blind to the perspectives we hold, and to their negative effect on everything from our business decisions, to our relationships with employees, vendors and family.

Understanding that perspective was the difference between success and failure, was an epiphany that would fundamentally change how I saw my business and ran my company—from employees to clients, financial strategy to communication. It would also lead to the successful sale of IncentOne, establish my company as the pioneer of the health rewards movement, and inspire me to do something I never expected to do: write this book.

The Lonely Entrepreneur *was born*!

I share my story in greater detail in Chapter 1, and after you read it, I think you'll understand why I was reluctant to relive it. I had survived the storm and tied a bow on that part of my life. I sold my company, am credited with helping to create a new industry, and, thankfully, made peace with my only brother after two years of daily screaming matches. I thought that something could be learned from this idea of "perspective," but, frankly, I was ready to take a break.

Then something happened. I started coaching entrepreneurs. Entrepreneurs that had the right stuff—great ideas, passion, smarts and an intense desire not only to succeed but to realize a vision. Despite everything they had going for them, they were overwhelmed, emotional, and inefficient. Smart, talented, inspired individuals were drowning in quicksand. I knew it all too well. They were experiencing the Four Ps and developing many of the same misaligned perspectives that I had, and it was clear that they were undermining their ability to succeed. After my own baptism by fire, I could not watch these intelligent, determined individuals go down in flames. I wanted to make it a little easier for the next generation of entrepreneurs. I hoped they would benefit from my struggle. I figured, if sharing my story could help even one overwhelmed entrepreneur, it would be worth it.

So I started writing. I wrote at home, on the road, at the dog park where I went to play with other people's dogs because I had been too busy building my company to get my own. The book chronicles IncentOne's story and our decade-plus fight to turn a radically new idea (offering rewards for healthy behavior) into a business despite an industry hostile to change. That was a major entrepreneurial challenge on its own, but of course, it was just the beginning. The book captures IncentOne's next and greatest challenge—the once-in-a lifetime financial crisis that turned the company's survival and the normal entrepreneurial struggle into a perfect storm. As most of us know, it's in the trenches and under the greatest of pressures that we learn the most. As I described above, this was the part of my story where real change began. I wanted other entrepreneurs to understand, and take heart from knowing, that the realizations I made about perspective during this time offered me, not just a way out of the trenches, but the power and freedom to do more than survive. I discovered that there were ways of "seeing" that led to better "doing" and the possibility of actually thriving—even when storm clouds are threatening.

The tools for each perspective change are drawn directly from my own struggle and experiences building IncentOne. It's one thing to get advice on being successful from a caring friend or professional colleague. It's another to get it from someone who has been on the front lines and understands the nature of the battle you're fighting. I hope that you'll find my story, and the perspectives change that resulted from my own entrepreneurial battle, a road map for your own change in perspectives. Being an entrepreneur will never be easy, but with a new vision, you might start to pull yourself out of the quicksand to solid ground where you can evolve and flourish even in hostile environments.

When you read this book, you may laugh, cry, drink, yell, curse, celebrate, punch, kick, scream or pout—so it's kind of like being an entrepreneur. Don't worry. I think you'll see I've already done that and more, and I'll be with you every step of the way. In fact, it would be an honor if this book helps just one of you. It would be a dream come true if this book helps all of you.

WHAT IS THE LONELY ENTREPRENEUR?
A Methodology to Help You Thrive

While writing the book, I realized that *The Lonely Entrepreneur* was much bigger than my personal story. It was a "methodology" that could be used by entrepreneurs everywhere.

The Lonely Entrepreneur *Methodology*

1. Helps entrepreneurs recognize the damaging perspectives that develop under the influence of the 4Ps (Pressure, Passion, Pleasure and Pain) and how they can seriously threaten the work of building a new business.
2. Teaches entrepreneurs how to change their thinking from perspectives that stifle progress to those that empower them to thrive.

Changing your perspective can happen in many ways—that is the beauty of it. Some changes are big and some are small. Some are strategic and some are tactical. Some are business and some are personal. Running the business isn't the only thing we have to tackle. The circumstances, risks, time commitments and personal investments create personal issues everyone wrestles with: family relationships, social lives, personal lives, not to mention, sleep, stress and mental health. Again, there is no personal life or business life. It's one and the same but it is important to notice how and where they overlap.

The Lonely Entrepreneur helps change your perspectives by identifying:

- **How You Feel**—learn to identify and acknowledge how you feel physically and mentally under the influence of the Four Ps.
- **Blinding Perspectives**—recognize the perspectives these feelings create and how they stunt the progress of your business.
- **Perspective Shift**—discover insights and tools to change these perspectives.

- **The Benefits**—understand how you and your business will benefit from the shift in perspective.

The Lonely Entrepreneur identifies a core set of perspective changes that address common business and personal issues we must solve:

- **CONTROL—RUNNING THE BUSINESS INSTEAD OF IT RUNNING YOU**: Tough love for gaining perspective on business management and process.
- **STAYING FOCUSED AND SANE**: Perspective change for mental and physical health, and maximizing your efficiency without being overwhelmed.
- **LEADERSHIP—LIKE IT OR NOT YOU NEED TO BE CEO**: Detailed guidance for a comprehensive perspective on being a leader in an entrepreneurial venture.
- **STANDING OUT FROM THE CROWD**: Learn how to outsmart the market and excel across industries by changing your perspective on competition and success.
- **COMMUNICATING IN THE CHAOS**: Learn how to be clear, concise and efficient in communicating so your organization and its constituents stay informed and aligned.
- **KNOWING WHERE YOU'RE AT**: Learn how the right perspective involves strategic timing, and honest evaluation of the market status and readiness of your business.
- **PEOPLE MAKE YOU CRAZY... AND SUCCESSFUL**: Perspective change to inspire and strengthen employees, build company culture, impress investors, and build relationships with vendors and other resources.
- **SURVIVING ON A PLANET CALLED "INVESTOR"**: Insightful perspective shifts for presenting your pitch, and communicating with investors, as well as, a detailed set of tools for ensuring investors have the best perspective of you.

These perspectives are constructed to help you thrive—even in the most challenging entrepreneurial environments—instead of feeling stifled. From running in quicksand to swimming in water. From walking up a mountain to running downhill.

A final note: the book and the perspectives it presents are designed to apply to entrepreneurial ventures of all shapes and sizes. From the "solo-preneur" to the venture-backed entity with twenty employees, to the small businesses with two hundred, every entrepreneur feels the impact of the Four Ps and the harmful perspectives they cause. As you read you may find that every perspective does not apply directly to your organization. However, all the perspectives will offer valuable insight into both the nuts and bolts of business building, and the unique experience of entrepreneurship that influences your vision and sense of identity. During the writing of this book I had many conversations and came to another conclusion: understanding these perspectives can be insightful not only for the entrepreneur, but for those around them—team members, family, friends and colleagues. For those of you non-entrepreneurs, young entrepreneurs and for the long-suffering and inspirational advocates in supporting roles, I hope this book offers a helpful, inside look at the mind-set and shared experience of entrepreneurs.

There are many days, no doubt, that you feel like a "lonely entrepreneur." But in reality, you share a special camaraderie with your fellow entrepreneurs who, like you, feel the daily impact of this challenging and fulfilling identity we call entrepreneurship: Pressure, Passion, Pleasure and Pain. You're not going it alone. All of us together—empowered by *The Lonely Entrepreneur*—are about to embark on a journey to change your perspective.

INCENTONE

*A Story about Invention, the Perfect Storm,
A Battle for Survival and Thriving in the Fight.*

Other than being shortstop for the New York Yankees, I always wanted to start my own business. I wanted to build something—and maybe change the world along the way. I couldn't see sitting in a board room with a spreadsheet at a private equity firm or investment bank and not be on the field spilling blood with everyone else. I was well equipped to start a business, more equipped than many first-time entrepreneurs. I grew up in a family that owned real estate. It was common to have conversations at the dinner table about "the business." While my brother and I fed our broccoli and Brussels sprouts to my golden retriever Fido under the table, we talked about our buildings in New York City, the property management company that managed them and the day-to-day of collecting rents, fixing repairs and working with contractors. Avoiding vegetables was no easy trick, but I learned quickly that managing a business was much harder. Why did the property management firm not do its job? Why were the expenses so high?

I got a business degree from Bucknell University and continued on to Northwestern University in Chicago for law school. After graduating, I returned to New York and took a job as a corporate lawyer at a well-known law firm. As a corporate lawyer, I was exposed to complex business issues: preparing financial statements, establishing new companies, the financing and merger process, intellectual property rights, employee benefits, contracts, audits and many other sophisticated legal and business concepts. While I had never run a business, when I left my firm to start IncentOne in 1998, I felt pretty confident—despite leaving the security of a great job for the dark side. Fortunately, unlike many entrepreneurs, my family gave me some seed capital to get going. Even so, when I left I knew we were likely a year or two from real revenue. Seems like a dumb idea when you really think about it. But no one said entrepreneurs had common sense.

But first: How did IncentOne happen? It was 1996. Like most New York corporate lawyers, I was working late on a Friday night and the phone rang. It was my brother Dan and he was ranting about gift certificates. He needed a gift for a christening and had called Baby Gap hoping to buy gift certificates over the phone, but was told they could only be purchased at the store. Back then, gift certificates were not like the gift cards or "e-certificates" of today. They were large pieces of paper that resembled the checks people held up after winning golf tournaments. They had to be printed, signed and individually recorded. My brother went to a Baby Gap, and by the time he was done, he had spent two hours at the store and still had to go to the post office and mail them. Three hours to send a simple gift to someone. Needless to say, he was at the end of his rope. When he called, he said to me, "Why isn't there a 1-800-FLOWERS for gift certificates? You could order and send whatever gift certificates you wanted."

I said, "Hey I've been working for twenty hours straight. Go ask Mom." But when I got off the phone, I thought, "There must be a service like this." I opened the Lexis Nexus application on my desktop. Back then, that is how lawyers got information. I searched for "gift certificates" and two things came up: popular retailers like Barnes and Noble and "corporate incentives." I had never heard of incentives. I was curious, so I started poking around.

When I looked at the "incentive" industry, I saw an industry ripe for a new player. There were companies spending billions on rewards, incentives and loyalty programs. The industry was not a new one—it had existed for over fifty years, going back to the old S&H Green Stamps that our parents knew. Other than the large credit card and travel reward programs, most of these incentive and loyalty programs were run by regional marketing firms that ran these programs on a one-off basis. There was little technology, data, analytics and no investment capital. I also noticed something else—in these programs, the reward was never cash or gift certificates—it was always merchandise or travel. In fact, the only credit card company that had a cash reward program in the 1990s was Discover, and they were an outlier. It seemed odd that all of the credit card companies didn't have programs that allowed people to choose cash or gift certificates as their rewards.

The gift certificate world kept going around in my head. The next clue happened a week later when I was on a date. She was a pharmaceutical rep and while I was waiting in her apartment for her to finish getting ready, I was flipping through a "rewards catalog" on her coffee table that featured page after page of travel packages and merchandise. When I asked what it was she said it was her "incentive catalog"—the reward options she got to pick if she hit her sales targets. I asked, "Why would they go to all the trouble of picking all these travel and merchandise items? Why wouldn't they let you get cash or gift certificates and pick what you want?" She didn't know.

Then I figured it out. The business model for incentive companies for the last fifty years was to make money on the "reward." The existing players in the market who ran the large loyalty programs would buy a television in China for $100 and sell it to Pfizer for $400, who would then give it to a pharmaceutical sales representative as a reward for hitting sales target. Why would you offer cash or gift certificates when you could make so much money on merchandise and travel? The incentive companies even used to publish surveys arguing that merchandise and travel rewards drove better performance than cash or cash equivalents like gift cards. I always thought that was bullshit. These companies made their money on the margin, and there was no margin to be made in cash or gift certificates. So even though most consumers would likely prefer cash or gift certificates if the established players actually offered them, it would decimate their business. I knew I was onto something big.

In my mind, it seemed like a moment so big that a band should have burst out of my closet or a showgirl should have jumped out of a birthday cake. EUREKA! What an opportunity? Large, fragmented, inefficient market. Billions of dollars being spent on rewards. A built-in competitive barrier to shield us from the largest players. It was *perfect* for a new player! And once we built a network of gift certificates, not only could we hit the corporate market, we could also solve the problem my brother had—ordering gift certificates through a phone number or website.

That was the beginning of my new life (or the end of life as I'd known it). My brother and I would meet at the end of the day at my law firm, usually around 10 p.m., and in the wee hours of the night we built our business plan and financial models. In January 1998, I left my law firm and we launched the company on October 15, 1998. In the beginning, I worked out of my brother's real estate office. On the consumer side, our plan was to create a phone number and website for consumers to order the gift certificates of their choice. On the corporate side, we were going to be the first company to offer cash and gift certificate-based rewards and incentive programs. Our model was not to make money on the reward, but rather to provide the technology and analytics to administer company reward programs and optimize their business results. For the next year, in addition to trying to launch our new business, I spent about two hundred days on a plane to convince the national retailers of the world (e.g., Target) to offer their gift certificates in our program.

On the consumer side, we wanted to create the 1-800-FLOWERS for gift certificates that enabled consumers to purchase the gift certificates of their choice from a network of national retailers through a phone number and the Internet. We believed it needed to be called 1-800-GIFT CERTIF-ICATE and we agreed on one thing if we didn't get the phone number that corresponded to the first seven letters of gift certificate, the business was not worth doing. We set out to see if anyone owned 1-800-443-8237 or 1-800-GIFT CER.

We called the number a few times to see what would happen but no one answered. After some digging, we found that the phone number was owned by a man who lived in Las Vegas. We used a connection at AT&T to see how much the number was being used and it turned out that there had been limited amounts billed to the number. While the number was already taken, at least it wasn't being actively used. We tried to get a different phone number for the owner but we couldn't find one.

My brother and I crafted a plan to purchase the number from the owner. We decided that Dan and I would take turns calling the number every other day. We agreed that if we did reach the owner, we would say that the number was the "800" version of a New York number that we used in our real estate business *and we wanted it. We debated how much we should offer for the number. We didn't want to seem too anxious or that the number was so valuable to us. Offer too little and he might not consider it. Offer too much and he might realize that there was something more here. We agreed to offer him $500. We would have paid much more.*

This went on for weeks and no one answered. Later that month, purely by coincidence, my parents were going to Las Vegas for an anniversary party. We joked that they should go to the owner's house and take the number at gunpoint. Not the best plan for my seventy-year-old parents. We continued our alternating calls and weeks went by without any answer. We were starting to think that this business idea was going to die before it even got started.

On the day my parents left for Las Vegas, my brother made his standard call to the number. The owner answered. Dan was a little surprised at first, but went on to explain to him why we wanted the number as we had planned.

The owner paused and responded, "Sure. Why not? We have not used it in years." Dan did not want to let him off the phone without making arrangements. In addition to paying him, we needed him to sign a document required by AT&T to transfer the number. Even though it was a long shot, because my parents were going to Las Vegas, we gave them a copy of the AT&T transfer document "just in case." We were grasping at straws but now it was real. We told the owner that by coincidence our parents were going to be in Las Vegas and asked him if he would meet them to exchange the paperwork and receive payment. Dan arranged with him to meet my parents on Friday at 6 p.m. at the sports book at Treasure Island casino. It felt like we were arranging a drug deal.

Dan got off the phone and immediately called me. My parents had already boarded their flight to Las Vegas. We didn't want to let any time go by so Dan started looking into flights to Las Vegas. We talked about it and decided that unless we came up with a form of travel that could get us to Las Vegas in three hours from New York, the best option would be to wait until my parents landed. My parents did not have cell phones back then. We called their hotel and left a message for them to call us as soon as they got the message. We waited for their call. It was the longest six hours of our lives.

Finally, my Mom called. Dan conferenced me in. We told her what happened and started to talk through the details. Dan explained to her that they would meet the owner at 6 p.m. at Treasure Island on Friday. My mom responded with an answer that only a Jewish mother could. "We can't meet him then. That's the same time as the party." We said "Mom, come on, that's ridiculous." She said "We are not missing the party. We have to be there." There was a pause and I think Dan and I said, in unison, "Put Dad on the phone."

Dad agreed. I have this picture in my mind of my Mom holding on to my Dad's leg trying to prevent him from going to the meeting. We gave my parents the details and called the owner back and confirmed. We told him my Dad would be at the sports book at Treasure Island and would be wearing a red hat. We asked him to bring his driver's license as it was required by AT&T. Drug dealers would have been proud.

We sat on pins and needles until the next day. The time came and my Dad met the owner as planned. Dad was to pay him, get the paper signed, give him his money and get out of there before the owner started asking questions. He immediately recognized my Dad with his red hat. Dad handed him the papers and they asked someone in the casino to make a photocopy of the owner's driver's license. They exchanged some pleasantries, the owner signed the transfer papers and Dad handed him an envelope with $500 in cash. They shook hands and started to walk away. Then the owner said, "Hey, by the way, you don't have anything to do with those gift certificate guys, do you? Those guys called me a few years back and said something about gift certificates." My Dad put on his poker face and shook his head, no.

A day in the life of the entrepreneur. 1-800-GIFT CERTIFICATE was alive!

FROM ITALIAN ICES TO HEALTH REWARDS

In the early days, it was just our first employee, Randy, and me. Believe it or not, Randy and I were in the same Management 101 class as undergrads at Bucknell. It was the first class that business students took at Bucknell. The course taught organizational behavior by having the students run a real business, beginning with electing officers, dreaming up a concept, and making a pitch for a loan. The grade was based on profit. Most of the businesses from this class over the years were t-shirts or hot dogs at fraternity parties. We came up with "Bison Ices." Bucknell's nickname is the Bison and the business was portable Italian Ices all over campus.

I was elected CEO and Randy was elected Director of Operations. A few engineers put their engineering degrees to work and rigged bicycles so we could pedal around freezers that could hold three vats of Italian Ices. We were everywhere. On a moment's notice, we could pedal our ices (literally) to a crowd. Sporting events. Fraternity parties. Association events. You name it. It was common for our drivers to call back to the home base and say "We've got an emergency. We are out of blueberry." Our delivery team would pedal their asses off and deliver product to the various locations. I think my tongue was blue all semester because every night the vats would come back to our office at the end of the evening shift and we would eat the last two inches of Italian Ices left in each vat.

Bison Ices was a huge success. From what I hear, it is still one of the most successful businesses from that class. Although I didn't know it then, it was also a snapshot of our future. Other than a chance meeting here and there, Randy and I lost touch for the balance of our Bucknell years. But one day, in 1998, I was working out in a gym in Hoboken, New Jersey, and noticed a guy wearing a Bucknell sweatshirt that looked familiar. I introduced myself and realized it was Randy. We started working out together, and although IncentOne was still a set of ideas swirling in my head, I told him about the incentive idea. He mentioned that he worked for a publishing company and they asked him to head their new division using this thing they called the Internet. I told him that I could not pay him anything but asked if he was interested in helping me flush this out and what role the Internet might play. He called me a few days later and said he'd love to.

We would meet after work, go to the gym, and then noodle and noodle and noodle. Boy was that fun. We felt like we were having a secret meeting of NATO and no one knew that we were about to change the world. After a year of noodling Randy became our first employee as Director of Operations. Go figure—CEO and Director of Operations from Bison Ices to CEO and Director of Operations of IncentOne. We were off to the races.

Over three years, we did everything to build the business. ***And then our first order!*** After nearly two years of travelling the country to create a gift card network, building our technology, creating our gift card fulfillment center and our customer service operation, raising money, and working twenty-four hours a day, Randy walked into my office with a huge smile and handed me the one page printout of the order sheet from our first order. It said "$100 Gift Certificate. Kenneth Cole. Diane Tapia."

On the corporate side, we created technology that would allow companies to administer all of their reward and incentive programs in one place and to offer every type of reward, including cash and gift certificates. Our solution resonated in the corporate market. Customers liked letting their employees and salespeople select the gift cards of their choice or cash, as opposed to travel or merchandise. They also liked having a single technology platform to run it all. We knew we had arrived when we beat the 800-pound gorilla:

> *NBC was a multimillion-dollar opportunity. They had incentive programs all over the country. We had been selected as one of two finalists in their vendor selection process. We were going head to head with the largest company in the incentive industry. The day before our finalist presentation, I learned that our competitor was not only bringing twenty people to the meeting, but that one of their senior leaders used to be golfing buddies with the president of an NBC division. We had a total of ten employees at the time. On the day of our four-hour finalist presentation, my head of IT told me that he needed to monitor our platform very closely throughout the demonstration of our product. When I asked him why, he said it was probably better if I didn't know. Since he was going to be on the phone, we agreed that if he needed to send me a message, he would chime in to the conversation and use a specific word as a clue. We had to pick a word that was distinct enough that I would notice, but common enough that*

it made sense in the conversation. After passing on ridiculous things like "blue horseshoe loves Endicott Steel" (from the movie Wall Street*) and "life is like a box of chocolates" (from the movie* Forrest Gump*), we decided on "universal." Our platform was designed to be a "universal" solution for all of NBC's incentive programs. The plan was that if I said the word "universal" it was because our demo platform was freezing and I would have to stall to give him about three minutes to do something on the platform. What we didn't realize was that NBC had just finalized a deal to acquire "Universal Pictures" and to create a new division called "NBC Universal."*

Our competitor had the morning session and we had the afternoon session. There were about ten NBC people in the room and another twenty on the phone from divisions around the country. Our presentation went perfectly. Our solution made sense, the attendees were engaged, and there was a good amount of joking around. Everything lined up with what NBC needed. Then we did our demonstration. Things were going perfectly. But during our demonstration, some of the people from NBC Universal started to ask questions. Both my head of IT and I heard the word "universal." I was afraid that my head of IT was going to start tinkering with the platform even though it was fine. I pretended that I didn't hear her question and asked her to repeat where she was from. I stopped her and asked what NBC Universal was, since we had not seen that name as one of the divisions that had sat in the many meetings during this process. I was stalling. I also asked her a couple of follow-up questions that took her about five minutes to get through. As she was answering, I jotted a note on the notebook of one of my colleagues to tell our head of IT that everything was fine and that the new word was "China." It was the first thing that came to mind. Then I thought, doesn't NBC do business in China? We made it through without an incident. At the end of the presentation, NBC told us that it would take a week or so for them to cull through the scoring of both vendors. We got a call the next day and the head of benefits called to tell me we had been selected the winner. I thought of calling our team into my office when he called, but I was afraid that he would hear us cheering in the background. I hung up, asked everyone to go into the conference room and walked in with a big frown on my face. I paused and said, "NBC picked us. We beat the 800-pound gorilla!"

People began to notice. Some of the nation's largest companies started to hire us to run their reward programs. Our clients included Deloitte,

Washington Mutual, Countrywide Financial, Safeway, British Airways and General Motors. Those names sound familiar, right? Partly because they are some of America's most well-known companies. Partly because they were some of he companies that were devastated by the financial crisis of 2008. More on that later.

Even though we were making progress, I wanted our solution, which was being used to run employee and sales incentive programs, to be something that was on every CEO's desk. It was 2002 and I was looking for a different vertical market for our solution. Sales and employee rewards were a good start, but I wanted something that was at the "C" level and directly affected the bottom line. Then it hit me. I was walking down the street in Manhattan and saw a billboard outside a Starbucks. It said, "We pay for healthcare even if you work part-time." I had never thought about healthcare before. Everyone got their healthcare from their company. I knew nothing about healthcare. Some say I still don't. I did some research and what I found blew me away. Every car that General Motors made had $2,000 in healthcare costs. Starbucks spent more on healthcare than coffee. Whoa!

I kept digging and found another statistic that sealed it for me—for every ten pregnant women who do not follow their prenatal care, it costs our healthcare system one million dollars. Wow! As I kept looking, all the research was the same. Americans don't do the basic health things they are supposed to do and it costs the healthcare system billions. Even pregnant women, who are as motivated as anyone, were not doing the right things. I thought, "If you gave each of these women $1,000 to do what they should be doing, the system would save $990,000." I may not be a healthcare guy, but I can add.

Now we were really off to the races. From that day forward, we were focused on being the first company to use rewards for healthy behavior. Not only would people get healthier, the system would save money. We would say: "Fixing the healthcare system, one activity at a time." We thought we could change the world.

Makes sense, right? Great idea. Great energy. Passionate belief. Huge market. Sure, in 2004, we were ahead of our time. In 2004, not only were rewards in healthcare nonexistent, they were offensive. People in the health industry insisted that they would never pay people to do the things they should be doing for their health. The head of benefits of a large waste management firm said to me in 2005, "It is offensive to me to pay my truck drivers to deal with their sleep apnea." We would respond, "But isn't it just math?" In every other industry if someone wants to get a consumer to do something, they use rewards. Would anyone switch bank accounts if they didn't get their $200 reward? Would anyone use an airline or a hotel that didn't have a reward program? We would remind them that healthcare was the only industry that was asking consumers to change their behavior without rewards. Needless to say, we felt—like many entrepreneurs do—that every customer should want to buy this tomorrow.

It became clear we were inventing an industry. I wished I could have asked Steve Jobs or Mark Zuckerberg if they had realized, when they first got started, whether they were inventing a new industry or just felt nuts for trying something radically new. We even approached American Express and told them that they could own healthcare. Imagine "American Express Rewards for mammograms." I told American Express that they already had the infrastructure we were about to build. They declined. Even without American Express and other naysayers, by late 2008 we were going strong.

To that point, the funding for IncentOne came from our family and about one million dollars from outside investors. But on October 15 of that year—ten years to the day that we started the company—we closed a financing deal with a private equity firm for millions of dollars. As part of the transaction, a portion of the money was to go to my family. After ten years of blood, sweat and tears, we had arrived. It was a huge moment! The sense of accomplishment that day was indescribable. It lasted about a week...

"EVERYONE HAS A PLAN 'TIL THEY GET PUNCHED IN THE FACE"[1]

October 15, 2008, fell in the middle of what would become the largest financial crisis since the Great Depression. Exactly one month earlier on September 15, 2008, Lehman Brothers filed for bankruptcy. The next day the Federal Reserve gave $85 million to AIG to rescue them. On September 25, the Office of Thrift Supervision closed Washington Mutual and shortly thereafter JPMorgan Chase acquired Washington Mutual out of bankruptcy. Our customer base consisted of some of the largest companies in the United States. Washington Mutual was our biggest but it was just the beginning of the avalanche coming our way. In a matter of months, virtually all of our top clients were bankrupt or on the verge of financial ruin. Washington Mutual. Countrywide Financial. General Motors. Capital One. Merrill Lynch. Fifth Third Bank. ADP. Deloitte. It seemed as if the *Wall Street Journal*'s "stories of companies facing dire financial fates" was taken from our client list.

It's one thing to have a company freeze or reduce their spending with a vendor like IncentOne. It's another when a customer is spending millions of dollars with your company one day and on the brink of bankruptcy the next. The impact on us was significant and abrupt. What took us a decade to build unraveled in days. My family had to immediately take the money they'd just received from the new financing and put it back into the company. It was like a kick between the legs. The pit in my stomach didn't go away for a couple of days. I kept thinking, "I just wish that I hadn't involved my family. I wish I could give them their money back and just take this on myself." I was always so thankful that my friends and family supported me with their money, and all I could think at this point was that I wished I had never let them put *any* money in the company.

I told my parents that I needed a week to figure out what the impacts were. A week later, I called them from the steps of the New York Public Library about two blocks from my apartment. I'll never forget people around me laughing and enjoying the beautiful scenery. I told my parents that it would take two years to save the business, that there was only a

---

[1] Mike Tyson

50/50 chance of survival and it was likely that my brother and I would battle through those two years, if not longer. I also told them that it would take me working twenty-four hours per day to make it happen and that I would have to make decisions that were not going to be popular. I got off the phone thinking, *It took ten years of working our asses off, and now we have to work for two years just to save the business.*

BIG BOYS AND GIRLS SHIT

But wait, that was only the beginning. Our investment came from a private equity firm. When the market crashed, they were understandably concerned. As the news about the financial markets hit, I received a call from a partner from the investment firm. He said, "How the hell could this happen with Washington Mutual and Countrywide and why didn't we disclose it to them?" I told him we were as shocked as they were. When he insinuated he had been "duped," I reminded him of a few things. First, as part of their due diligence process, they had talked to every one of our major customers including Washington Mutual and Countrywide. I reminded him that they brought in two separate outside due diligence firms to evaluate our financials and our technology. Finally I said, "With all due respect, you read the same *Wall Street Journal* that I do. As Washington Mutual and Countrywide were collapsing to the tune of billions of dollars, they didn't call us to talk about their five-million-dollar employee reward program. Nobody duped you. You have the same information that I had. The bottom line is the country's going through something we've never seen before."

To this day, I feel like it was my failing to not see the collapse of our customers coming. After all, as CEO, you are supposed to be ahead of these things. It was understandable for our investor to be upset. They had just invested and our top customers were disintegrating as the world's finances fell apart. Apparently our investor felt the same way. From that point forward, our investor was determined to remove me as CEO.

There's more. We were in the reward business and our programs required us to distribute gift cards to the employees of our clients who earned incentives. We had built relationships with hundreds of national retailers and their gift card departments. Those relationships involved extending us credit for the purchase of gift card inventory to the tune of about two million dollars per year. With all companies facing a potential financial crisis, our retail partners suspended credit to IncentOne almost instantly. Our two million dollars in credit was gone in a matter of days.

Not done yet. Our banking customers not only stopped their business with us, they demanded refunds. Washington Mutual and Countrywide were both acquired and once they were, the acquiring companies were looking to squeeze the most from their acquisition. While I was dodging bullets from our investors, watching customers collapse, seeing revenue disappear, and battling with my brother, I got a phone call from a lawyer from JPMorgan Chase. JPMorgan Chase had acquired Washington Mutual out of bankruptcy. He barely introduced himself before he said, "You owe us five million dollars." As part of our contracts, including the one with Washington Mutual, incentives that were not redeemed expired in one year. He said that because Washington Mutual was in bankruptcy, they had the right to void contracts and that the bankruptcy court would require us to return the dollars associated with expired rewards. His team's estimate was that we owed them five million dollars. He was also nice enough to let me know that he had an army of lawyers whose only job was to squeeze as many assets out of Washington Mutual as they could.

Where were we? Ten years of hard work gone in a fraction of the time. Customers asking for refunds. Customers gone. Revenue gone. Credit gone. Investors pissed and after me. Daily battles with my brother. Business on the brink. Family money and relationships hanging in the balance. Economy in shambles. Making payroll was dependent on collections from companies like General Motors and the United States Postal Service— companies the *Wall Street Journal* were reporting as "running out of cash." Every day a new bullet would fly over my head.

To say the days were long and hard would be an understatement. The time definitely took its toll on my family. My brother and I would often end my twenty-hour day with a screaming match. What was the loneliest day for me? There were plenty to choose from.

One of the most painful was a conversation with my Dad that almost broke up our family:

> *We were scrambling to survive. Every time we reforecast revenue and cash for the business, another customer of ours would go bankrupt. We tried to take a worst-case scenario approach but kept getting it wrong. I was on the phone one night with my Mom and Dad giving them an update. My Dad had just gotten off the phone with my brother who was upset about what was happening. I explained to my Dad what was happening. We always had calm, reasoned conversations. This time he said, "Mike are you being truthful with us about the numbers?" I lost it. I told him if he thought I would bullshit my family about the numbers, he wouldn't have a son for long.*

And the time that my brother and my Dad confronted me in a Florida parking lot:

> *I was on vacation at my parents' place in Boca Raton, Florida. My brother, his wife and two kids and I would go there around Christmas each year. It was hardly a vacation with what was going on in the business. That time of year was particularly busy because the health industry launches programs like ours for the first of the year. My brother had gotten a call from my head of technology. I had been riding our head of technology hard, as we were having lots of technology issues for the past six months. Nonetheless, I was working with him to get through the end of the year. He knew how much my brother and I were battling at the time. He called my brother and told him that the entire leadership team was ready to walk out the door because of me. After hearing this, my brother was understandably upset and asked to meet Dad and me in the parking lot of our hotel. He told me that I was bringing the company down and pleaded with my Dad to reason with me. I assured him this was bullshit and was a way that my head of technology was trying to save his skin, but I could see the look in my brother's and my Dad's eyes and they were thinking to themselves,* Mike is taking down the whole family. *My brother and Dad screamed at me for an hour and told me that I had to change.*

It also started to take its toll on me:

> *Things seemed like they were spiraling out of control. We put together a dinner at a steakhouse with some board members and other colleagues. My board consisted of my brother Dan, my friends Marc, Fran and Dave, a few professional colleagues and we were joined by our accountant, Mark. During the dinner conversation, our accountant made the comment that we would have net operating losses to carry over for the next ten years. Someone made the comment, "No one is better at losing money than IncentOne." It was a joke, but not really. Everyone at the table should have been catching up and talking about the Knicks game or what was going on with their families but I had the feeling that everybody was thinking, Mike better get his shit together.*

And it made me do some things of which I am not too proud:

> *It was right in the middle of the financial crisis. My assistant walked in my office and closed the door. She said she was concerned about me and asked if I was okay. I told her I was fine. She then said she wanted to ask me something but she was embarrassed to do so. She said she only was asking because she was concerned about me. She told me that one of the crew who cleaned my office the night before founded a soda bottle full of what seemed like urine. She paused, and asked me if I had done that. I lied. I told her of course not. My brother asked me the same thing a week later. I lied to him too. During the day, I had peed in an empty soda bottle so I didn't need to leave my desk to go to the bathroom.*

But at least it forced me to learn about bourbon:

> *It was a Tuesday and I had to pick up something from a friend in Midtown Manhattan. I was near the bar owned by my brother's college roommate, Chris. I stopped in. Before I did, I called my brother to give him a daily update. The pressure was intense on everyone at that point. What resulted was a screaming match of about an hour, which, unfortunately, wasn't rare back then. When we were done, I sat down at the bar and started talking to Chris. Chris was quite a character. He was someone who lived in the bar business. Conversations with Chris didn't talk about lack of liquidity or credit. They were about the new waitress and how long it would take Chris to sleep with her. In one sense, it was the perfect antidote to the seriousness of my day. It also made me think what it*

would be like to be able to think about fluff like that. He said, "You look like shit. How about a bourbon?" I said, "You mean Jack Daniels." He said, "No, like Bulleit or Blanton's." I tried it and not only loved it, but now also understood what it meant to "take the edge off." This was the first time I drank alone. It wouldn't be the last but at least I fell in love with bourbon.

Two years. Groundhog Day every day. Gym at 5 a.m. Work by 7 a.m. Leave work at 10 p.m. Screaming match with my brother until midnight. Lather, rinse, repeat. It was hard but I got us into this and I was going to get us out of this. I just wish I could have given my family and friends their money back and let my Mom, Dad, Dan and Dan's wife Alyse go back to a normal life. I'm a guy, so I'll put it this way—I got kicked in the balls so many times that I stopped noticing.

THAT MORNING IN THE GYM

The issues going on in the world were so big and complex. Investment banks were collapsing. Companies were going bankrupt. There was even a report that General Electric wasn't going to have enough cash to pay its bills. The normal solutions to problems weren't working. If even the biggest companies didn't have solutions, how would a company like IncentOne survive? There were so many nights that I sat up thinking about the business at 2 a.m. with the realization that the "math just wouldn't work." That we could do all the things people do in these situation—cut costs, cut back growth plans, look for financing—and it still might not matter.

I was in the gym one morning and it hit me. The normal solutions were not going to work and I had to start to think differently. If I was going to save IncentOne, I was going to have to change my thinking entirely, universally. I was going to have to change my perspective on every part of the business. We were going to have to come up with new ways of thinking about everything—customers, people, expenses, investors, technology, revenue, financing, negotiation. After all, it was no longer about thinking outside of the box—the box was long gone and there seemed no point in replacing it.

For some reason, I felt like I had discovered plutonium. I remember walking across the street after I left the gym that morning and almost getting hit by a bus. My mind was in a different place. And it reenergized me. It gave me a new opportunity. I mean this is what entrepreneurs do right? We think differently. I spent nearly three years doing just that. I worked like a dog, made many mistakes but also found success, insight and humility. I also made many shifts in perspective that helped me save IncentOne. The events of these years are no longer simply the details of my story. They are the foundation for **The Lonely Entrepreneur**—and will hopefully become part of the story for many more entrepreneurs to come. How do you change your perspective when you are under the pressure, chaos and burden of being the entrepreneur from the ones that stifle progress to those that empower you to thrive?

You already know how my story ends. We successfully sold IncentOne to Welltok in 2013. By then, rewards for healthy behavior were everywhere and I was acknowledged as a pioneer of the movement to use rewards to drive healthy behavior, and one of the nation's experts on the topic. In 2014, *Forbes* named five megatrends with the power to transform healthcare and two of the five were related to rewards. Eighty percent of employers use them. They are part of every health plan, Medicare, Medicaid and your local retailer. As of November 2015, Walgreens had 85 million people enrolled in their Balance Rewards program. A provision increasing the use of rewards for healthcare was even included in Obamacare. In fact, it was one of the few provisions in Obamacare that Democrats and Republicans agreed upon. It is only matter of time before every health plan will have a rewards program like your credit card, airline or hotel. Remember the benefits manager? Not surprisingly, he called me back years later and said, "It is still offensive to me to pay my truck drivers to deal with their sleep apnea, but they keep crashing trucks into buildings so what does it matter what I think?"

I was fortunate enough to sell IncentOne, and I am hardly poor, but IncentOne should have been a billion-dollar company. Think of it this way, if the 110 million people in the Walgreen's program earned a $100 reward, this would amount to $11 billion dollars—and that's just Walgreen's. It could have been much more if I had learned how to change my perspective earlier. It could have been much more if I had this book!

PART ONE

Pressure, Passion, Pleasure, and Pain Make Us Blind

Introduction

Congratulations! You are the entrepreneur. You get to be president. You get to write off your expenses. You get to set your hours. You get to pursue your passion. You also get an unlimited pass on a perpetual rollercoaster. Being an entrepreneur is exhilarating, humbling, challenging, inspiring, mind-numbing, nerve-racking, exciting, life changing, exasperating, maddening, irritating, encouraging, discouraging, exhausting, motivating, debilitating, exciting, tiring, energizing, empowering, disheartening, uplifting, depressing and enlivening—usually all in the same day!

Once you have made the decision to be an entrepreneur, it is as if you have stepped into a telephone booth to turn into a superhero. The difference between an entrepreneur and a normal superhero is this—normal superheroes possess one or two amazing skills (e.g., Superman can fly and has x-ray vision, Spiderman can leap tall building and spin a spider web). But the entrepreneur must possess an almost endless set of skills. Imagine if there were a superhero that could do all of it. Well, that superhero is you—the entrepreneur—and you possess traits that are not found in mere mortals:

- Vision—the ability to see an opportunity where others cannot.
- Courage—the guts to leave stability, or comfort or normalcy, to take a risk.
- Passion—a desire to not settle for the status quo and create your own idea.
- Creativity—the talent to see solutions where others see roadblocks.
- Individualism—the independence of spirit to take an idea and run with it.
- Belief—the ability to believe when many tell you not to believe.
- Grit—firmness of mind or spirit and unyielding courage in the face of hardship or danger.

Think about the premise of many entrepreneurial ventures. The entrepreneur gives up her job, invests her money, convinces her family and friends to invest, never sleeps, works twenty-four hours per day, and cries, drinks and laughs about her business. Like many of our famous superheroes, entrepreneurs struggle with having a "normal life," and with interacting with "normal people" who don't share or understand the burden of carrying the world, or a new business, on your shoulders.

But like most superheroes, the entrepreneur has his or her kryptonite and it is this:

> *Entrepreneurs naturally develop certain **perspectives** that are damaging to the progress of the entrepreneurial venture—even when they have a great idea and the talent to execute it.*

Ask yourself: Why does one company succeed, and another with the same idea fail? It's how we manage the struggle of being the entrepreneur. When we are under the pressure, chaos, and burden of being the entrepreneur, we develop damaging "perspectives" on the business and personal issues we face. While it is natural for us to develop these perspectives, they blind us, obscure solutions and undermine our progress.

Why do we develop these damaging perspectives? Because we are under the influence of the "Four Ps" of being the entrepreneur—**Pressure, Passion, Pleasure** and **Pain**:

PRESSURE	PASSION
The enormous burden of responsibility and daily stress of a new business makes us overreact, make hasty decisions, and have a hard time seeing past the next thirty minutes.	Our obsessive belief and commitment to our vision makes us plow ahead in the face of obstacles but also makes us ignore things we see along the way. Entrepreneurs say, "I know nine out of ten restaurants fail, but no one can cook like me."

PLEASURE	PAIN
The energizing feeling of seeing a vision come to life and of satisfaction, accomplishment, achievement empowers us but also makes us fail to address problems staring us in the face.	The angst over the disappointments, frustrations and mistakes makes us doubt ourselves and feel it is just too hard when we face constant setbacks or are picking ourselves up off the ground every day.

When we are under the influence of the Four Ps, we develop these damaging perspectives. We

- Don't think we can set priorities
- Believe we have to do everything
- Expect others to live and breathe the business as we do
- Think others don't understand what we are going through
- Get frustrated that others don't work as hard or as well as we do
- Don't know what a weekend or holiday is
- Don't take a day off or get a full night's sleep
- Fear missing payroll
- Feel like the world is resting on our shoulders
- Feel like we are running in quicksand even when we have a great idea
- Feel very, very alone.

> *How many entrepreneurs have said, "No one can do this except me"? Despite the fact that we have visited outer space, mapped the human genome, developed driverless cars, and invented car service companies that don't own cars, the entrepreneur thinks he or she is the only one on earth—I'm sorry in the universe—that can do the job.*

Think about how many times you have sat across from an employee you were about to hire, knowing that they were wrong for the job. But your passion for your idea, the pleasure of being able to have some help, and the pain of working twenty-four hours a day makes you say to yourself, *They are perfect for the job.* You think, *I know they got arrested a few times, but they were never convicted. And I like that they have had to work through some challenges.*

Entrepreneurs not only develop these perspectives, we also fail to recognize when we are exercising them—and can't take corrective action. Any one of the Four Ps alone would be enough to skew our perspective. Mix them all together and it affects our ability to see that we are developing these perspectives in the first place. In the thick of things, we become blind to the perspectives we hold, and to their effect on everything from our business decisions, to our relationships with employees, vendors and family. Once the Four Ps have had their effect, these damaging perspectives can hold our progress hostage.

UNDER THE INFLUENCE: THE ENTREPRENEUR AND THE FOUR Ps

In this section, we outline what it is like to be the entrepreneur and how the Four Ps affect us. We lay out the things you think and feel each day as an entrepreneur and how to recognize when we are acquiring or exercising perspectives that harm both personal and professional growth.

When you read this section, you are likely to say, "That's exactly how I feel." Remember, I learned these the hard way in building my company. While each entrepreneurial venture is different, and not all these perspectives will apply to you, I think you will find that we have many shared experiences. Once we have identified these perspectives, we will be prepared for the second section of book, and the heart of **The Lonely Entrepreneur**: the change in perspective is key to your personal and professional progress as an entrepreneur.

When you read these perspectives you may feel like you're part of a secret club...or someone is reading your mind. That's because I've been there, and after all, we're all in this together.

Chapter 1
No One Cares as Much as You Do

We lose perspective as entrepreneurs. One of the reasons I wrote this book, was to help people recognize this and manage our teams and ourselves through it. We lose sight of the fact that the rest of the world does not wake up with the passion, determination and focus that we do. Something has spurred us to take this wild journey to create our venture. Our heart and soul are in it. Our business life and personal life (if you have one) are intimately intermingled. We think about it twenty-four hours per day and our dreams are not of sipping piña coladas or a relaxing day at the spa, but rather having our first real paying customers. It is unlikely anyone else is losing sleep, shunning their personal lives, or investing their heart and soul.

A problem develops, however, when we have the expectation that anyone associated with our venture wakes up with the same visceral desire to see it come to fruition as we do. Our business may be our oxygen, but for even the most dedicated employee or supportive spouse, it will never be what gives breath to their lives. We must accept that this is a unique place that we occupy, and if we expect others to have the same perspective, we will be disappointed. Bottom line—no one cares as much as we do.

This comes to life in many ways:

Work Ethic

I had a hard time reconciling this feeling when I first started IncentOne. My team didn't lack a good work ethic. I was simply lacking perspective.

When we started IncentOne, I had been a corporate attorney at a New York law firm for a few years. For anyone who knows anything about New York corporate lawyers, they work long hours. When we started IncentOne, even though I was working around the clock, I might have been one of the few people that did not work longer, crazier hours when they started their company. My expectations were that anyone who saw the vision that I saw—to fix the healthcare system with rewards for healthy behavior—would be as driven to work as I was. I became disappointed by their work effort, even though they were working their asses off. I expected that everyone would work till ten o'clock every night. I'd get frustrated when people would be leaving the office at 6 p.m. to get a drink with friends. I would think, How the hell can they leave early when we have so much to do?*

Imagine that. Going for a drink after work with some friends.

An entrepreneur was talking to me about an employee she was paying $20,000 per year. She said, "I'm not sure she is right for the team." When I asked her why she said, "I was talking to her and said that she needed to have her week-ends. She liked playing volleyball at the beach and she wanted to spend time with her boyfriend. I'm not sure she is cut out for this."

If we had our way, we would ban volleyball. We might even ban boy-friends.

We usually understand this when it comes to people who are tangentially involved in our business—like family, friends and team members that aren't involved in the day-to-day. While we might accept and even understand this for friends and family, this skewed perspective is hard to overcome when it comes to our team. We say things like, "So what if they are only working for equity?" or "Did they think sleep was part of the job description?" When we don't recognize that **no one cares as much as we do**, we not only become frustrated, but we alienate our team members that *are* working hard, and usually for below-market compensation. We must have realistic expectations not only about their work effort, but also about how much they care about the long list of things that run through our mind each day. Our teams aren't failing to care enough—we as leaders are failing to recognize and accept that ***no one cares as much as we do*** and take measures to bridge this gap.

Money

Lack of attention to money used to drive me crazy. Especially when it was my money. If you left a career or job with a regular paycheck, you understand how incredibly sensitive to money entrepreneurs can be. It's not that your team is insensitive, but they don't have the same obsession with it as we do. Imagine watching your bank account shrink when you know you are at least a year from revenue. Imagine getting a parking ticket for $150 when you are burning through your savings. Imagine having to ask friends and family for money. It runs through your mind every minute of every day. It drove me crazy when people going from New York to Philadelphia, Boston or Washington, DC, would take the Acela instead of taking the standard train. It would cost about another $100 to save thirty to forty-five minutes. Don't they know we are a startup?

We are always thinking about saving money and it often gets a little ridiculous:

> *When we had a team travel to trade shows or to finalist or investor presentations, I wanted team members to share rooms together even though most of them were in their forties. In retrospect, not sure this was realistic when it comes to grown professionals over the age of thirty-five but it was my perspective at the time. When they questioned it, I questioned their dedication to what we were doing.*

We just can't seem to understand why no one else is willing to drive six hours in the snow versus taking a ninety-minute flight. We think that no jury would convict us for killing a team member who ordered the $100 bottle of wine at the client dinner or used an expensive software when there was an open source version. Remember, ***no one cares as much as we do***.

Attention to Detail

It is inconceivable to entrepreneurs that a team member would send a document or presentation to us without every single line being perfect. We keep saying to ourselves, "How could they not proofread it?" or "Why couldn't they do the little extra research?" The entrepreneur is willing to leave no stone unturned, to proofread a document at midnight when we have already been working for fourteen hours and to redo a presentation despite spending hours on it.

The sooner we accept that there is no one out there who **cares as much as we do**, the better off we will be. It is our perspective that is off, not theirs. This flawed perspective can be detrimental to team members, and other resources, who are working hard, and still criticized for not being committed. Telling someone who has just worked a long day or a weekend that they aren't committed enough is a great way to turn them into an ex-employee. Our entrepreneurial passion can blind us to negative and inefficient perspectives, but that doesn't mean that we shouldn't be proud of our passion. We just need to recognize how it works and how it affects others.

Not everyone has what it takes to bring the energy to create something from nothing. I always felt lucky not only that I stumbled onto something that might turn into a good business, but that I was working on my passion every day. People will say to you, "Work is fine but it's not like I wake up passionate about credit card marketing. I wish I woke up every day working on something I really believed in." We are lucky to have found our idea or our vision. We are lucky to have that glow in our eye. What goes with that is the reality that no one will care about it as much as you do. How we handle that perspective, and the other perspectives in this book, is what **The Lonely Entrepreneur** is all about.

Chapter 2
Overwhelming Is an Understatement

In the movie *Bachelor Party*, Tom Hanks and Tawny Kitaen are sitting in bed the week of their wedding. Tom feels his fiancée's neck and notices how tense she is. He asks, "What's bothering you?" She responds, "The wedding. My parents. Your parents. Our friends. My job. The future. Our relationship. The caterers. My gown. Your tuxedo. The honeymoon. Our apartment. My shower. Your bachelor party." He responds, "How about the Middle East? You all right with that?"

Welcome to Monday, Tuesday, Wednesday, Thursday, Friday, Saturday and Sunday for the entrepreneur. This is the life of the entrepreneur. ***Overwhelming is an understatement.***

Every entrepreneur faces an overwhelming set of tasks to be accomplished. The list is endless. Strategy. Technology. Team. Business models. Plans. Tactics. Functional areas. Branding. Staff. Money management. Offices. Fundraising. For every ten hours of time, there are one hundred hours of work.

Put aside the passion, energy, emotion and pressure and think of all the things that need to get done.

It's like standing in front of a dam holding back a river of water. Your first issue of the day arises, and pokes a hole in the dam and you plug it with one finger. Then the next hole and you use another finger. After a few hours, you've encountered ten issues and you've used your ten fingers. Problem solved. Then another leak springs and then another. No problem, you are an entrepreneur and you are creative. You use your toes. Soon it's only lunchtime and you have used

39

all ten fingers and all ten toes. Then one more hole comes and you figure out a way to use your tongue.

Sound familiar? It's not only the number of holes to fill, but also the nature of the holes. Some of the holes are little holes—a hundred small tasks that need to be done. Some holes in the dam are larger and more complex. These are things like business strategy, business models, technology, vendor selection and fundraising that require deliberation, multiple perspectives, as well as the time to vet and implement the right solution.

With all of these issues on your mind, and holes to plug, you must still run a business and manage the chaos of the day-to-day:

> *When we started IncentOne, we built a national network of gift card retailers. We felt that a network of gift cards would be a differentiating reward portfolio that did not exist in the marketplace. I spent two hundred days on a plane in 1999 convincing retailers that we could bring them a new channel in corporate rewards and in the healthcare arena that would increase their sales.*

> *One day, I got a call from FirstUSA, a well-known credit card company with about ten million cardholders. They were interested in offering their members a discount on the purchase of gift certificates for the holiday season. Our focus was business to business so this did not seem like a good fit. But they made a compelling offer. If we offered their cardholders a 10 percent discount on gift cards, they would publicize our brand to all ten million cardholders at no cost to us. We got a 15 percent discount on gift cards so we could get exposure to ten million people basically for free. At the time, we were building the company and had no dollars for marketing. It seemed like a great way to put us on the map. Even though it was a consumer opportunity, we decided to do it.*

> *FirstUSA told us that for these offers, they would normally get a 0.25 percent response rate for established national brands. They told us we could expect 25,000 orders. 25,000 orders spread over about forty-five days. Seemed manageable. We had a small call center set up with our vendor to take phone calls. If there were overflow calls, five of our staff in New Jersey were set up to take calls. We also had a fulfillment operation for gift cards in our office. On November 1 we were ready. We stocked about $500,000 in gift cards and had credit*

relationships with retailers that would allow us to restock quickly. Also, because the orders were placed on credit cards, we would get payment from FirstUSA within two days of the order so we had cash flow. We had a plan.

FirstUSA sent out the mailers on November 1. Then the shit hit the fan. From the moment the mailers were sent on November 1 until Christmas Day—55 days—the orders plowed in all day, every day. In addition to all the daily orders on the Internet, the phones rang from the minute the lines were open at 8 a.m. until the moment they closed at 8 p.m. Order after order after order. The call volume was so high that not only was our vendor's call center overwhelmed, but the five phone lines set up for overflow in our New Jersey office rang constantly. We needed more phone lines. We bought old school phones at the local store and wired them from the ceiling to everyone's desk. Every employee in our New Jersey office had two phones on their desk—their regular office phone and a red "bat phone" that had been bought at a local retailer to take orders. Order after order after order.

Not only did we have to take orders, we had to fulfill them. We had a small fulfillment staff prepared to handle the 25,000 orders over fifty-five days, but not this. The volume was so much that we couldn't keep up. The minute we got off the phones at 8 p.m., we would all go into the fulfillment room and stuff envelopes with gift cards. We asked many friends to help. Old pals from our hometown, classmates from high school, and new friends from New York City would show up at 8 p.m. and we would have a nightly fulfillment party.

We had two big problems. First was shipping. The last Federal Express pickup at our office was at 7 p.m. The local Federal Express office closed at 8 p.m. We didn't even stop taking calls until 8 p.m. I knew from my law firm days that Federal Express allowed certain customers to extend those hours as late as midnight. I went over to the Federal Express office at Newark Airport and had a discussion with the night manager. I asked him if there was a way for us to drop off packages at the airport location up until midnight. He said no. They were not allowed to accept packages that did not come from a Federal Express location. After some dialogue we struck a deal. Since we were in the incentive business, I offered to provide rewards for his staff for the holidays if he agreed to allow us to drop off packages until midnight. He agreed as long as we followed a specific procedure.

41

What about inventory? We had started with $500,000 in inventory and had credit lines with our national retailers but not nearly enough for the volume. In addition, we had deals with Barnes & Noble and our other retailer partners for a discount off the face value of the gift certificates (We paid $85 for a $100 gift certificate). With all of the volume we were doing, I wanted a bigger discount. When I approached our retail partners, they were happy to help us with larger credit lines and larger orders, but most weren't willing to negotiate a better discount.

We got creative. Near our office on Route 3 and Route 17 in New Jersey are strip malls with virtually every retailer and national restaurant in the country. I went on a shopping spree. I went to every retailer and asked, "If we bought x in gift certificates, what discount and credit terms would you give us?" Since many of these locations were managed locally or regionally, they were happy to accommodate.

I'll never forget walking into Applebee's on Route 3. I walked in and asked the teenager at the front desk if I could talk to a manager about buying some gift cards. I knew that we needed about $250,000 in gift cards over the next month. She said, "That's great because we are running a contest for the holidays and the restaurant that sells the most gift cards would get a trip to Hawaii for all staff." She said they ran the contest last year. I asked what the winning amount was and she said, "A little more than $25,000." I needed $250,000.

The manager came out and I asked her what discount she could give me for $25,000 in purchases. The team went to the back room like a car salesman does to talk to her "manager" and came out with a number. I told them it was not good enough and it was a short drive to another Applebee's. They ran back into the office and came back with a better offer. I said, "What if I increased it to $50,000." They ran back to the office and came back with two things, a better offer and a plate of hot appetizers—chicken wings, potato skins, mozzarella sticks, the works. We continued this back and forth until we got to $250,000. Great deal for them. Great deal for us. The manager was concerned about how she was going to get that many gift cards. I told her if she wanted the business she needed to figure it out.

Once a week, one of our employees would run to these various retailers to pick up gift cards. For our employees, Applebee's was a unique experience. Regardless of the time of day, as soon as we showed up with big checks (about $50,000 per week), they would scramble around and make the appetizer platter for our employee. Employees used to come back to the office with lots of gift cards and marinara sauce on their face.

For some retailers, the gift certificates actually had to be signed. A few times, our retailers and restaurants forgot to have their managers sign the gift certificates. When we called and asked what to do, they would say, "You can sign them. Once they are in our system they are valid but they must have a name in the signature line or the restaurants won't accept them." They told us to sign the Applebee's manager's name but that the name on the signature didn't matter. So much for corporate controls. A few of our employees would sit and sign gift certificates at midnight when we were done fulfilling. At first we were signing the Applebee's manager's name as they instructed us to do but with all the days of no sleep we got a little punchy. We would sign Joe DiMaggio, Marilyn Monroe, Roseanne Barr, Martin Luther King, and Ronald Reagan.

The orders never stopped. When one of our employees would refresh our fulfillment application that showed us the list of orders, he would say, "It's like the mail. It just keeps coming." Every once in a while he would be fulfilling an order and shout, "Jeanette Smith from Erie, Pennsylvania, you're going to Applebee's."

Every day and night, the phone would ring. All day. Day after day, after day. Twenty-hour days. Order taking. Stuffing envelopes. After our fulfillment party every night from 8 p.m. to 11:30 p.m. we would drive one hundred miles an hour to the Federal Express office at Newark Airport. Almost every night we didn't have time to label all the packages. It was common for us to be labeling the last packages in the cars on the way over. On one of the first nights we did this, we were ready to leave our office and asked who would drive. My right hand man, Randy, offered to drive. We started driving and asked him to turn on his light in the car so we could keep labeling. He said, "Oh, that light hasn't worked in years." I said, "Why did you offer to drive if you knew the light didn't work?" We continued labeling by sticking our heads out the window like overheated puppies trying to grasp for fresh air to use the light from passing streetlights to finish our labels.

When we arrived at the Federal Express office at Newark Airport each night, it was like a covert operation. The packages had to be stuffed into special bags that the Federal Express manager gave us. We had to drive our cars into the packing area and would knock on a back door of the location. The door would open and the manager would help us unload our bags. Then we would drive back and do it again the next day.

To say that it was chaos would be an understatement.

Wait, there's more. While you are filling little holes and trying to address bigger ones, and actually dealing with running your business, there is the one issue that has you looking over your shoulder every day—competition. It's like a large alien spaceship that hovers in outer space, sees everything you do, waits for you to do the hard work, and swoops in after learning from all your mistakes and does it better, faster and cheaper. The level of competition for any business is staggering. Every entrepreneur has to constantly ask herself, "Is there a competitor that is further along, better financed and ready to pounce?" In days past, that might have been confined to the competitor across the street or across town. Now you ask yourself if there is a competitor in Shanghai, Bahrain, or Mumbai that wants the same market. This doesn't just apply to larger companies. The local jewelry store used to compete with the jewelry store in the next town. Now they can be put out of business by an online jewelry store from halfway across the globe. Did any taxi driver think that they would be competing with anyone who could drive a car? Seen any Blockbuster stores lately?

Some even argue that if a business model is already out there, it is too late. In their book, *Blue Ocean Strategy*[2], professors W. Chan Kim and Renée Mauborgne argue that companies can succeed not by battling competitors, but rather by creating "blue oceans" of uncontested market space. Competition comes from everywhere in this day and age. Like the black cloud that sits over the haunted house, you have this feeling there

[2] Chan Kim, W. and Mauborgne, R. (2015) *Blue Ocean Strategy* (Harvard Business Review Press)

is someone out there with more money, more people and a better model than you have. The thought creeps into your head that you could work tirelessly and execute flawlessly and still lose.

> *I was at a restaurant at the beach one summer and a friend came up to me and said there was someone that wanted to meet me when she heard I was an entre-preneur. She introduced herself and said she was interested in my opinion of her business. She had created a product for women that was a tiny gel cushion that would be placed under the heel of a woman's shoe. It would cushion the heel and make it more comfortable to wear heels. I told her that while I was probably the least qualified person to discuss women's shoes, I thought it sounded like a great idea. I also told her that my concern was that Walmart could copy it and have it in the hands of half of America in a month.*

Imagine that. Working for years on your baby and Walmart mass pro-duces your baby in a month. Thinking about the prospect of how compe-tition can dash your dreams is overwhelming in and of itself.

One hundred hours of work and ten hours of time. Complex business issues to resolve. Competition waiting to pounce from across the street or around the globe. No guarantees that hard work and smart ideas will equal suc-cess. As entrepreneurs we are subject to a constant pressure and intensity that is hard to imagine. That is on Day One. What happens on day one hundred or two hundred or five hundred? When we started IncentOne and I was distracted, I used to think, "We are a year away from revenue. Wait, we were a year away from revenue if what we are doing works." Not exactly a comforting thought. When you add together the pressure, the tasks, the business issues, the competition, the money, the uncertainty and the risk, it doesn't feel like we have a full plate, it feels like we are spinning plates. I remember a quote from astronaut John Young, after being asked if he was nervous about making the first Space Shuttle flight in 1981:

> *"Anyone who sits on top of the largest hydrogen-oxygen-fueled system in the world, knowing they're going to light the bottom, and doesn't get a little worried, does not fully understand the situation."*

It's not that the astronauts do not appreciate the gravity of the situation. It's that they choose to have a perspective that allows them to manage through the pressure. Overwhelming is par for the course for all entrepreneurs. If you can find an entrepreneur that says, "We've got everything under control," then I have some unicorn hooves I'd like to sell you. When "overwhelmed" is the norm for entrepreneurs, why is one business able to make progress and another can't? What we need to learn is how to have the right perspective and to apply the right tools and insights when we feel overwhelmed. In the second half of the book, which directly addresses perspectives, you will gain access to detailed tips and strategies for managing the entrepreneurial experience, and perspective shifts that will empower you to overcome the feeling of being overwhelmed.

Chapter 3
Not for the Faint of Heart

Regardless of whether you face a perfect storm like IncentOne did during the 2008 financial crisis, or simply the daily challenges of starting a business, being an entrepreneur is not for the faint of heart. It's big boys and girls shit, and it will likely be the most humbling experience of your life.

First, many entrepreneurs leave stable jobs. Salary, health insurance, expense reimbursement, infrastructure—here today, gone tomorrow. When we started IncentOne, I left two great jobs: my position as a corporate attorney in New York, and the opportunity to join my family real estate business. When I left my law firm to start IncentOne the math looked like this: salary on Tuesday = $150,000. Salary on Wednesday = $0. That's financial planning.

Second, many entrepreneurs put their own money into the venture. Running a new business is hard enough but when you risk your savings, or other assets, it only adds to the pressure. But it doesn't stop there. In addition to your own money, it's common for "friends and family" to provide seed capital or a private loan. When we receive this money, without having to go through the formal process of raising capital, it seems like a blessing. When it is your own money, there is pressure. When you ask friends and family to trust you with theirs, not only does your sense of responsibility grow, your sense of what's at stake grows too—including relationships with those closest to you.

Leaving a stable job and shouldering the financial risk of a new business can create a pressure that is hard to fathom. And you may not have even started the business. Yet, big decisions must be made, and a million details completed with little or no capital, few (if any) team members, and in the face of a brutal reality: most new ventures fail within a year. Finally, you might struggle through all of that only to discover there is no market for your product or services.

But let's say you get the business up and running. What happens when you get actual customers, employees and vendors?

> *When we started IncentOne, we needed technology to administer incentive programs. At the time, it was Randy and I working around the clock. We hired a consultant who helped us source technology vendors to build our technology platform. We wanted a company that had both software development and a call center because, while our service was to be web-based, we wanted callers to be able to talk with a human if they wanted. We had very little money so we looked outside the New York/New Jersey area for inexpensive vendors. Randy was from Rhode Island so we started looking in that part of the country. We found a company in Vermont. Our main technology criterion was that the vendor build the platform from an Oracle database. We had six months to build the platform. We had countless calls and drove many times to Vermont for meetings with the vendor. We had invested two months with this vendor. After many trips and phone calls, we made the last trip to Vermont to finish the details of the contract. We asked to have one final discussion with their head of technology development. When we asked how many Oracle resources they had, the head of technology said, "Oh we don't use Oracle that much." Our jaws dropped. We had discussed Oracle from day one. They also communicated that the pricing which we had been negotiating for some time was not based on using Oracle and that the price would double if we required Oracle. After some intense discussions, we left with no vendor and a huge gap in our plan. It felt like a surprise left hook to the face.*

Just when we feel like we have things under control in one area, the shit hits the proverbial fan. We were no different. This makes sense—you don't have the capital or resources to properly manage or execute. For example, with the right resources, we would have had a primary technology vendor and a backup vendor in case something didn't work out. Nonetheless, we dusted ourselves off from our Vermont debacle and moved forward. Or so we thought.

We left the meeting with our Vermont vendor and immediately turned to alternative vendors. Randy researched some and we came across a Florida-based company that had both the technology and call center services we wanted. After a few weeks of discussions, visits and negotiations, we struck a deal. They would develop our technology infrastructure and serve as our call center. We only had a few months until our launch. Whew! Disaster averted. Or was it?

Our vendor was unique. They had been successful in developing the backbone for one of the Internet's early successes: pornography. They developed a scalable technology platform that could transition an old school business—pornography—with heavy dependence on online photos and videos and a call center to deal with customers. Given this success, their parent company established them as a separate development subsidiary to find the next big idea. They fell in love with incentives. Incentives were used in every sector of the economy and they loved the idea of bringing scalable technology to another industry that, like pornography, was going to be prevalent across the US economy.

We worked together for months and were about 70 percent done with our technology backbone when the bottom dropped out. We were thirty days from launch and I got a call from the president of our vendor. He said, "I'm not sure how to tell you this, but our parent company is shutting us down." He explained that while the pornography solution had been a success, their parent company didn't think that having a development arm was in line with their company direction. The president, who I still know to this day, told me that they fought to stay in place, and when it was clear that the entity would be disbanded, even fought to finish our project. Their parent company emphatically "said no." He also told me that this news was not public, that his team didn't even know, and he called me because he wanted me to know before his team started scrambling for jobs. I'll never forget the president putting his neck on the line to tell me about this news before he even told his team. With thirty days to go, the countdown began.

I asked the president if his team was going to lose their jobs. He said it was likely. A few of them might be offered jobs with the parent company but it was speculative at best. I asked him if I could hire the team. He thought that was a great idea. He arranged a conference call between his team and I immediately following his own meeting with them, where he'd have to break the news of their layoff. His team was unemployed for a total of about five minutes. We offered to pay them the money that would have gone to their parent company, which was far more than they were getting paid individually. Within a day the entire team had accepted. They flew to New Jersey for a week. We didn't miss a beat. We were in better shape because the team was now dedicated solely to us.

You can't make this shit up. This is the life of the entrepreneur. So what happened with the launch?

The day had come to launch our platform. The entire technology team had come back to New Jersey to manage the process. It was a success. On the last day of their trip, in the parking lot of our Carlstadt, New Jersey, office, the team's lead technologist said to me off the cuff, "Who is going to be your chief technology officer (CTO)." I said to him, half-kiddingly, "You, if you happen to know anything about incentives." He laughed and replied, "Make me an offer." Bada Bing, Bada Boom. Just like a scene from a mob movie, (which was apropos given our location in New Jersey miles and its proximity to Sopranos *territory), I walked over to my car, took out a piece of paper, jotted down a number, and handed it to him. He turned it over, added a little, passed it back to me and said, "For this we have a deal." We shook hands and I had my first CTO.*

I recently saw a twenty-something millennial wearing a t-shirt that read: "I Can't Adult." Come to your entrepreneurial venture with your helmet on. Come ready to work hard, and to struggle harder than you probably ever have. If you scare easily, or faint at the sight of blood, or get uncomfortable when everything doesn't go as planned, maybe you should think about another profession. Being an entrepreneur is one of the most rewarding things you will ever do. It is for those that dare to dream, and dream about the work. It is not, however, for the faint of heart.

Chapter 4
You Won't Get It Unless You're Concerned about Payroll

Cash is like that foot injury from years of ballet. We feel it in every step. We feel it every day and at least once a day it flares up. It clouds our judgment to the point it can be debilitating. There are many days when we say to ourselves:

- Are we going to make it?
- How long can we go on like this?
- When is my savings going to run out?
- Are we going to make payroll?
- How can we think about strategy when we can't pay the bills?
- Are we ever going to have the money it takes to bring this to life?

Unless you've been there, and been there with your money, it's hard to imagine the feeling. One of the reasons entrepreneurs get frustrated with people trying to give them advice is, if you haven't had the experience of what it feels like to be on the brink, it's difficult to imagine.

There were about ten times during the history of IncentOne that I wondered whether we would make payroll. I remember one instance when one of our healthcare customers owed us $700,000 and the thought crossed my mind to drive to Connecticut to collect the money because we were desperate. Think of how ridiculous that would have been—me walking into a national health plan like it was a local check loan operation and saying—"Hi, would you mind cutting me a check for $700,000?"

When we don't have cash, it is difficult to make good decisions, and even more difficult to make strategic decisions. When cash is the central driving factor, we make inappropriate decisions such as not paying dedicated people, pushing vendors to the brink and creating imbalances in relationships. What to do tomorrow to survive constantly clouds our judgment. This often goes too far:

> *Randy and I were looking for office space near New York City in New Jersey. The least expensive spot we saw would have been generously described as a basement. I was excited about the space because it was inexpensive and gave us what we needed. All I could think about was cash. Fortunately, Randy talked me out of it because he said if we worked in that dungeon, we would develop lung disease and that would cut into our productivity.*

He was right, but all I could see was how were we going to pay for it. There are many bad decisions I made because we didn't set up the business with the right amount of capital. Time after time I would hire people that were less qualified than what I needed for a business of our complexity. Spending another $25,000 per year for an employee seemed like a fortune at the time, but not doing it was one of the biggest mistakes I made. The lack of judgment that comes from a lack of cash can be debilitating.

Every day great ideas come across your desk. The idea might be carefully researched and presented with thoughtful analysis, but as soon as that idea requires cash, your mind immediately shuts down. It ignores all the facts that were just presented so persuasively and thinks about nothing else except, "How are we going to pay for that?" This is the case even when we know the idea is the right one, or the best path to follow. When all we can think about is cutting hotel costs at the trade show, instead of considering our three-year business goals, we have a problem. Making strategic decisions for the future instead of today's cash balance, seems absurd to the entrepreneur who left a well-paying job to pursue their vision, and now has no salary or health insurance and only $8,000 left in the company bank account—half of which is already spoken for.

People that run successful businesses understand that the answer to good strategy is not, "We don't have the cash," it is asking the question, "Does the business have enough money to take advantage of the strategic opportunities that exist in the marketplace?" Most of us entrepreneurs just think about the cash we have in the bank today.

The lack of cash most entrepreneurs face does have a silver lining. It makes you a good negotiator. After all, you have few other options:

> *The dot com world was all the rage. Companies in Silicon Valley and all over the country were popping up with crazy valuations on a daily basis. One of those companies, Netcentives, was not going after the consumer like most dot coms of the day. They were going to provide an Internet-based platform to run the big loyalty programs in the country. They approached us about being their gift card reward partner. It was good fit because we had no interest in the loyalty market. Netcentives started running some of the largest loyalty programs in the country like programs for airlines, credit card companies and banks. They had garnered a huge valuation and hired thousands of employees. Individuals in their programs earned a lot of gift cards and as their reward partner we would ship gift cards directly to the individuals. They were doing close to one million dollars in gift cards per month. As a result, at any time they might owe us north of $500,000, a huge amount for a company like ours.*

> *Like many other dot coms, their day of reckoning came. They had grown to three thousand employees and the press release came out that they were laying off a third of their staff. I got a call from their CFO assuring us that this was merely a "cost correction" and that it would result in a more rational cost structure. This is generally finance speak for "The shit is hitting the fan and we can't cut staff quick enough." I thanked him for the call, and candidly communicated that while I understood he was calling to reassure us, we had to interpret the information that they were having financial trouble. I communicated that their outstanding balance would be immediately due and until we received payment, we would suspend shipping gift cards. He said, "I don't control the accounts payable department." I pushed back and said, "I don't ship the gift cards, but I can get someone who does to stop shipping them."*

Part of this was prudent judgment on our part. Part of it was if they defaulted, it would be a huge blow to our cash flow. Lack of cash makes you bold. Without cash you don't have options.

"More money, more problems" was an incredible insight from Notorious B.I.G., but anybody who believes that has not stared at their computer on a Saturday night and realized there's a good chance you're not going to make payroll next Friday. Sure, when there's money in the bank, the issues do grow. More hands in the pot. Dealing with investors and private equity. Employees want more salary. Even so, that does not compare with not being able to buy health insurance or a cup of coffee. More money, more problems is bullshit.

The lack of adequate cash is one of the most debilitating and stressful parts of being an entrepreneur. When we are worried about whether we can afford the gas to drive the car, it is hard to determine the most efficient driving route. Recognizing the impact this has on you does not put cash in the bank today, but it certainly allows you to think more clearly about your decisions. Thoughts like, "how are we going to pay for this?" can be coupled with, "if we *did* have unlimited cash, would this be a priority or a good idea?" In either case, recognizing the impact that cash, or the lack thereof, can have, is an important step to changing your perspective.

Chapter 5
Your Balloon Is Full

We've all been at a birthday party where one of the guests barely touches a balloon and it pops. It explodes because the balloon is full. That is the way we entrepreneurs feel all the time.

Entrepreneurs are "full balloons." The pressures and activities of early stage businesses ventures constantly add air to the balloon. What also inflates the balloon is that we experience every detail of every aspect of the business on a daily, visceral level. We have hundreds of conversations with others and thousands with ourselves about every part of the business. I used to say to my dear assistant Carol at IncentOne, "I start my day with 95 percent of my brain full." Part of that was certainly due to the limited grey matter of my gender, but most of it was the overwhelming number of things on my plate. I told her that unless something was important, anything she told me had an excellent chance of bouncing off my skull.

When your balloon is full, you need a place for the air to go or the balloon will pop. When given an opportunity to do so, we will eagerly take the chance to let air out of the balloon. Ask an entrepreneur how the business is going, and you will be lucky if you escape before hearing thirty minutes of details about the business. Ask us about the price of our product, and you are likely to get theories of products, philosophies of products, and the long sordid history of the product.

Have you seen entrepreneurs participate in a demo day or *Shark Tank* where they have five to ten minutes to present their business? After their presentation, they take questions from the judges. Notice how many entrepreneurs can wait until the judge finishes asking the questions before they answer. Not many. Ask an entrepreneur, "What's the weather for the weekend?" To your surprise, the answer won't have anything to do with Doppler radar or the chance of rain, but rather the latest jewelry design and the details of why the rhinestones aren't fitting properly.

Try asking a simple question like, "What is the price for the product?" The answer, which should be something like "$25,000 per year," sounds something like this:

> *"We considered several pricing models and bounced back and forth between an advertising model and a subscription model. One of our investors was a big proponent of a subscription model because of the valuation implications. When we ran our financial model, which still needs a lot of work, our assumptions were based on customer growth of 20 percent and customer attrition of 5 percent over the first two years. Keep in mind that we have not done a cost of goods sold on the product so we are making educated guesses. We won't be able to do that until we get our finance team set which we hope to do as part of our Series A raise."*

So what was the price of the product?

Full balloons make us give silly answers to simple questions:

> **Questioner:** *"Do you prefer Michael or Mike?"*

> **Entrepreneur:** *"When I was growing up no one called me Mike or Michael—I always had a nickname. It eventually landed on "Derm" but along the way it was dermatologist, which is interesting because I thought nicknames were supposed to be shorter than the actual name. Anyway, Derm was a win because other nicknames were words that rhymed with "Derm"—use your imagination. Anyway, Mike never worked because there was a commercial when I was a kid when they were trying to get a family to try a new cereal and they had a son—Mikey—that would eat anything. The commercial said, "Give it to Mikey. Mikey likes everything." I think if people called me Mike it would be too much like being a kid. After all Michael is one of the most popular names in the nation every year. It is always in the top ten. Truth be told, my Jewish name is "Moshe" which is Moses. I guess Michael or Mike is better than Moses.*

Questioner: *I'm sorry, which do you prefer Michael or Mike?*

What are the consequences of all this trapped air that is dying to escape?

- **We create confusion by not giving simple answers.** It's critical to create clarity and simplicity in a chaotic and unstructured environment. When we give simple responses, we make things easy. Unfortunately, simple answers do not release air from the balloon. When we give long complicated answers to simple questions, those we interact with lack the clarity they need to help the business.
- **We mismanage time.** Issues that come across our desks that don't need attention are tended to anyway. This distracts us from our priorities. We tend to jump in and out of email, text messages and other communications throughout the day to help release air from the balloon. Needless to say this is counterproductive.
- **We drain our teams and others with whom we do business.** During the early days of IncentOne when my parents, board members, or friends asked me a question, I'm sure they dreaded the long, complex, nuanced and boring answer. I am also sure that when my three-year-old niece asked, "How are you, Muck?" (what she used to call me), she quickly regretted it. More than likely, I responded with an explanation of why we thought biometric screening partners would be a good strategic fit for incentives. When we "brain dump" this behavior weighs on our resources, and can make interactions with employees, vendors, clients, and investors awkward and inefficient.
- **We react inappropriately to issues.** With all the tension, we tend to react quickly, emotionally, haphazardly, aggressively or inappropriately. For example, we had spent long hours building a financial model for our health rewards business. The model was based on the total number of lives on our platform, which would interact with assumptions to drive five-year income statements, balance sheets and cash flow statements. It was all based on the number of lives. We asked our Board and advisors for feedback on the model by a certain date. One of our Board members provided feedback a week after we asked for feedback. My reaction should have been, "This is a perspective we need to consider." My reaction was to let

air out of the balloon with a long and somewhat nasty explanation of our process and that while we appreciated the feedback, we asked for feedback on the model a week ago. The response I gave was more a reflection of the air in my balloon than anything else.

- **We struggle to make deliberate decisions.** We react instead of act. Careful analysis, weighing multiple opinions, and balancing risk often don't get the attention they deserve in the decision-making process—especially when letting the air out quickly provides immediate relief.

- **We negatively impact the investment process.** Investors want to understand a business quickly and want the leader to briefly and efficiently communicate the value of that business. When we unload unnecessarily detailed and circular answers, it lets some air out, but the lack of brevity often conveys a missing clarity about our own business.

- **We impact our team's perception of our leadership skills.** When team members see calm, thoughtful, reasoned and deliberate action, they feel secure and reassured. When they hear conversations that are reactive, rambling and unfocused, and lead to unclear decision-making, they start to feel like the ship could sink at any time.

I recently got this phone call from an entrepreneur. I said "What's up?" and she said

> *"I'm fine. I'm fine. I'm fine. I'm fine. I'm fine. I'm fine. I'm fine. I'm fine. I'm fine. I'm fine. I'm fine. I'm fine. I'm fine. I'm fine. I'm fine. I'm fine. I'm fine."*

Recognizing that our mind is full almost all of the time is key. Once we understand that, we can catch ourselves letting out too much air, and take the time to be more thoughtful and deliberate.

Chapter 6
There's Nothing Like Your First...

I remember so many "firsts" like they were yesterday. I certainly remember our first order more vividly than my first kiss. These firsts are not just events in time, but a culmination of countless hours of work, ranges of emotions, overcoming doubts, and plowing through the challenges. Firsts are validating—customers want our stuff, investors believe in our vision, employees want to be a part of something. Without firsts, we might just be another entrepreneur toiling in his or her garage or basement. I wonder if Steve Jobs wondered if he would ever have his first.

I'll never forget our first big customer win.

We knew that winning the Deloitte account would be a long shot. We were barely a year old and few knew about us. During our meetings Deloitte had about twenty people in the room and another twenty from countries around the world. We had a total of twenty employees at the time. Meetings were held in Wilton, Connecticut. Meetings, conferences calls, presentations, more conference calls—all to win their internal multimillion-dollar reward program. Deloitte informed us that their selection process had narrowed the field from ten down to three. They would not tell us the competition. Their decision was to come on the Monday after the Fourth of July holiday and, once made, the solution would have to be in place by January 1.

Deloitte would be a great client, and having the opportunity to run their reward programs would send signals to the marketplace. They did not tell us when we would be informed. We sat on the edge of our seats all day. Three o'clock came and went and I went downstairs to the little coffee shop in our office building. Of course when I was gone they called and left a message and said, "Hi, it is Donna, the procurement manager from Deloitte; please give me a call back when you get a chance." I returned to my desk and called her back. She started by thanking us for participating in a grueling selection process and telling me that it was a very difficult decision. The one thought that kept running through my head is that these are the things that a company says to the vendors they don't select. She paused and said, "This was actually quite an easy decision for us. It was clear to us that you were the best vendor in the market. If you are okay with that, we would like to enter into negotiations to finalize a contract for you to be our worldwide reward and incentive vendor." We were on the map.

I remember it like it was yesterday. All those memories of leaving a law firm, working in a barren office, working twenty hours a day—they all came back. And it all seemed worth it.

There were so many firsts that made the effort and pain seem miniscule in comparison:

- The launch of our first technology platform
- The hiring of our first chief technology officer
- The closing of our first investor
- The first press coverage we got
- The first time we saw our logo in print
- The first check we received from a customer.

When we achieve, it seems as if the loneliest days never happened. The best days not only unlock boundless energy, they tap into our spirit. So many people say every day, "I wish I were working on something that I was passionate about." When you have great days, or even a few great hours, you experience passion and pleasure while pressure and pain take a backseat for a bit.

What did you feel when you won your first customer? Did you feel a chill up and down your spine? Did you call your spouse? Did you scream something ridiculous like, "You can't handle the truth?" Achievement in the face of challenges—financial, emotional and visceral—inspires, enlightens, and energizes. That energy can last for days, weeks or months. The challenges of yesterday no longer seem like insurmountable obstacles. They seem like mere speed bumps along an inevitable path of success.

As John F. Kennedy said, "We chose to go to the moon...not because it is easy, but because it is hard."

So what is wrong with this perspective? Nothing. Absolutely nothing. In fact, what often happens to entrepreneurs is that we fail to appreciate the accomplishment because there is so much to do. Soak in the victories— even the small ones and especially the first ones. When you do, you start to see a balance between all of the challenges and the successes. The famous tennis player Jimmy Connors once said, "I hate losing more than I like winning." We tend to move on past accomplishments too quickly. We all know that this rollercoaster will climb to great heights and take us through a nauseating series of gravity-defying loops. And if we don't stop to enjoy the view, the challenges can overwhelm us. Of course you have more to do. Of course you need twenty more customers like the first one. Of course one press mention does not make a marketing plan. But they all sure feel good. And they should.

Chapter 7
Your EKG Looks Like a Rollercoaster

Every day has its highs and lows. It's very possible to win a big sale and have your head of technology quit in the same day.

Like pregnant moms, when entrepreneurs start a business, they go through three trimesters:

- **First Trimester.** The excitement is palpable. You wake up energized and focused. The challenges you face are there, and you know there will be more, but success seems inevitable. You think it is just a matter of time before you get there. Troubles are just speed bumps along the way.
- **Second Trimester.** You feel fat and ugly. Reality has set in. You're not moving as fast as you'd like. You haven't lost passion for your vision, but you are realizing just how much hard work and sacrifice it is going to take. Like the pregnant mom, you wish you could drink, and that sometimes getting out of bed wasn't so difficult.
- **Third Trimester.** You're excited and scared. Now it's about balancing the anticipation of giving birth to your child with the fear of being a new parent, of the unknown.

Here's another way to think about this: a day in the life of the entrepreneur is like a boxing match. Win or lose, you get hit in the face a lot. Each time you take a step forward, you get energized and at almost the same time, you are exposed to new challenges. It is not uncommon that in the same month, day, week or hour to experience all of the following:

- Win a deal. Lose a deal.
- Hire an employee. Lose an employee.

- Great investor meeting. Terrible investor meeting.
- Prototype looks perfect. Packaging is terrible.
- Marketing person is great. Marketing materials stink.
- Customer wants to use you more, but wants a new account manager.
- Your presentation was well received, but had two typos.
- A customer decided to do a pilot, but your main contact is leaving the company.
- A customer wants an onsite presentation with your whole team. The trip will cost you $10,000.
- Your new office space is perfect and your monthly cost went up $8,000.
- You got a check from a customer for $25,000 and a bill from a vendor for $26,000.
- Your investor wants to put in all the money, but only at a valuation that lacks enough zeros.
- Your husband is happy to see you, even if it is for an hour a day.
- You discovered bourbon and bourbon discovered you.

This is your day:

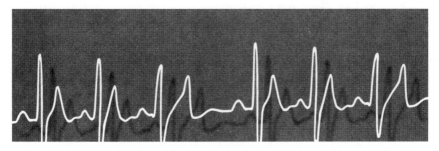

Your day is a series of ups and down. When you don't have the resources or the capital you need, there are often more losses than wins. When you do get wins, they are energizing and reinforcing, but they always seem to raise other issues. I remember when we won our first big customer:

> *We were high-fiving in the parking lot. We had won the health incentive business of a large national health plan and just signed the contract at their offices. It was a two-year process and winning a national health plan would likely ripple throughout the health community. The ride from Connecticut down Route 95*

back to New York City was packed with traffic. Who cared at this point? The team was on cloud nine. Then it hit me. Did we have the resources to support them? What if this one health plan went poorly? Were the account people we had sophisticated enough to manage a complex health plan? Would we end up customizing our technology and throwing our technology road map off course?

Celebrate your wins. There are many times during the meeting, the hour, the day, the week, and the month that you will get punched in the face. At early stages, wins tend to be small and incremental. Nonetheless, celebrate them. At the same time, be prepared that when the wins come, they naturally raise issues and concerns. It's like this: just as you are relieved and happy your teenage daughter is all grown up, you realize she is about to start dating.

Every day you work to make progress and get wins. When your organization still doesn't have its foundation, these wins expose the shortcomings of your organization in terms of capital, resources, technology, operations and people. For example:

- **You get your first big order.** Your customer wants twenty of your jewelry design? How are you going to buy all the materials for the jewelry?
- **You win your first big customer.** Who is going to handle the day-to-day relationship? How are we going to manage a customer with 50,000 employees when we have ten?
- **You sign your first office lease.** Gone are the days of working in your "workspace." Whew! Who's paying for all this?
- **You finally have employees who are helping advance the business.** You now have a payroll, greater risk and a financial obligation you must cover each month.
- **You hire your first big management team member.** Current employees feel slighted. You pay more attention to someone who has been with the business two weeks than you do to the people that have toiled with the business since the start.
- **You close your first big investment.** Employees want more reasonable salary. Vendors want more commitments. You need

to manage your board and investors. Is your CFO experienced in talking to investors and creating the financial reporting they need?
- **You release your first version of your software.** Your competitors now see it. Your customers are banging on it.

We work every day to make progress. When we make progress, we expose weaknesses. The questions that come with the evolution of a business are natural. The immaturity of your business gets exposed. While the business challenges that arise can be difficult, the greater challenge is what this dynamic does to our psyche and the psyche of our organization if we don't handle it properly.

In our daily entrepreneurial life, the gas in our tank moves from full to nearly empty. When that gas level is a slow, constant movement toward empty, our faith in the business wanes. Fortunately, that is not how it normally works. It doesn't look like a slow decline in our gas level. Rather, it looks more like an EKG—up and down. The gas is being alternately choked and throttled. Our tank seems to sputter out and then all of a sudden you get an employee to join the company you didn't think you could afford. We win that customer. We launch a product. We close an investment. We bring on a team member. We get our company in the paper. When any of these things happen, we hit the gas. The daily grind, with all the pressures and risks that come with being an entrepreneur, seems worth it when you get those wins and helps you deal with growing sophistication of both your company and the challenges success brings.

If your organization is fortunate enough to be making progress, your business gets more complex and more challenges arise. Be thankful for that. It means you are succeeding. However, this exposes deficiencies—often ones that are personal. We may have been perfectly well equipped to manage a few people in startup mode, but do we have the skills to manage and lead a larger company?

This is particularly true when it comes to investors. Securing an investment should be a day of celebration. It is a validation. Whether it is $10,000 from a family friend or $10 million from a private equity firm, it represents progress. At the same time, investors present challenges. If you secure an investment, especially from a sophisticated venture or private equity firm, the dynamic changes. We need to have the experience and resources to manage a Board and investors.

With wins and successes come concerns and doubts. Imagine someone who won a $50 million lottery saying, "Sure but I must pay twenty million in taxes." As an old law school professor used to say, "Taxable income is better than no income." Some say, "Be careful what you wish for." Don't ever forget how lucky we are to be making progress.

Your perspective on this is critical. Even though there is pleasure and pain at almost every turn, you must move the organization onward and upward. You must celebrate wins. You must appreciate being challenged because it means you are successful enough to be growing. Investors, customers and employees are attentive to your venture because you are bringing something that is valuable to them. Don't forget that. Make sure you and your team take time to remember the alternative: sitting in your bedroom writing business plans no one cares enough about to create problems for you.

Chapter 8
What Is a Holiday?

The month of August and the holiday period around Christmas and Hanukkah are supposed to be time for relaxation, downtime with family and friends, and a little fun in the sun or snow. It's a time for the world to relax before the start of the new year or to enjoy the final days of summer. Sounds great. These are all normal and well-deserved periods for downtime. In fact, many countries take the whole month of August off and can't be found in December. During these months, the US workforce works more than most countries globally, but even they take time to unwind. But not everyone is excited about taking time off. In fact, entrepreneurs hate Christmas and August.

Entrepreneurs aren't thinking about their vacation plans, they're trying to cope with an additional load of stress. Investment deals slow down. Customer deals die. Employees go on vacation. Vendors take a break. Family obligations and events proliferate. Kids are out of school and need extra attention. For the entrepreneur, these months can be torture. They may be scrambling to close a deal by the end of the year. They may be working hard to prepare the company for the upcoming year. The entrepreneur's calendar is put on hold until the rest of the normal world comes back from recess.

As entrepreneurs, we have enough stress throughout the year trying to win customers, bring on employees, raise money and sign deals with vendors. We may have enjoyed, or even taken advantage of these breaks in our "past lives," but once you become an entrepreneur we can't understand how this ever made sense. We also don't understand how the world could be so insensitive to our efforts by taking time off when we need to get shit done. We console ourselves by feeling lucky we don't live in France, where many can't be found for the better part of the summer. We say to ourselves, "How can a whole country can take off weeks at a time?"

It used to bother me to no end that customers, vendors, employees and investors would say, "Well, it will be hard to get something done in August," or "We'll have to wait until the new year because December really slows down." Don't they understand what we are going through? Don't they understand how important it is to keep the ball moving forward?

Come to think of it. This doesn't only apply to August and holiday time. How often do friends and colleagues ask, "Are you off for Columbus Day?" Or Martin Luther King Jr. Day? Or Presidents' Day? Or Good Friday? No disrespect to history or religion and the reasons we celebrate these holidays, but do people not get it? There are no days off. Even when the rest of the world has the day off, we do not say to ourselves, "No one is working anyway so it would be a good day to take a break." Quite the contrary. We say to ourselves (because no one else is around), "This is the perfect time to get work done. The phone won't be ringing and there will be no distractions."

If in the interest of celebrating the entrepreneur, the country declared an "Entrepreneur Day" and offices throughout the world were closed, none of us would take it off. Even if they made it a federal crime to work on Entrepreneurs' Day, we would sneak around with disguises like a beach bum sitting on the beach with our laptops covered in palm fronds or hidden in the shadow of a low umbrella while we work on the new sales plan.

I used to say that my next venture would be to extend the twenty-four-hour day. If we can't do that, we could try to eliminate all holidays—or at least Christmas and August—and get back to work. After all, we have a business to build! It's difficult to let this perspective go—working harder than everyone else is part of our job, part of who we are. But think of a little time off as accomplishing something else: a change in perspective and environment can boost your creativity and energy, present a new solution to that unsolvable problem you've been battling, and give you the chance to do some very important work—strengthening relationships with the people who are supporting you the most.

Chapter 9
Advice That Drives You Crazy

Friends, family and colleagues see our struggle and offer help in the form of advice, pearls of wisdom or a good drinking partner. What emerges is a common set of messages that are meant to be helpful, but instead make our blood boil. We say to ourselves, "They just don't get it":

- **You get to make your own hours, write off expenses and take vacations.** That's right. We get to make our own hours—all twenty-four of them. We get to write off expenses but the money for expenses comes from our pocket. We can take vacation whenever we want—but we aren't getting paid for it, and we haven't used the word "vacation" in years.
- **Take a few days off.** It's the best advice we'll never take. Do they understand all that needs to be done? Do they think the marketing materials will write themselves? It is incomprehensible that we could take a day, much less a few days, away from the business. To the entrepreneur, it is the equivalent of abandoning a baby in the middle of Central Park on a Saturday afternoon in August.
- **Even if it doesn't work, you've already been a success.** Boy this pisses us off. This is what people say to losers. "Even if you lose, you are winners in my book." In the mind of the entrepreneur, success has to be measured by an event or an achievement. This could be positive cash flow, going public, or selling the company. It can be many things, but it is not the fact that we have moved through the process. When people say this, it makes us feel like they are preparing us for an impending failure.
- **It should be easy to raise money.** This is only spoken by people who have never raised money. It's never easy to raise money. It is hard even for a well-established business. For a company in the

69

early stages, it is even harder. Combine new business models and unproven concepts with anything involving lawyers, and "easy" is hardly the first thing that comes to mind. PowerPoint presentations, financial models, talking points, consistency with team members, valuation of a new business in a new market—let me know what part of that is easy.

- **Go slow to go fast.** This is great advice but who has time to go slow. If we slow down, the competition will pass us by.
- **If it is killing you, you should quit.** Easy for you to say that. It's not your oxygen. You haven't invested your heart and soul into this.

Most of these suggestions make sense, yet they can still drive you crazy. Yes, this advice may be coming from non-entrepreneurs, but it is coming from people who care about you. The fact that they have a different perspective, and some distance from your experience, can actually be to your benefit. We *should* be saying to ourselves, "I really ought to listen to some of these people who care about me and who want me to be successful." Instead, we often think, the next time someone says to me, "take a few days off" I am going to kill them and as long as the jury includes a few entrepreneurs, I will never get convicted. Even if you do escape with impunity, I hope you'll remember that if you are getting advice, it usually means someone cares enough to worry about you and genuinely wants to help. As I (eventually) discovered, their suggestions might even hold some truth.

Chapter 10
Your Dysfunctional Family

We've all sat at our family Thanksgiving table and said to ourselves, "I wonder if every family is this dysfunctional?" If it's any consolation, there are dysfunctional families that come with every entrepreneurial venture. Our early teams will almost always be dysfunctional. The criteria for early team members is not what needs the business has, but who is crazy enough to leave their job, or has enough free time to spend on your idea. It is like the movie *The Replacements* in which NFL players go on strike and a motley group of new players, led by Keanu Reeves as their quarterback, are brought in as replacements. There is a convict, two drug dealers, bouncers from a night club, a Fijian wrestler, a chain-smoking placekicker, a deaf wide receiver and a psychotic police officer. Welcome to your dysfunctional family.

If someone gave us enough money, we would recruit based on need, and at a level of experience commensurate with the size of our vision. Unfortunately, that almost never happens in the early stages of businesses. Our initial team members are often those whose level of experience is below what is needed. They may work their asses off, but there will be gaps.

Our teams are going to have missing skills and experience. Our teams may also have members who are not used to the pace or the pressure. These may be ongoing skill gaps for our team or just a lot of blips along the way. Our team had plenty:

Did your CTO quit again?
I will be forever indebted to my first CTO. We are still friends to this day. He runs his own business now and one of the nicest things he ever said to me was, "Now that I run my own business, I find myself thinking some of the things you

used to say when I told you that you were crazy." Back then, however, it was different. He used to quit once per week.

To say the market was new would be an understatement. When we started selling our incentives model, we tried to include the most important features for a platform serving this market, but we were not sure. My CTO had come from a traditional software development world with a waterfall development process and software releases. You didn't "kind of" release software. You scoped it, built it, tested it and released it. Once you did, right or wrong, it did what it did. I would regularly come back from meetings with Fortune 500 companies with a high level of interest in our solution but each had requests for different features and functionalities. When I communicated this to my CTO, he would give me analogies like, "When Crest launches a new toothpaste, do you think you get to go back to the store and say, 'Can I get more fluoride?' When Microsoft releases an operating system, do you think you get to call them and say, 'Can you move the Edit menu to the left?'"

We had this debate over and over. Of course we wanted to get to the point that the market was defined (hopefully by us) and our software releases were strong enough to not require major change. But the market was very new, and we needed to be flexible and willing to adjust to market feedback. These debates were no different than any other early stage company delivering a new product into the marketplace. Unfortunately, these debates not only became fruitless but they led to him quitting once a week. I would talk him off the ledge, and then we would do it again the next week. I used to date a girl on and off at that time and when he called in the middle of a date, she said, "Did your head of IT quit again?"

This is experienced?

We had prepared for an important meeting with Blue Cross Blue Shield of Florida for several weeks. We were finalists for their request for proposal (RFP) to be their reward vendor. I traveled to Jacksonville, Florida, with one of our salespeople who had spent fifteen years selling to health plans like Blue Cross Blue Shield of Florida. One of the things we wanted to know in preparation for meetings like this was who were the major employers that a health insurer like Blue Cross Blue Shield of Florida insured. This was standard operating procedure for any meeting with a large health plan and would be so for any experienced health plan salesperson. We met in their lobby for him to brief me on details. I asked him who their major employers were and he looked at me like I had three heads. I got angry that this simple request had not been fulfilled by an experienced salesman. As my blood started to boil, I think the entrepreneurial gods were mocking me because when I looked over his shoulder in their head-quarters lobby there was a big wall with the logos of all the major companies that they insured. I told him not to ever show up for a meeting without doing his homework, and then to "Turn around."

Knock-off?

We hired a Chicago marketing firm to help us with our branding. They came recommended through a colleague. We were launching our brand to help Fortune 500 companies with their corporate reward programs. One of the pieces of our engagement contract was that they would create our logo for that market. We settled on an interlocking "C" and "R" surrounded by a circle of lettering that repeated "Corporate Rewards."

A week after we had settled on that design, I was walking down the street in New York City. For all of us that are entrepreneurs, when you walk down the street, you rarely take in the scenery. You have a million things on your mind and rarely notice what is going on around you. I walked past a New York Health and Racquet Club with their logo and name on a large awning and happened to look at it. I was stopped in my tracks. The logo that our marketing firm had proposed was a carbon copy of the New York Health and Racquet Club logo, even down to the font.

The "C" and "R" that represented "Club" and "Racquet" were the "C" and "R" that represented "Corporate" and "Rewards." No jury would have con-victed me.

Who is CEO?

We were attending a healthcare conference at Coronado Island off the coast of San Diego. Our booth at the trade show portion of the event was across from a company whose booth was run by an attractive woman in a doctor's coat. She turned out to be their Chief Medical Officer. During the event, a few of our sales guys would flirt with her. As usual, I was running around talking to customers, prospects and potential partners and was rarely at our booth. Two nights later, I had finished dinner and walked to the bar and ordered a bourbon. The Chief

73

Medical Officer was sitting at the bar with a colleague of hers that I happened to know. She mentioned she saw me across the aisle at the show at the IncentOne booth. She asked what I did for the company and I told her that I had founded it and was CEO. She said, "That's strange, because one of your guys came over to talk to me and told me he was founder and CEO." After validating my credentials, I told her we should screw with my sales guy the next day and I would come over when they were talking and ask him what it was like to found a company.

What will you do for me?

When we had about twenty people on payroll, we hired a developer to help us with internal systems. He understood business concepts and could quickly translate them into technology we needed. His job had him rolling out frequent enhancements to our internal systems. He interacted with our client services team that consisted of five women ages twenty-five to thirty-five. Every time he would deploy something, he would train them and when they thanked him he would say, "I would do anything for you. What are you willing to do for me?" I guess this went on for several months before anyone brought it to my attention.

Accept it. Our teams are going to be dysfunctional—not the least of which is you.

I was driving to a meeting with ADP with one of our female sales reps and we were late. I've been known to put the pedal to the metal and we were buzzing through the streets of New Jersey trying to get to there on time. I was also talking on my phone. In the midst of casual conversation with her, she said, "Can you pull over for a second?" She opened the door, stuck her head out the window and threw up. She leaned back in the car with a look of horror on her face. This is when the ridiculousness of an entrepreneurial mind takes over. My first reaction should have been, "Oh my god are you okay? Can I get you something to drink?" I looked at her for two seconds and said, "Are you okay?" She said, "I'll be fine." I slammed the car into drive and started speeding back toward ADP. We ran into the building and she went into the bathroom and collected herself. I remember thinking, "I wonder if we are going to blow this meeting because she smells like puke." What I should have been thinking is that I should have planned better, left more time, driven slower and been more sensitive to the person in my car.

Despite our appreciation for their commitment and dedication, the people we consider our early stage team—whether they are employees, consultants, or vendors—may not have the skills or qualifications to advance our business. This is not to say that they can't be effective members of the team. For us to remain sane, and not be frustrated every day, we must accept that the team is dysfunctional—it just happens to be *our* dysfunctional team. Try not to drive yourself, or them, crazy along the way.

Chapter 11
My Baby Won't Be Ugly

Eighteenth-century French historian and philosopher Voltaire was known for his wit and coined many quotable phrases including: "Perfect is the enemy of good." Even though we have more tasks than time, we lose perspective and become perfectionists about every detail. It's like new parents who used to scoff at other moms and dads for buying their children designer clothes and baby gear, and fussing over everything—only to find themselves doing the same. When it is our baby, we want everything to be perfect.

> When we started IncentOne, the head of our marketing firm had a connection at a radio station and got us inexpensive radio spots because a sponsor backed out at the last minute. We had little budget so the voice-over was done by someone at our marketing firm. He went to the studio to create the radio spot. They completed the spot and it was surprisingly good given how much time was spent on it. I listened to it and approved it. Then something struck me. How would people remember it? Then I remembered the sound that came at the end of every Intel commercial. What if we created a similar sound? My agency guy had already left the studio. I made him go back and add a sound to the end. It took almost as long to add the sound as it did to do the ad. This was my baby and my baby was going to have the perfect rattle.

Talk about a loss of perspective. A company like IncentOne who few had heard of, that had a few random spots on the radio we got nearly free. What was I thinking? We lose perspective when it is our baby. Unfortunately, this is not a once in a while lapse. It happens every day.

This is debilitating enough when it is just you. But it can be disastrous when you develop a disdain for anyone who works with you who doesn't bring the same intensity to every detail. Regardless of whether the people we are working with have slept or been paid a market salary, we expect perfection at every step of the process. We develop a mania around perfection and attention to detail that is misplaced.

> *During IncentOne's early days, we had to convince national retailers that integrating their gift cards into our incentive program was a powerful opportunity for them. To do that, we created a slick marketing package that highlighted the values of being part of our service. The package mimicked the blue and gold color scheme of our logo. In those days, when marketing packages needed to be printed in large quantities, they were run on huge presses like the ones on Varick Street in New York City we were using. The first run of the materials seemed a bit off in the colors and my brother and I asked the company to adjust them. We asked them to adjust the colors over and over. I am sure a few times they never changed the color and just represented the same ones to us to make us stop. At one point, they even told us that it depended on the lighting, even though the lighting had not changed. Every time we asked for a change, we went cross the street to the twenty-four-hour diner and Dan and I debated the color palate. I think we hold the record for the most food eaten between midnight and 6 a.m. By the end of the night, which was around 6 a.m., the production guys in the print shop were trying to figure out how to kill my brother and I and hide the bodies in the vats of paint. No jury would have convicted them. Needless to say, we had lost perspective.*

Watson-Watt, who developed early warning radar in Britain to counter the rapid growth of the German Luftwaffe, propounded a "cult of the imperfect," which he stated as "Give them the third best to go on with; the second best comes too late, the best never comes."[3] No one wants an ugly baby. While attention to detail is a good thing, taking it too far can stifle progress, and doesn't make the baby any better looking.

---

[3] Brown, L. (1999) *Technical and Military Imperatives: A Radar History of World War 2* (CRC Press), p. 64.

Chapter 12
Differentiated Means It Hasn't Been Done Before

The reason your new venture has merit is the also the reason it's difficult to build, and what makes the entrepreneur's task so challenging. The more differentiated a business opportunity is compared with the status quo, the more it is undefined. While some may see undefined as an opportunity, others will interpret undefined as "There is no evidence that a market exists" or "If this is such a good idea, why hasn't it been done before?" On the other hand, if your business is like other existing businesses, others may respond positively to valid proof points and at the same time remain skeptical about whether your product or service is just different enough to be viable.

While differentiation bodes well for the success of a business, it also (by definition) means that the business is unproven. Some of the most novel concepts—Starbucks, Amazon, Uber—were the most difficult to develop. At their inception, many of these brand new industries were considered not much more than technological voodoo or witchcraft. Even our business—rewards for healthy behavior—was nonexistent in the mid-2000s. Every industry other than healthcare—airlines, credit cards, banks, hotels and retailers—rewarded consumers for the behaviors that they wanted to drive. In fact, healthcare was perhaps the only industry trying to drive consumer behavior that didn't use rewards. At the time, if you remember from my story, customers in the health industry said, "We are never going to pay people to do the things that they should be doing to be healthy." Today, rewards in healthcare are everywhere and whenever there is an effort to drive behavior in healthcare, rewards are always a part of the solution. Differentiation is a necessity but it also comes with the reality of charting a new frontier.

Think of all the novel concepts that would not exist today had the entre-preneurs behind them been deterred by this reality and not plowed ahead. Can you imagine:

- Buying all of your books in a bookstore?
- Renting all of your movies from a store?
- Waiting for a yellow cab for a ride?
- Buying coffee from your local grocery store?

You will walk into two investor meetings an hour apart. One investor will say, "Your concept is not different enough from what is out there." An hour later, another investor will say, "Your concept is too different from what the market has seen and there is no proof it will work." This is the nature of the beast. One of the hardest things to do is to strike the balance between sticking to a firm plan for your business, and adjusting as you get feedback. You must understand *why* your solution is or is not different enough—not just that it is or is not different enough. Is it the market you are going after? Is it the business model? Is it your pricing model? While it is always important to listen to feedback from customers, investors and others, expect conflicting responses and don't let them sway you from your goal. Get used to being *damned if you do and damned if you don't*. No one said entrepreneurism is fair.

Plenty of people have said, however, that there are no new solutions out there. With so many entrepreneurs, so much capital and so much new technology, it is almost impossible to do something that stands out. Yet, on a daily basis we are amazed by another new business springing to life and we say to ourselves, "Why didn't I think of that?" Remember, if you are doing something different, you are going to have to deal with the fact that it has not been done before—but when has that ever stopped us? After all, we made it to the moon.

PART TWO

Perspectives

Introduction

You have an amazing opportunity to transform your business. Reading about the "Four Ps" should have been a wakeup call that helped you recognize how the perspectives you develop can stunt your progress. You now have a greater recognition of the nature of the beast—of the unique and extraordinary planet called Entrepreneurship. It is supplying your oxygen, but also clouding your vision.

In this section, you'll move from recognition and acknowledgment into action with a detailed set of Perspectives to help you shift mind-sets, thinking patterns, and habitual behaviors you acquired under the influence of the ***Four Ps (Pressure, Passion, Pleasure and Pain)***. Again, the goal is not simply to help you survive or muscle through by tightening your bootstraps—you'll do that anyway. The goal is to help you acquire the ability to change your perspectives from those that stifle your progress to those that will enable you to thrive in a tough but exhilarating environment.

The Perspectives that follow cover many areas—running the business, leading the company, differentiating your product or service, staying focused, managing your time, prioritizing, people, investors, creating efficiency, negotiation and your sanity. While we could certainly write a book on each of these individual areas we cover, we have selected a set of foundational Perspectives that most entrepreneurs must address. As you move through these chapters, you'll learn the critical shifts in perspectives you need to make, and acquire the tools and insights to make these shifts in real time, for you and your business. The guidance offered here comes directly from my own experience at IncentOne, as I've mentioned before, but it also draws on hundreds of hours coaching, mentoring, consulting—and drinking bourbon with fellow entrepreneurs.

We've established that your personal life and professional life are intimately intertwined. It's hard to even think of them as separate. Have you ever been out on a date with someone that you begin to lose interest in personally but once you learn what they do, and how it might help your business, you all of a sudden want to share another drink with them? For that reason, some of the Perspectives are geared toward you, and some are geared toward the business. But we all know that in the end, they are really one and the same.

The Perspectives are designed for businesses of all sizes. They are designed not only for the entrepreneur, but also for their teams and friends, family and other people who support them. When your team, family, and friends better understand these Perspectives, you will find yourself saying, "They just don't understand" less often. Have them take a look and take some time to share, discuss, argue, or laugh about what it's like to be in your shoes. As they understand better, they will be a valuable resource, as opposed to a source of frustration.

Remember, not every Perspective will apply directly to you. For example, you may not have any investors and aren't looking for them but the perspective change and strategies presented, which help entrepreneurs gain the trust of investors, present themselves confidently, and communicate their business assets and goals clearly and efficiently, are critical to anyone who has ventured into entrepreneurship. So I would encourage you to read each Perspective in its entirety. You may be launching a major tech startup, a local Amway group, or running a one-woman show on Etsy. You may be entering the sharing economy of Uber, Lyft, Airbnb, Task-Rabbit and others. You might be a "lifer" in the freelance media world. Regardless of what "kind" of entrepreneur you are or the size of your business, these Perspectives will help unleash the potential of entrepreneurs of all stripes.

The Foundational Perspective

The Perspectives that follow all play an important role in unlocking your entrepreneurial greatness. The first and foundational perspective is particularly important, and perhaps the most challenging one you will encounter: **The Brutal Truth: It's Not Them. It's You**. Let me begin by saying—first and foremost, you have to accept a harsh reality. Despite the fact that you are the only one that cries, loses sleep, invests his money and truly sacrifices, many of the poor perspectives you have developed and the shortcomings of your business are your fault. You heard me. Pretty unfair—but true.

You are going to have to accept this. It is easy to blame the circumstance—no money, wrong people, too much to do, lack of time. The reality is that you must look at yourself, and accept the brutal truth that you must change what you are doing. I made the same mistakes, and while we are under the influence of the Four Ps, it is easy to do. You need to separate yourself just enough to see how your actions, feelings, health, sanity, sleep (or lack thereof) directly affect your business—both for better and worse. It was not until I looked in the mirror, and discovered the need to change, that I really broke through. You must take responsibility for your own feelings and actions and their effects. This may be the hardest Perspective of all, but you can't move forward without it. It is essential for your progress.

Being an entrepreneur is a life-altering experience. I've made many mistakes but also stumbled onto numerous insights. The most profound discovery I have made is this: your Perspective changes everything. It determines what we see, how we see it, how we solve it, and whether we succeed or fail. I truly believe that the difference between success and failure is your perspective. As an entrepreneur shouldering the weight of a new venture, that realization can feel like an enormous responsibility or burden, but it also embodies everything you need to succeed. You need look no further than yourself. There is incredible freedom and empowerment in that discovery.

Are you ready?

PERSPECTIVE #1: THE BRUTAL TRUTH— THE TRUTH THAT SETS YOU FREE

What I am about to tell you is as unfair as it gets. If your company is struggling, or not progressing as quickly as you would like, whose responsibility is it? Yours. You work the hardest. You care the most. You put in the most hours. You are the most dedicated. You are the most passionate.

You put in the money, strain your personal life (if you have one), deplete your finances (if you still have any), strain your relationships (if you have any), cry, drink, don't sleep, don't date and spend every waking moment on the business. Is anyone else willing to make the sacrifices you make every day? No one said being an entrepreneur was fair.

Early stage companies need to accomplish a lot with limited resources, and this can lead to organizational chaos. This chaos is characterized by common problems:

- Too much to do
- Lack of financial resources
- Lack of human resources
- Lack of established priorities
- Lack of clarity with internal and external constituents
- Emotional and reactive decision-making
- Frustration with existing resources
- Reactive day-to-day management.

The definition of *chaos* is:

1. "Complete confusion and disorder: a state in which behavior and events are not controlled by anything."
2. "The state of the universe before there was any order."

Starting a business is like driving in New York City. All taxi drivers swerve from lane to lane. Taxi drivers with passengers drive fast and erratically (to get their passengers to the destination as quickly as possible). Taxi drivers without passengers drive slow and erratically (to be in a position to pounce on an available fare). Now add the constant wail of sirens from police cars and fire engines and the inevitable garbage truck. Crazy. Imagine if you took away all structures of order—lights, lane lines, speed limits and traffic signs—and threw in jaywalking pedestrians, a couple of skateboarders, a dog walker with an unwieldy pack of hounds and a good oil slick. It becomes a game of Frogger on steroids. Chaos!

Now you know what it feels like to be an entrepreneur—if you didn't already. Without the appropriate tools to manage, entrepreneurship is a like driving in New York City without any lane lines, speed limits, stop signs or traffic signals.

Sounds about right, doesn't it? You probably believe the cause of this chaos is that your business is unique or faces a unique set of obstacles, you're developing a new market, or you don't have the resources to operate like a more established business. It is common for us entrepreneurs to blame the chaos on others, the lack of money, the lack of resources, the lack of a defined market, or one of the many other excuses for not fixing the chaos. When you believe passionately in your idea and chaos ensues, it's easy to blame everyone and everything else. After all, you think you are doing the right thing. This may be ego, insecurity or over-confidence in your ability. The natural reaction is, "How dare you challenge me? Without me, this business would be nothing." We all say, "It's not me, it's you." Customers don't understand. Employees don't work hard enough. Employees aren't talented enough. Vendors don't perform. Advisors aren't committed. Investors haven't seen something like this before. Friends don't care as much as we do. Family can't understand what it feels like to walk a mile in our shoes. There may be some truth in each of these complaints, but what is important is why you are getting negative results in the first place.

Want to know the cause? You may be ticking off a hundred reasons in your head as you read this sentence, but ultimately, there is only one, and that is You. Why? In addition to being the most dedicated, you are also the most emotional, the most tired, the most reactive, the most frustrated, the most _____ (insert what you are feeling right now). You get the picture.

The pressure, emotion and intensity of being the entrepreneur is often accompanied by a lack of perspective, and a failure to apply to your own behavior a set of basic principles that will prevent a chaotic business environment. The same drive, self-assurance, and creativity that enable you to create a vision, are often the same characteristics that prevent you from bringing that vision to life.

Isn't that a relief? You thought you had hundreds of problems to fix and you only have one—You. At first glance, this may seem like a huge slap in the face. On the contrary, it is the realization that will unlock your potential and create new skills and opportunities to move your business forward.

Don't look at this as fixing something that is wrong with *you*. It's natural that you are in over your head. Being an entrepreneur is a humbling experience. Your friends say to you, "You get to be your own boss." You think to yourself, "It must be cool to make the donuts at Dunkin Donuts." Accepting that your company is flailing because of you is a tough pill to swallow, but once you take the medicine, and put the job of "learner" on your resume, you can do great things. Accept this truth, and it will set you free.

With that in mind:

Why is there too much to do? Because you need to set the priorities and align your resources to those priorities.

Why do you lack financial resources? Because you need to raise enough money to keep the company properly funded.

Why do you lack human resources? Because you need to raise the capital necessary to build the right team.

Why do you not have established priorities? Because you need to understand how a company that has to do everything, can still prioritize one thing over another.

Why do internal and external constituents lack clarity? Because you need to avoid communicating in a way that is confusing and verbose.

Why are you frustrated with existing resources? Because you need to understand their role, establish their job, and align their skills to the appropriate tasks.

Why do you make reactive and emotional decisions? Because you are reactive and emotional.

Why is the management of your company reactive? Because you need to build a plan.

It's tough, but once you realize the power of changing your perspective, the challenge becomes exciting, and the responsibility becomes liberating and not so different from the satisfaction you feel being responsible for inventing a great idea or trendsetting product.

Great Leaders Are Great Learners

There's a powerful book called *Leading at the Speed of Growth: Journey from Entrepreneur to CEO*[4] by Katherine Catlin and Jana Matthews. It addresses the long-standing belief that entrepreneurs who start a business do not possess the skills to help a business grow. It challenges this notion and argues that entrepreneurs have enormous talent that simply needs to be applied differently at various stages of the business. In other words, the unique talents entrepreneurs possess—drive, passion, creativity, the stomach for risk and uncertainty—can't remain static or be applied with cookie cutter repetition to distinct and evolving stages of your business. No matter how much talent you bring to the table, to achieve success you can't remain satisfied with your own status quo. Your skills and perspective must be adaptable and flexible as you grow your business. This had a profound impact on me. It was as though someone said to me, "If you are as good

---

[4] Catlin, K. and Matthews, J. (2001) *Leading at the Speed of Growth: Journey from Entrepreneur to CEO* (Hungry Minds/John Wiley).

as you think you are, you need to change." Initially, this really challenged me—though I'm sure it was my ego talking.

Then I realized how much a change in my own perspective could help my company. What an opportunity. I also didn't realize was how empowering it was to be challenged, to acknowledge shortcomings and to grow. Change in the midst of calm seas is one thing. Change in the middle of a hurricane is another. If you can come out the other side, imagine what that would feel like? When someone asks you, "How is your company going?" you probably answer with a description that includes the word *crazy* or *chaotic* or *nutty* or something unprintable. Wouldn't it be something to be able to say, "We have our shit together"? When my company was acquired, one of the sales team members of the company that acquired us said to me, "Every time I interact with your business or your people, you are organized, structured and efficient." What a message to be able to share with your team. It still makes me proud.

There is a famous line in the John Lennon song "Borrowed Time"—"The more I see the less I know." Once you accept this, it is easier to see that your perspective is both the cause of your company's problems, and its best opportunity for success! Embrace the gift of growth and learning. You may tap potential you didn't know you had.

Bottom line—it is *your* job to fix these issues. You are the leader, and must manage the chaos, whether it is the pressure, passion, pleasure or pain, a lack of experience or a lack of perspective doesn't matter. It is your job to fix it. But while you're doing hard work, remember that *you* are the greatest tool you have to transform chaos into order and to bring your vision to life—and to see it grow successfully.

SECTION 1:

RUNNING YOUR BUSINESS INSTEAD OF IT RUNNING YOU

Introduction

Every business has more to do than it has time and resources. For the entrepreneur, this reality is exacerbated by the fact that it may only be you—or a few of you—doing everything. When you start a business, or even when your business starts to grow, you always feel like you are running on a treadmill that keeps going faster and further out of control.

Even though you were not formally trained as one, you've become a juggler. The difference is that the juggler gets to pick which objects he or she wants to juggle—and how many of those objects he or she wants to juggle. Not so for the entrepreneur. The entrepreneur starts out most days juggling at least three things. Then someone from the crowd throws a fourth knife into the mix. Then another. Even if you are organized enough to know what enough to go into the day knowing what you want to juggle that day, when the business starts throwing new knives at your head, it's hard not to drop one of the knives while you're dodging the next one.

How many entrepreneurs would describe themselves as "in control" each day? Without an active effort on your part to control the business, it will control you. When this happens, it is even more difficult to focus on priorities, and keep your team moving forward and your business evolving. If you think chaos is just the "nature of the beast" or proof of you bootstrapping your business from the ground up, you're engaged in a perspective that can do a lot of damage to the foundation and progress of your business.

The Perspectives in this section will help you take control of your business by challenging many of the conventional (and flawed) beliefs entrepreneurs hold:

- "My challenges are unique to my business."
- "I can't prioritize because everything has to get done now!"
- "I have to do everything myself."
- "Process and procedure are for IBM."

It will take commitment on your part to overcome these and the other flawed perspectives many entrepreneurs hold. Once you do, you will see that changing your perspective about how you run the business will allow you to take control and feel like you get to set what, when, how and why you decide to juggle.

Chapter 1
Your Problems Are the Same
As Every Entrepreneur's

What We Feel: *No one can understand our challenges because they are so unique to your business. People say they have been through our problems but what we are doing is unique. What the hell do they know about my business?*

Your problems are not unique. The first time someone told me this I thought they were insane. But it's true. Every startup shares the same problems. First and foremost, we all suffer from the issues endemic to new and developing businesses—lack of capital, lack of qualified team members and a lack of time to execute across all parts of the company. You are faced with creating the building blocks of a business, building a business model, gaining market acceptance, creating operational capacity and doing so with strained or nonexistent resources. In addition, we all have to build the functional areas of a company—sales, marketing, finance, operations, technology, human resources and the list goes on. This is true whether you are opening a pizza store, launching a clothing line, building an online store or selling jewelry. These same problems exist in virtually every newly launched venture.

Suggest to entrepreneurs that their dilemmas aren't unique and they are offended. Their first reaction is that you are insulting their business. They don't want to hear that their business is "like every other business." Instead they'll interject: "Our product has never been created." After all, they believe they are doing something special. If they have this perspective, they also believe that the problems they are experiencing are unique. They think that others don't understand the issues they are experiencing.

95

They confuse their passion for their business with the notion that these problems exist for virtually all entrepreneurs.

The key task for entrepreneurs is to separate their vision, product, or service, and the entrepreneurial experience of building it. In other words, you may have the most innovative new idea in the world, but the day-to-day challenges of bringing it to life are shared by many others. Additionally, the basic business principles you need to succeed, while sometimes applied differently in traditional companies, still remain basic road signs for everyone.

Why does this distinction matter? Imagining your struggle is incomparable with anyone else's is a damaging perspective for a number of reasons. When entrepreneurs believe their issues are unique, they shun support and direction from experienced businesspeople offering valuable advice. They believe they are operating under a different set of parameters. As a result, they isolate themselves and hunker down in their perspective. It's a bunker mentality. As more people try to help, they feel more isolated and hunker down further.

What keeps running through the entrepreneur's head is, "Unless you are here every day, you can't understand our issues." It's true—people who have only worked in larger organizations or have not put their money, career and lifestyle on the line may not understand what the entrepreneur goes through on a daily basis. Yet, responding with a bunker mentality or defensive attitude prevents you from taking advantage of established tools, business principles, guidance from others and supportive mentorship. More importantly, your belief that no one understands your specific situation isolates both you and your team, not only from the knowledge of the larger business world, but of those in the entrepreneurial community.

Your Change in Perspective

As we have noted, the reality is, in fact, quite the contrary. There are many experienced entrepreneurs who have "been there, done that" and can lend valuable support. Other entrepreneurs also understand the natural insecurities that can take over, especially in the early chaos of launching your business. We are not insulting the uniqueness of your business. No one is questioning the dedication it takes. However, when it comes to accessing much needed resources and direction, defending your "difference" is not only incorrect, it is not in the best interest of your company. Here are some strategies to shift this perspective:

- **Create Building Blocks.** Accepting this perspective allows you to start implementing basic business tools that help all businesses run well. Setting priorities, creating process, making communications efficient—basic building blocks that advance all businesses and will help do so for yours.
- **Advice from Others.** You will start to see advice in a different light. You may still be thinking: "That advice makes sense for most businesses, but our problems are unique, different." But if you stop and take notice, you'll see far more similarity than difference in the problems you're facing. Take advantage of that shared knowledge. It enables targeted support and advice from other entrepreneurs who have been in the same trenches as you. You welcome advice and can take advantage of the wisdom of others.
- **Benefit from Experience**. Others have been exactly where you are now, and where you will be in two weeks, worried about an upcoming investor meeting. Let their experience help you prep for the unknowns you're facing. It will save you valuable time and energy that you can put toward keeping your product and vision unique rather than wasting time defending your experience as unique.
- **No More Bunker Mentality.** When you understand that you are part of a community with shared experiences, it changes your point of view from a bunker mentality to, "How can I interact with and learn from others who have these experiences?" It helps you get you out of your bunker and into the light.

Your vision is unique. Your problems are not. Once you accept this, you have a much better chance of bringing that vision to life with a strong business foundation under it.

Chapter 2
Everything Can't Be at
The Top of the List

What We Feel*: There is no way I can prioritize. I can't turn my attention to one thing or another because it all has to be done and all has to be done now.*

Most entrepreneurs are in a state of chaos. Everything needs to be done at the same time. Financing, people, product, customers, business models, technology, operations, finance, cash and the list goes on. Entrepreneurs are in a constant state of hole plugging because you lack financial and human resources. That is the *nature of the beast*. But what you *can* change is, how you manage the overlapping tasks that are demanding to get done. Setting priorities is the first and foundational step. But ask entrepreneurs to "set priorities" and they will scoff at you. "We can't set priorities. We have to do everything to build the business." This perspective, while understandable, prevents entrepreneurs from making meaningful progress. It becomes Whack-a-Mole, with you taking a hammer to the next issue that raises its ugly head instead of implementing a focused strategy.

For example, if you asked an entrepreneur, what would you do if your pizza business could make ten slices of pizza and you had three customers that each wanted four slices? They would likely say, "We either need to prioritize which customers get pizza" or "We would need to be creative to expand our capacity by two slices." Ask an entrepreneur about their business, "Given the scarce resources of the company, how are you going to prioritize?" Their answer often is, "How can we prioritize when we have to do everything at the same time?"

Think about it. Is there any business that doesn't have more to do than they have time? Doesn't every business need to set priorities and figure out what has to come first, second and third or what can't be done? Would anyone in corporate America have a job if they said, "We need to do everything." Entrepreneurs fail to see this. This is a recipe for failure. Especially with limited resources, you must decide the organization's top priorities and align what resources you have to processes those priorities. Does that mean that you neglect the rest of the business? Of course not. It does mean, however, that when you set priorities, you treat them distinctly and with more focus and energy than other activities. When you set something as a priority, you create an operating structure (such as the one outlined below) that brings the organization's focus and accountability to that priority. In addition, these top priorities require your best thought and the inputs and expertise from various constituents. It is not only about setting priorities, but building the processes that bring the focus, substance, expertise and accountability of your organization to these priorities.

Your Change in Perspective

How do you accomplish this?

Communicate to the Organization. Communicate to all team members and constituents that you are going to develop a process to set the priorities for the company. This process might include employees, consultants, advisors and, if you have one, your Board. This communication should go something like:

> *It is an exciting time for the company. We continue to make progress on our vision. In order to operate more efficiently and leverage the resources of the company most effectively we will be running a process to set the top priorities for the company. We will be seeking your input and when concluded, we will have a finite set of priorities and will align our resources to those priorities. We expect this process to be completed by February 1. Once we set those priorities, we will communicate them with all members of the team. Stay tuned.*

Set Your Priorities. Lay out the top five priorities of the company. Start with everything in your head—this will lead to a list of at least twenty. Pare it down to five. This will (and should be) a difficult exercise. You need to make tough decisions. This may require debate among the team. It's important to remember that you are not ignoring other activities in the company (we will get to that later). You are setting a lower focus for those other activities, not cancelling them out.

The result must be no more than five priorities. Priorities might include:

- Getting the company properly funded by raising $1 million
- Delivering our beta product
- Hiring our sales leader
- Expanding our customer base.

If possible, go through this process with team members. Involve advisors. If you have a Board, use a formal process with them. Working through the process with your team helps build consensus around your selected priorities as well as the items that don't make the list.

Be realistic about your priorities and consider all resources at your disposal. Don't think only of employees. Include consultants, interns and friends. If you have a small resource pool, set your priorities as smaller tasks you can realistically accomplish. If you have more resources, the priorities can be larger strategic or longer-term items. The items that end up on this list should be awarded the special attention and focus of the organization. Once set, operationalize these priorities.

Set a Goal for Each Priority. Establish a goal and/or schedule for each priority. Goals for the priorities listed above might be:

Priority	Goal
Raise $1 million	Close by January 1
Delivery our beta product	Launch by March 31
Hire our sales leader	Hire by December 31
Expand our customer base	Close 5 customers by April 30

These goals must be specific, measurable and visible throughout the company. The organization should know, live and breathe these goals.

Assign an Owner for Each Priority. The owner will be the one accountable for achieving the goal. A few guidelines. First, each priority can only have one owner. This ensures a single point of accountability. Second, the owner does not act alone. It is their job to lead, but they will be supported by others. Third, you can only own one priority. Don't worry, you will be a contributing team member for other priorities. Fourth, owners do not have to be employees of the company. But when you look for an owner for each priority, be realistic—consider their relationship with and time commitment to the company. For example, someone has agreed to be an advisor, but you also need to determine, could they own a project? If a friend has agreed to help, is it more appropriate for them to create your marketing plan or look at some marketing resumes?

We would assign owners to the priorities we set above:

Priority	Goal	Owner
Raise $1 million	January 1	Amanda Smith
Delivery our beta product	March 31	Bob Jones
Hire our sales leader	December 31	Kelly James
Expand our customer base	Close 5 customers by April 30	Michael Wilson

You will need multiple owners, but be realistic about who can own what. I know what you are thinking. "My team members are not experienced enough to own these things." That may be true. This is a leap you are going to have to take. You can't own everything and if you try to, you are setting up your organization for failure. You will have to assign people that might be under qualified and then use the process defined below to help them. Challenge them, tell them that they will make mistakes, and let them know you will be there to help. This is hard to do. Even though you know that you could manage this better, let your resources own things.

When you settle on an owner, two things must happen. They must "own" it—meaning that they will be the one driving the initiative and reporting on its progress. You can't make someone an owner and then take over. Second, "owners" must be committed. You can't have individuals "own" something only to come back later and say their outside life got in the way. Have candid dialogues with team members about what they are interested in, whether they are willing to own a priority and what that means. For example, it might be realistic for an advisor to run your interview process for a new head of sales, but unlikely that an advisor would be in a position to own delivering your beta product. I know what you are thinking, "How is this going to work if I am not involved?" If you are not an owner, you are still involved. You will likely be part of every priority, might have the final say on decisions and your input will be needed.

Assign Resources to Each Priority. This will require your creativity. Look to your entire resource pool. This not only includes employees and consultants, but it might include advisors, interns, even family members or friends. Assign resources to each priority:

Priority	Goal	Owner	Resources
Raise $1 million	January 1	Joe Smith	John A. Jim C.
Delivery beta product	March 31	Sue Jones	Adam B. Randy W.
Hire sales leader	December 31	Jennifer James	Chris B. Phil T.
Expand customer base	5 customers by April 30	Michael Wilson	Patty B. Mary P.

Since you are asking people to simply contribute to a set of tasks (as opposed to own), you should be able to garner support from your network of resources.

The Owner Sets Tasks for Resources. The owner should set the tasks for each team member assigned to their priority. The owner must take into account the role of the resource. A paid employee could be asked to do more than an unpaid advisor. For example, for your "Hire a sales leader" priority, you could ask each team member to interview three candidates over the week.

Set a Process to Monitor the Priority. Set a schedule and method for staying on track. Without regular assessment, items that start out as priorities lose focus and fade back into the chaos. When everyone knows that the "Fundraising Meeting" will always occur on Thursday at 5 p.m., it sets the tone for accountability and follow-through. The owner of the priority should be responsible for setting up this process and for reporting on the priority. This should include a regular status meeting (weekly or biweekly) with the following elements:

- Set agenda.
- Designate someone to take notes.
- Report from the owner on progress toward goal and measurement tools.
- Report from team members on their assigned tasks.
- Discussion of issues and obstacles that must be addressed to reach the goal.

While the purpose of the meeting is designed to create accountability and to keep your team on track, it is also designed to bring your team's best thinking to the priorities of the business. By having resources focus on a particular issue, in a constructive and regularly scheduled collaboration, you bring the full force of your team's creativity to bear on solving difficult problems.

Set Up Each Priority in an Online Project Management Tool. Use an online project management tool (e.g., Basecamp, Bitrix24) and set up each priority as a separate "project" with each owner and resource assigned as "users" in that project. Many of these tools are free or have minimal costs. These tools allow you to add to each project with the following:

- the specific project
- the specific tasks
- the resources assigned to the task
- the date each task is due.

Use the tool to post meeting agendas, and all weekly reports and updates. This allows everyone to use one tool, access it from anywhere, and find all relevant documents, conversations and information about the topic. Team members should use this tool for all activities related to the priority, including task status and any accompanying notes. Your team should understand that "If something doesn't happen in this tool, it didn't happen."

Publicly Announce Priorities, Owners and Goals. One of the toughest parts of an early stage company is holding people accountable. Setting the priorities of the company is only the first step in the process. Achieving the goals of each priority is the rub. Once you have completed the steps above, send a communication to all constituents that includes the following:

Priority	Goal	Owner	Resources
Raise $1 million	January 1	Joe Smith	John A. Jim C.
Delivery beta product	March 31	Sue Jones	Adam B. Randy W.
Hire sales leader	December 31	Jennifer James	Chris B. Phil T.
Expand customer base	5 customers by April 30	Michael Wilson	Patty B. Mary P.

You accomplish several goals with this communication. First, you align the business and its team members to the organization's priorities. If you involve team members in setting priorities, you create alignment that you may not have had before. Second, you create accountability. Owners know they are responsible to a larger group. In smaller companies, owners often don't actually "own" or take responsibility for their assigned priorities, and, regardless of your business size and number of resources, making the expectation of ownership public enhances accountability. Third, it demonstrates the organization's movement to a more disciplined management structure. You change your "chaos" to a more structured approach. Finally, it demonstrates your leadership. It's easy to keep doing what you did yesterday. It takes leadership to challenge your organization, to help them make tough decisions, to align priorities with people and drive accountability.

Meanwhile...

What happens to the tasks that didn't make your first priority list? You cannot ignore them. Secondary priorities don't require the same level of process as top priorities, but you can apply some of the same techniques. Set a regular meeting. Use the online project management tool. For example, you might hold a weekly meeting to address all client issues. One meeting. Set agenda. Same topics. Same team.

By setting your top priorities, and creating a process for executing them, you eliminate wasted effort and unnecessary communication, reassessment, and conflict. Setting priorities is the first step to managing what's most important to you and your business. You can continue to react to the chaos or make a move to control it. Holes are going to appear in the dam from time to time, and if you manage what's most important, you'll know which holes stop the most water. You won't be rushing to plug all the holes with every finger and toe you have. You might actually start to feel like you are running your company instead of it running you.

Chapter 3
Doing Everything Isn't Dedication—
It's Bad Leadership

What We Feel: *You know you need to delegate, but you are not sure anyone can do it the way you can. When I give things to others, it comes back with pieces missing or poorly done. If I read one more PowerPoint with a spelling error, I'm going to lose it. It will take me longer to train someone than to do it myself.*

Most entrepreneurs feel that they have to do everything. They feel that they are the only ones who know exactly how to get things done. It is a telltale sign of bad leadership. Of course you know more about your business than anyone. You live and breathe it. You dream about a better way to deliver your product. In the beginning, every activity probably could be done more effectively by you. You probably also feel that only you will provide the necessary attention to detail. This may all be true, especially in the early stages of your business. If you are lucky enough to have a team, you say to yourself, "It will take me much longer to teach someone to do this than to do it myself." This starts with one issue, but then becomes the mantra for all issues. This perspective can stunt the growth of your business for years.

It is one thing to acknowledge this feeling and understand that it is impossible for a business to be successful with this mentality. It is another thing entirely to actually *believe* you must do everything. Too often the entrepreneur's passion and desire for perfection outweighs reason. You may be thinking, "With the team I have right now, I know that all of this can't run by me, but until I get more experienced team members, I have to do it all." This perspective is concerning but is at least starting to move in the right direction. Unfortunately, many entrepreneurs hold a much more

106

damaging perspective. They believe there is no one in the galaxy other than themselves who knows or cares enough to get the job done right. I once had an entrepreneur say to me, "I'm not sure there is anyone who can do this stuff." My response was "How about Carly Fiorina? Would she do?"

Don't get me wrong, when you have inexperienced resources on your team, you get frustrated. Sometimes they can't act on simple issues. Other times they will not meet your expectations. Other times they will do well on the substance of an issue but not bring the attention to detail you expect. How often have you said to yourself "I can't believe that they didn't even proofread the PowerPoint." There are times when you start to pass a task to a team member and stop yourself and do it yourself. There are other times when you pass along a task, it comes back unsatisfactory and you say to yourself, "I will never do that again."

If you looked at a friend's business, and they said to you, "There is no one else that can do these things and when I give it to others they don't do it with the quality I expect," your first reaction would be that they are destined for failure. It is hard to see this so frankly in your own business.

This flawed perspective can have many negative implications:

- **Your business will not grow**. You become the bottleneck. It is impossible for a business to gain any momentum when everything waits for you. You see your passion, dedication and attention to detail as a huge plus. Others see it as detrimental to the growth of the business.
- **Employees, investors and customers will question your leadership.** When sophisticated individuals hear "I'm the only one that can do this," they question your ability to lead the company. At early stages of the business, many people you are interacting with are putting you in one of two buckets:
   - Passionate entrepreneur that can't ultimately lead the business.
   - Entrepreneur that understands how businesses grow.
- When you say, "I'm the only one that can do these things," people put you in the first category. It is not that they don't appreciate your

passion—it is one of the reasons they want to work with your company. However, these individuals are getting involved with your business because of the potential for growth. When they hear this perspective, investors think, "How are we going to get someone that can run the business going forward?" Employees think, "We won't grow if he needs to have his hand in everything." Customers will not see your passion. They will see you as a single point of failure: "What happens if he gets hit by a bus? Does that mean I am left out in the cold?"

- **It will undermine your ability to engage employees.** Senior employees will question whether your management style will give them the authority and accountability to execute, or will they be micromanaged instead. Senior employees don't want to work in a company that looks like a "solar system"—where you are the sun and everything revolves around you. They want to join a team with a chain of command that allows them to naturally execute in their area of expertise.

- **Your productivity will suffer.** Junior employees will become less productive as they wait for you to weigh in. When you do weigh in, you will likely change what has been done. While an edit may be in order, returning their work with 99 percent of the content in your pen, is discouraging and invalidates both the employee and the mentorship process. If you don't allow them to make mistakes and learn, they will never grow and improve.

- **Your business will have significant risk.** While early stage entrepreneurs are almost always indispensable, once you are fortunate enough to have customers, employees, and investors, you have to minimize this risk. What would happen to your employees if you got hit by a bus? What would happen to the money your family invested? What would happen to your investors? Would your customers continue to do business with your company? When everything revolves around you, you create risk for your constituents that they must weigh when doing business with your company. Would customers purchase an Apple product if they thought that when the world tragically lost Steve Jobs their products would no longer work?

When you do too much, you are setting your company up for failure. Regardless of why, if you operate this way, it will stunt your business for a long time. You need to get your organization to the point that resources other than you can operate with efficiency and up to your expectations. At that point, you will be convinced that not everything has to be done by you.

Your Change in Perspective

How do you shift this perspective to a belief that you can have others take on significantly more than they do today? Try the following:

- **Recognize That This Will Not Happen Unless You Drive It.** You must make a concerted effort to manage your company to the point where others can do the jobs you need done. If you don't make a commitment to this, everything will continue to be on your to-do list.
- **Understand That Wanting Quality and Creating Scalability Can Coexist.** Entrepreneurs invest so much in their venture and sometimes believe that no one else on the planet will nurture their baby like they will. That is commendable. My brother runs a property management business and has always felt that no one could provide the personal property management service that he could:

When I was a business student at Bucknell, my mind was constantly thinking about the type of business I could start. I was home with my family for Thanksgiving in the fall of my freshman year. At all family occasions, religious or not, my Mom would make her famous Rugelach. Her secret recipe (yes, my next business is to commercialize her Rugelach) is to die for. It is impossible not to eat a dozen at a time. It is rare that you can get ten Jewish people to agree on anything. At my family functions, the only thing that everyone agrees upon is that my mom's Rugelach is indescribable.

I tasted one at Thanksgiving and started asking questions. What are the ingredients? How much do you need for a batch? How many does a batch produce?

What is the cost of the ingredients for a batch? What do people pay for a dozen? My Mom answered the questions and then said, "You have to make them by hand." I said, "Oh, I understand that you make them by hand now, but if we commercialized them we wouldn't need to." She said, "Yes you do. If you don't they won't be the same." I said, "Mom, Entenmanns' doesn't have one hundred ladies sitting in a kitchen baking doughnuts and crumb cakes. They use machinery." She said, "You can't do that. It won't taste the same." While I have to admit that the thought crossed my mind of putting one hundred Jewish grandmothers in a bakery and cranking Rugelach out day after day, the idea was ridiculous. Two things crossed my mind—that I appreciated my Mom's commitment to quality and there is no chance a business like that would grow beyond our holiday dinner table.

- **Understand the Risks.** Understanding the risks of this mis-aligned perspective should be enough to change your point of view. After all, if someone described a business strategy as "having the potential to stunt your business's growth for years," you would immediately change it. The same is true of this perspective.
- **Accept The Fact That You're Part of the Problem.** You also have to accept the harsh reality that your own lack of managerial experience is a likely cause of this issue. Managers everywhere are tempted to dip their hands in every issue. It is not until they teach their teams to "fish" that they operate more efficiently. The same is true of the entrepreneur, but for some reason it seems almost to be a badge of honor—as opposed to a management flaw—for the leader to take on everything.
- **Focusing on Non-Critical Items Demonstrates a Lack of Leadership.** With the limited time and bandwidth most entrepreneurs have, it's important to focus your attention on, and to preserve your energy for, priorities. When you allow yourself to spend time on non-critical items, you begin a domino effect that harms your entire organization. Imagine saying to your employees, "I can't pay you anymore because I didn't focus on financing for the last three months because I had to proofread the PowerPoint."
- **Be Clear about Expectations.** Clearly communicate your expectations about substance, attention to detail and everything that is important to you.

- **Teach.** You know more than anyone about your business. Without imparting some of this knowledge to others, employees can't take over functions. In no time, you've created the very situation that you are trying to avoid—you doing everything. When you teach, don't do it five minutes before something is due or you will simply take on the task yourself. Schedule time each week that is dedicated to teaching. You are not "allowing" people to take on more, you are "enabling" them to do so.
- **Have Employees Work as Teams.** When two or more employees work together, they have the opportunity to not only improve each other's work, but to learn more effectively. If your employees work as teams, you will have fewer individuals to train on distinct tasks and your mentorship will become more efficient.
- **Expose Employees to Issues Outside Their Core Areas.** Let employees sit in on meetings, conference calls and dialogues that expose them to the various issues of your company. This helps employees get a context for the different tasks and prerogatives of your company.
- **Let People Make Mistakes.** If you want things off your desk, you are going to have to accept some errors in the process. Let your team know that you expect this as part of the learning process.
- **Be Honest about Your Own Ego.** Ask yourself, do I really believe that I am the only one that can do this, or is that my ego talking? I am concerned that others might do it better? Am I concerned that I will lose control?

If you are able to shift your perspective, and enable others to do more, the benefits will be exponential. More focus on the right things. More engaged employees. More people that can bring their ideas to the resolution of an issue. The ability to apply your talent to areas that need it. The ability to contribute your knowledge to an area without having to own everything. As we noted above, this does not happen on its own—you must drive it. As soon as you see some success in this area, you will think to yourself, "Letting go goes a long way."

Chapter 4
Know What Inning You're In

What We Feel*: The market needs your solution now. You can't understand why it is taking so long to get investors, win customers or attract employees. Doesn't everyone see what you see?*

R. Buckminster Fuller, architect and inventor, once said:

> *"I just invent, then I wait until Man comes around to needing what I've invented."*[5]

Wouldn't that be great? See the future, invent, and watch them come. What a pure, insightful, and powerful perspective. Also a great way to run out of energy and money.

Have you ever looked down the strip in Las Vegas and seen your hotel and decided it was not too far to walk? The backdrop of the strip creates an optical illusion. As you walk, you realize how far away it is. Had you known, you would have prepared differently.

As entrepreneurs, we believe our solution is unique. Otherwise, we would not leave the stability and sanity of the real world to enter this parallel universe. Once we make the leap, we are convinced that our idea is unique, necessary and the missing solution in an underserved market. Our perspective is, "I'm surprised that the market isn't clamoring for my solution now! Once we get it out there, we will be off to the races." While this perspective can be exciting and invigorating (there's that passion taking over again), it can also create misalignment of people, financial resources and expectations.

---

[5] Buckminster Fuller, R. (1981) *Critical Path* (St. Martin's Griffin).

Uniqueness is both a blessing and a curse. When an idea or product is unique, it is new to the market. This may be what makes it sell, but it is also what makes the market slow to comprehend and adopt your innovation. So, one of the perspectives we must develop is the ability to clearly judge how ready the market is for your solution. Put another way, if you have a nine-inning baseball game, you must know what inning you are in so you know how to align your resources. If you believe you are in the ninth inning, you would bring in your closer to end the game. If you are actually in the second inning, you have used the wrong pitcher at the wrong time. It would be like putting on your wedding dress at 9 a.m. for a 5 p.m. wedding. Seems like a good idea at the time, but by 3 p.m. you'd be crying for your jeans and t-shirt.

Understanding what inning you are in is critical to:

- establishing the right pace for your company
- setting expectations for your team and other constituents
- aligning capital and other resources.

For example, knowing how long it will take for the market to accept your idea is critical to aligning the early employees of the company. Communicating that you are six months away from revenue in a market that really requires eighteen months sets bad expectations for your team, vendors, and especially, investors. Six months in, there will be disappointment from all sides. For example, employees will get frustrated and worn out when you pass the six-month mark and you can't offer the raise your promised them for sweating the hard, early months.

This is also important when it comes to investment capital. The amount of capital you need for market viability, and the point in time that you raise it, are largely based on what inning you are in:

At IncentOne, in the mid-2000s, it seemed like a no-brainer that health organizations would adopt incentives for healthy behavior. After all, every major consumer industry did, and the cost savings was clear. Get ten more pregnant women who were not following their prenatal care to follow it, and the health industry would save $1 million. We said, "You mean if we gave ten women $1,000 each and *they followed their care, the system would save $990,000." What we failed to realize was how old school the health industry was. They already thought they had incentives in the form of co-pays in health plan designs. Because we thought we were in the fifth inning when we were in the second inning, we misaligned our capital needs and underestimated how long it would take to get to market. Today, people say, "You guys were way ahead of your time." In entrepreneur speak, that means two things: that it was visionary, but you should have recognized the inning you were in and aligned capital needs accordingly.*

There are many factors that go into this determination: the nature of the industry, established players, competitive solutions, pricing models, market influences, nature of the disruption, and the list goes on.

A good friend spent his career in the claims world of the insurance business. He started as a lawyer and moved into the internal processes used by insurance companies to manage insurance claims, including settlements and law suits. He worked for a company that bought several other insurance companies. What he found was that the claims process was manual, which led to many inefficiencies, a lack of reporting, an inability to spot claims trends and the use of high-priced lawyers to perform claims functions that could have been done at a lower cost. For example, lawyers were being used to perform basic claims reviews and file reports instead of administrative personnel. To solve this issue, he worked with some internal developers to build an "audit portal" that put all claims activities in a single place. It allowed for reporting, insights and the assignment of tasks to appropriate resources. The solution delivered efficiency and saved time and money.

Several years later, he started an entrepreneurial venture to bring the audit portal to market. Virtually all insurance companies managed the claims process the same way his old company did prior to his efforts. He built out a prototype and took it to market. No-brainer, right? It turns out that the insurance industry was as old school as it gets. Bucking the trend and moving to a more technology-driven solution would have been a leap. Also, the same people he was selling to (e.g., head of claims) were the ones that had put in place the inefficient process that existed for years. He was essentially selling to people that at the least would look bad and at worst would lose their jobs. Needless to say, as he struggled, it became clear that a market that should have been in the eighth inning was in the second inning.

The same is true in raising capital as well as mergers and acquisitions. Raising capital and buying or selling a company is complex stuff. When you think you are in ninth inning and coming down the home stretch, you get more frustrated when things don't finish as quickly as you had expected. This can also have an impact on your negotiating strategy. There are issues to be raised and levers to be pulled, but only at the right stage. You have a certain amount of political capital with your investors, your management, and the party with whom you are negotiating. You may have to horse trade with the other side on issues. Using this lever too early or on the wrong issue leaves you with no reserve of political capital when you need it in the future. Being realistic about what inning you are in during the investment or acquisition process is key to pulling the levers you need to pull at the right time.

Your Change in Perspective

But how do you change your perspective to understand where you are at and which levers to pull and when? Try asking the following people: "Using the analogy of a baseball game, what inning are we in terms of the industry's acceptance of our solution?"

- **Ask Someone with No Horse in the Race.** Find someone who doesn't have interest in you or your company and ask them about your product or service. Ask them what inning they think you are in. You are more likely to get an unbiased opinion, especially if they know nothing about your market and don't have a vested interest in you succeeding or failing.
- **Ask Your Investors.** Investors tend to have seen a lot and may have a more sophisticated or nuanced frame of reference against which to measure your offering. For example, they may be able to compare other companies they have invested in and how long it took to get to market.
- **Ask Other Entrepreneurs.** It might be an entrepreneur you know, or one whose work you respect. You will likely get a candid assessment from other entrepreneurs that don't have the emotional attachment that you do.

- **Ask Industry Experts.** While it is beneficial to get views from unbiased and uninvolved people, they often lack the knowledge of your specific industry. People in your industry understand the normal selling process and when and how products are brought to market. For example, in healthcare many products and services are sold during the third quarter so they can be put in place for the first of the year. In fashion, new collections are presented during fall and spring events to showcase the new look for the upcoming season. If you are launching an infomercial, you may need a two- to three-month lead-time. If you are writing a book, you need to be teed up many months in advance to submit your work to publishers for their next round of publication.

In addition to gathering this feedback, you must understand the impact that your financial resources can have on timing. While new solutions always take time to come to market, this can be accelerated if you have significant financial resources. Blockbuster aggressively went across America and bought out all the video rental stores. If they had not had the capital to do so, it would have taken many more years for that industry to evolve. Without the proper financial resources, it may take longer than expected for your solution to be adopted by the market.

In any event, be conservative. Take the opinion of your most skeptical employee, advisor or investor, and subtract three innings. It is better to set the expectation that your film will take two years to complete and deliver it early, than to suggest it will be finished in eighteen months and have it take a full two years or longer. Understanding what inning you're in goes beyond the adage: "Under promise and over deliver." Remember that you are under the influence of your passion. You have a personal investment in seeing that your vision gets to market as fast as possible, but that doesn't mean the market is on your schedule. Strengthen your perspective by acknowledging the tendency to skip a few innings in your assessment, and be conservative about which inning you are actually in. This effort will help you set appropriate expectations for vendors, investors, your team, and you. It will also strengthen their trust and support of both you and your business.

Chapter 5
No Process, No Progress

What We Feel: *Process is for IBM and General Electric. We have to be nimble. We don't have the resources of large companies so we've got to be able to move fast and respond quickly. Who has the time to build process?*

I started working with a first-time entrepreneur who felt she was drowning. I told her she needed some structure and process to run the business. I told her she could benefit from regular meetings, set schedules and standard operating procedures that didn't require scrambling every time the company had an issue or met with investors, customers, vendors and other resources. Basic stuff. The stuff that mature businesses use as the foundation for running their business. Her reaction? She looked at me like I was crazy. She believed that her latest issue was simply a "personnel issue" that had to be handled and was not indicative of a lack of process. The next day it was the product. The next it was investors. The next it was the marketing plan.

While each day can be different, the fundamental elements of any business are the same—sales, marketing, operations, finance, people, etc. Establishing processes to deal with the common issues of a business, seems like a waste of time to most entrepreneurs. Process is the fuel that energizes progress, yet many entrepreneurs view *process* as a dirty word reserved for General Electric and Six Sigma classes. This visceral reaction is based on the faulty perspective that the entrepreneur's job description is to innovate, upset the rules, invent new markets and simply do things differently. In other words, the entrepreneur's prerogative is precisely to *not* operate like big companies with set procedures for everything that move at the pace of battleships. The entrepreneur has to move, and move faster—not slower.

The feeling is understandable. As entrepreneurs, we pride ourselves on our independence, creativity, risk taking and willingness to chart the unknown. Scheduling meetings, defining accountability and discussing process may feel like a step backwards or a step in the wrong direction; after all, many entrepreneurs feel they left the status quo behind on purpose—along with org charts, mandatory meetings, and "corporate speak"—when they fled their cubicle to join the "dark side." While this gut feeling makes sense, it is a perspective that can harm entrepreneurs' endeavors from day one and fundamentally disable their progress. The entrepreneur's perspective that process is meant for larger companies, and the wave of activity is just the nature of the entrepreneurial beast, can hamper your organization for years.

There are many consequences that result when entrepreneurs avoid putting process in place. We'll focus on three scenarios here:

- **Plugging Holes as They Come.** Most early entrepreneurial ventures face a rising tide of incomplete tasks, decisions, and resources. As the pressure builds, holes begin to appear in the dam. When a fledgling business has no structure in place to manage common business issues and conflicts, the entrepreneur is left to plug the holes with whatever is on hand. Your "go to" strategy is to plug your fingers and toes into as many holes as you can, as fast as you can. If the day's crises are particularly bad, you might need your tongue or an elbow. After all, we entrepreneurs are pretty resourceful. You may slow the tide for a day, but it's very likely that more holes will show up tomorrow—more than you can manage with your extremities.
- **Reinventing the Wheel.** Even though an activity (e.g., sales call) has been done many times, when entrepreneurs and their teams lack operating process, each task or action is being executed as though it were the first time. This means starting from scratch—a significant and unnecessary use of time and energy. Think of it this way—you drive to work on the same route every day. When you do this, it is easy for you to manage different nuances such as weather, traffic, being late and a myriad of other issues that affect your drive. Imagine if you took a different route every day.

- **Communicating Inefficiently.** When entrepreneurs neglect to establish forums for regular company dialogue, or fail to schedule planning and progress meetings, communication ends up in a tangle of email replies, forwards, CCs and BCCs from multiple parties. This swirl of email can take longer to unravel than to reply, and quickly uses up hours, if not days. You've just wasted an enormous amount of time that a simple protocol would prevent.

Developing and implementing "process" *does* take time. For many entrepreneurs, the concept of "slowing down" to put that process and structure in place (e.g., create a standard sales PowerPoint presentation, set a standard pricing meeting), seems absurd—at least initially.

Throughout the day, entrepreneurs are fielding questions from vendors, customers, investors and employees. For example: "How are we going to price our solution for the RFP?" What if the response were, "Let's address this in the weekly pricing meeting; please send an email to all attending so we can be prepared to discuss"? The alternative is likely twenty emails, texts and phone calls that chew up an hour without a resolution. Process maximizes your scarcest resource—time.

Even established companies struggle to operate efficiently and effectively without good process. You hear stories about this from the fashion world—usually around the time couture houses and leading designers are launching new lines and presenting their collections on a global stage. Consider two different scenarios with identical resources and time:

- **First Scenario:** The team prepares samples of the collection for the "big meeting" with the president a month before the launch. In the meeting, it is clear that the president is not satisfied with the workmanship or fit. Hardware has been altered or replaced incorrectly. A cheaper fabric has been substituted for a key design. The President's standard of quality has not been met, and now there is an expensive scramble to repair six months of work.
- **Second Scenario:** The team holds weekly meetings in which the president is presented with tactile examples of hardware, fabric, and pattern construction—key concepts that are refined over months

prior to the event. As the collection comes to life, numerous alterations are made, and are reviewed with the president during the weekly meeting. By the time the launch is a month out, there are no surprises. Additionally, the team has time left to iron out the small, precise details that make the difference between ready to wear and haute couture.

Same staff. Same event. Different results.

Without process, the entrepreneurial landscape becomes even more challenging. Think about your normal day. It is common for an issue to arise and for emails to fly back and forth between multiple people. If this were one issue per day, it would merely be a distraction. When it is twenty per day, it is debilitating. A marketing issue is just as likely to arise at 10 a.m. as it is at 5 p.m., and as likely on Tuesday as it is on Friday. This becomes unmanageable quickly. The lack of structure makes it difficult not only to manage the business but also to create any progress. What's the solution?

Your Change in Perspective

First and foremost, you must recognize and understand that *process* is an enabler that accelerates not decelerates your activity and is not a dirty word. You are going slow—but you are going slow so you can go fast. Think about it. What if you had a sales presentation that could be used in a variety of customer meetings by changing just one slide? Or a clear structure for determining pricing that all your managers share? Or even if you're running a solo business, having a process set up for shipping— labeling software, postage meter, scale, FedEx materials and scheduled pick ups—is much more efficient than digging for supplies and running to the post office every time you need to ship your product. Process also allows you to be productive, efficient and to focus on the substance of your business. It's not a dirty word—it's a secret password that gets you into the club of successful businesses.

Once you recognize the benefits and consequences for your business, you are ready to implement or improve processes across your organization.

The suggestions below may initially appear designed for larger companies. If you are a small organization or a solo venture, there may be some action items that aren't applicable, but many of the process concepts will be of direct benefit to you as well.

Basic Process: Getting Started.

- Distribute a one-page business summary each week.
- Regular meeting schedule for major departments and other significant topics.
- Establish a consistent communication process for departments, employees, management and other organizational intersections.

Each of the above process items is described in more detail below.

Weekly One-Page Business Summary

Things move fast and it is hard to keep everyone informed. Distribute a one-page business summary at the same time each week that updates company constituents on the business. (I used to send it Sunday night before the week started.) This will allow you to communicate with all relevant constituents and eliminate repetitive conversations and ad hoc summaries. Your summary also keeps your team on the same page and provides answers in advance that eliminate unnecessary inquiries to you and other managers. Even if you are a one-woman show and have one consultant, one vendor and one advisor, you can benefit from simple repeatable tools like this. Summarizing the week's progress also helps you analyze and remain aware of your company's evolution.

The Business Summary details three bullets (no more) for each department or major area of the company. Tailor it to your organization. It might look like the following:

Area	Update
Financing	• Final materials being reviewed for 5/1 • Third-party broker hired • Obtaining feedback on financial model due 4/25
Marketing	• Developing sales collateral • Interviewing PR firms. Decision March 30 • Implementing CRM solution for 6/1
Sales	• Sales training 6/1 • RFP finalist for ABC Company • Looking to hire two salespeople by 6/1
Technology	• Hired two new developers • Implemented Rally to track IT deliverables • Building 2015 road map – due 9/1
Clients	• Launching ATT on 5/1 • Onsite meeting for expansion of Honeywell program • Training client services managers
Finance	• Accounting system online as of 4/1 • Implementing new expense policy effective 6/1 • Budget process starting 7/1
Operations	• Hired two new call center reps. Online 4/1 • Office lease signed through 2016 • Working on disaster recovery plan. Date TBD
Human Capital	• Need to clarify options policy for employees • Health benefits session on 9/1 • New employee policies in process. Due 6/1

This update will be unique to your business. Remember that this document is a summary, not a place to vent or a catalogue of details. It should not be longer than one page. The goal is to provide an efficient mechanism for high-level updates and to eliminate this communication from your midweek responsibilities. By consistently distributing this summary, your weekly reports help create efficient information flow. You may decide to distribute to all constituent—employees, consultants, investors, advisors, Board members and others—or you may decide to focus on core members of your organization.

Regular Meeting Schedule

Every company has the same basic functions—sales, marketing, product, operations, finance, etc. Organize regular meetings for each department or for major issues that require attention (e.g., pricing, customer relations). This becomes the process through which you manage the business. These meetings should be held at regular intervals (e.g., weekly) with a set agenda. I have suggested the agenda items, and the length, frequency and attendees for these meetings. If possible, these meetings should be held at the same time each week. Pick a day of the week when the team tends to be in the office.

These meetings have multiple purposes:

- Provide a consistent process for topics, updates and addressing issues.
- Create a consistent mechanism for communication.
- Remove ad hoc conversations about topics that distract you during the day.
- Provide a forum for negotiating and solving challenges, especially when a trend develops.
- Provide a forum for new issues and dialogue about where the company is headed.

By having these meetings at regular intervals, you ensure that issues are addressed without harmful lag time. Tinker with the length and frequency to suit your business. I tend to err on the side of frequent meetings that provide a rhythm to the flow of information. As your process implementation improves, you may find that you can decrease the frequency. Similarly, you may find that some departments or topic areas require an additional weekly meeting. You can further increase your efficiency by combining meetings for different departments or topics if the inclusion is appropriate. Your goal is to keep at least 80 percent of your communication within the organized process of established meetings, and not allow the black hole of spontaneous emails and impromptu conversations swallow your time.

Here is a sample description of each of these meetings:

Meeting	Agenda Items	Attendees	Frequency	Duration (mins.)
Management	• Review of metrics or reports for each department • Review of major initiatives with status reports • Issues from prior meetings with status • New issues that must be watched at the senior level • Decisions to be made or actions required	• CEO • Senior team members	Weekly	120
Department	• Review of department metrics or reports • Review of major initiatives with status reports • Issues from prior meetings with status • New issues that must be watched • Decisions to be made or actions required	• Department lead • Key department personnel • CEO (optional)	Weekly	30
Pricing	• Decisions on prices • General pricing topics	• Finance lead • Sales lead	Weekly	60
Client	• All client issues • Implementations • Client issues to address	• Client lead • Delivery lead	Weekly	60
Business Review	• Business Direction • Strategy	• Senior team members	Monthly	120

Department meetings are used for marketing, sales, product, technology, product and other major departments. If your business is not mature enough to need all of these department check-ins, combine meetings and handle multiple departments at once. In addition to department meetings, there may be other areas that come up frequently and deserve a regular meeting that fall outside a department or that involve multiple departments. Some examples:

- **Pricing Review:** Weekly. Duration: 60 minutes. The goal is to discuss and make necessary decisions on all issues related to pricing.

- **Client Issues:** Weekly. Duration: 60 minutes. The goal is to discuss and make necessary decisions on all issues related to keeping customers happy.

I know what you are saying, "Who has the time for all of these meetings?" I said the same thing. Try this: for a week, calculate the amount of time and correspondence you have for a particular issue or decision your company must address. Given the haphazard way that most early stage companies communicate, there is a very good chance you are spending more time in ad hoc discussion than an hour long meeting. You are also less able to make decisions efficiently when issues are dealt with at random, and without the necessary personnel in attendance.

If you are the entrepreneur who fled your corporate office hoping to never have another departmental meeting, there are going to be some process growing pains. But the more efficient your meetings run the better your results—and your incentive to keep strong processes in place. So make sure your meetings don't turn into the kind of ad hoc communication you're trying to avoid. Keep your team on the agenda items, set time frames for topics, use key points to guide discussion instead of open ended dialogue. Keep updates brief (department heads should give their update in ten minutes, using the same structure) and then use the lion's share of these meetings to address and resolve issues, hold discussion, and make decisions.

Create a Regular Pattern of Communication

Establishing a standard process for communication helps to keep various constituents informed and brings consistency to your messages. Tailor the content of the communications to your business. Assign ownership for the creation of specific reports or items of communication. Create a set schedule for communication that everyone knows. This will not only create clarity but saves time and energy responding to ad hoc requests for information. When an employee asks, "What new customers did we bring on last month?" You can respond, "We publish that information each week in our customer review summary." Here is an example of a regular communication process:

Communication	Purpose	Frequency
Business Summary	• Updates from departments and on major initiatives	Weekly
Employee Summary	• Overview of all employee items such as new employees and benefits updates	Biweekly
Customer Developments	• New customers, customer deployment and customer feedback	Monthly

Establishing this regular process will reduce wasted time and create consistent flow of information to various constituents.

I remember my first thoughts about creating **process.** Our perspective was that too much process would stifle innovation. I found the complete opposite to be true. Process is not a dirty word. This is a critical perspective to address but even if you're not convinced, add process to your business anyway, and the results will change your perspective. You'll find that process actually improves innovation, creates the stability and opportunity for creativity, and provides the organizational structure to meaningfully implement both. Process also ensures another critical result: an operating structure that helps you manage your business and transforms your daily experience from chaos to control. Once this occurs, you won't be asking, "How do I have time for all these meetings?" but "What am I going to do with all this free time?"

Chapter 6
Tools to Stay Organized —
And They Are Free

What We Feel: *You feel disorganized and as your business progresses, it becomes harder to keep track of what you've done, what you're doing now, and what you should be doing. I'd love to be tracking and reporting on all of the activities of the company, but with all we are working on, we can't take the time to track every task and every project. When we get bigger, we will put in place all the tools to be more efficient.*

You feel disorganized every day but you are not really sure how to change that. Certainly many of the other perspectives in this book (e.g., setting priorities, creating process) will help, but even when you get those tools in place, keeping track of the activities of the company seems impossible.

Many entrepreneurs are unaware of the available tools to manage this issue. I was sitting next to an entrepreneur and she was keeping track of her to-dos in her notebook. She was reviewing her to-dos from past days and transferring the ones she didn't finish to a new page to help her organize her day and effort. I asked her how long that took each day and she said about an hour. She was unaware of the numerous new tools, applications, and software design that automate your to-do list and track agenda items in an economy of time. These tools are mostly free, and are designed for both larger companies and the one-woman show.

One of the reasons that entrepreneurs often feel overwhelmed is simply the raw amount of activity that is going on at any one time. Although you may feel the same way about tracking as you did about process—that it's a waste of time—tracking, planning, and structure reduce significantly more time in the long run than the brief and immediate satisfaction of moving from task to task. Eventually, that "long run" is another day in the future. It can be busier and more stressful than the one you're facing today, or it can be a hell of a lot easier.

Entrepreneurs often get stuck in the present tense—after all this is where creativity and innovation live—but if you want to turn your vision into a successful business, then you must operate in all tenses. Track past work, communication and goals. Maintain priorities and balance your time in the present. Establish ongoing processes to ensure accurate and efficient communication and goal achievement in the future. Without simple management tools, organizing incoming information and tasks will continue to feel like herding cats all day, every day.

Whether it is a lack of knowledge or access to these tools, or a failure to appreciate their benefits, dismissing these tools and the end goal they are designed to help you achieve is a perspective that needs a critical shift. Making that shift will yield big results and the daily relief you need.

Your Change in Perspective

Once you are aware of these tools and their advantages, take some time to find the ones that seem best suited to your needs. Many of these tools are available online and are free (or very low cost) and allow multiple people in your company to access them at an appropriate level of authorization. You may not need all of them, but they will help you create order.

- **Project and Task Management Tools.** New ventures lack administrative support positions. Tracking to-dos, plans, and larger initiatives is time consuming. Online project management tools help organize your company and its tasks. They create a single, central source for all company activity. In addition, team members can dialogue and store all conversations in one place. To this end, set up a folder for each department (e.g., Marketing) and for other major projects and initiatives (e.g., New York City Launch Event). You will likely have multiple projects under each functional area. Get disciplined in your use of these tools. When a new initiative or project is commenced, set it up in the application. Populate these tools while you are in meetings. Use the tools to post meeting agendas, weekly reports and updates.

- **Simple Task Tools.** For simple to-do list items, there are free applications that keep track of tasks you must accomplish. Look at Google Keep, Wunderlist, Todoist and Habit RPG. You can also use the task management tools in your email program such as Microsoft Outlook. These tools allow you to track tasks and to assign tasks to other team members. Pick one and get disciplined about keeping all your to-dos in one place. The use of these tools may seem overly tactical, but they create efficiency and put time back in your day.

- **Accounting Package.** You may be spending time creating invoices, tracking expenses and trying to keep track of money with individual spreadsheets. Online small business accounting packages are efficient at managing the basic financial elements of the business including creating invoices, purchase orders, and keeping track of customers, employees and vendors. Also, if you track all financial activity in the package, you can produce the standard financial statements (i.e., income statement, balance sheet, cash flow statement) with the press of a button.

- **Sales Pipeline/CRM Package.** Online customer relationship management (CRM) tools allow you to keep track all sales opportunities and their size, stage, and likelihood to close. While primarily designed for sales, this can also be used to track potential investor opportunities.

- **Document Management.** You generate documents as your business evolves. Use an online document management tool that allows you to house all documents. Set up a section for each department and other major area of the company. This tool can also be used for your "data room" to manage your investment process. If you set up this central repository early on, you will not have to take extra effort to prepare your data room for investment materials.

You can obtain separate tools for each of the above, but there are software packages that offer one or more of these from a single vendor. Each of these tools are Internet-based, integrate seamlessly with common email programs (e.g., Outlook), provide updates and reminders, and act as a single place to manage various elements of the business. They also allow you to run reports on the business with a push of the button. In addition, they create an efficient method for presenting data to new employees, and for sharing information with third parties, such as investors.

In addition to reporting, these tools will allow you to identify the activities that need your focus. A project management tool can alert you that an activity is due in two days. A finance package can generate automatic reports on the status of your revenue budget. A "task" tool can remind you of the tasks of the day. While part of the benefit of these tools is tracking and organizing, an equally important benefit is making sure you stay on track.

However, these tools don't run themselves, and they are meaningless if you're the only one using them. In other words, your change in perspective has to involve your entire team. These tools will become less effective for your business if your organization is not committed to using them on a regular basis. You must drive your organization to use them religiously. They should be a fundamental part of your communication and content development. Once your team learns how to maximize their functionality, you'll build a remarkably clear map of how your business is running, what's coming next, and what current priorities are at any given moment. A single tool, accessible from anywhere, that contains all the relevant content for your company's daily activity, is a valuable source and incomparable advantage.

If you told entrepreneurs, "We have a tool that will show you all your company activity, map your progress, and alert you when a change of direction is needed," most would take you up on it. Yet many entrepreneurs still persist in the perspective that tools are not for startups, or small businesses, or are simply not worth the time to get them going. If you're one of the skeptics, start with one tool, do it right, and let the result change your perspective. If you're ready for your organizational makeover, by all means, get started. It won't be long before you see increased productivity *and* creativity. Then you'll ask yourself, "How did I manage before this?"

Chapter 7
Negotiating When You Have No Cards

What We Feel: *It is so hard to negotiate good terms because I feel we need customers, vendors, employees and other resources so much that I'm afraid to push at all in any negotiation.*

In an entrepreneurial venture, you often don't have negotiating leverage. You are anxious to get customers and even more anxious to complete an investment. When it comes to vendors, you don't represent a large volume of business. In these scenarios, you need them more than they need you. Unfortunately, this puts you at a disadvantage when it comes to negotiating. You can't let this limitation cause you to strike deals that are not in the best interest of the company.

Your Change in Perspective

Of course you need customers, vendors, employees and vendors. What entrepreneur doesn't? But you need to change your perspective in order to increase your chances of securing these important relationships. Instead of negotiating from a position of weakness, you must come to the table with tools and insights that put you more in the driver's seat. Think about the following:

- **Negotiate from a Position of Strength**. Don't allow any customer, investor, employee or vendor to hold your size or stage against you. Put differently, even though you really want (or need) a relationship, always negotiate from a position of strength. How do you do this when you have little leverage? It will require your entrepreneurial creativity to create leverage when little exists:

It was a day every entrepreneur dreams of. One of the largest health plans in the country, just completed its RFP process and had informed us that we were the winner. Normally when you win an RFP, it's an acceptance of both the solution and the price you have provided. There is, of course, always the normal contract negotiation that has its challenges, but generally once you "win" deal has been accepted. In this case there was a wrinkle. The health plan communicated that while we had "won" the RFP, they were not going to pay us anything for our service. They said, "We think you have the best solution, but at our stage, to have the opportunity to offer your solution to our members, it is worth it for you to invest the money to implement and support the solution to garner that opportunity." Imagine that. They were a multibillion-dollar organization, with no shortage of cash, and they thought we should invest. They lose more money in their break room couch every day than we had in our bank account.

As we discussed earlier, it was pleasure and pain. While I was raising my hands in the air celebrating, someone took the opportunity to punch me in the stomach. I got off the phone with the health plan and reached out to a few health-care colleagues. They said this was not uncommon. Large insurers working with earlier stage companies would ask (and sometimes demand) them to invest in the relationship to have access to their business. It didn't matter that they had virtually unlimited financial resources while we had the minimal resources of an early stage company. It was par for the course.

I understood their perspective but thought there could be another way. I reached out to other colleagues in healthcare and asked the question, "What makes a health plan do something?" In other words, what influences makes a large health plan take action? My colleagues informed me that large health insurers were responsive to the demands of the large companies for which they provided insurance. One of my colleagues informed me that this health plan had an advisory group of employers that consisted of their top twenty-five largest customers— companies like Federal Express, MassMutual, and Safeway. My colleague told me that when these employers talked, they listened.

I reached out to the employers on this advisory board. Safeway, who was on the advisory board, was also one of our customers. Other than Safeway, we did not have relationships with any of the other companies on the board. It's likely they had never heard of IncentOne. This was in 2007 when many employers and health plans were just becoming aware of the concept of using incentives to drive health behaviors. I started with Safeway. I reached out to them and asked them two questions. First, would they be interested in learning more about incentives for healthy behavior? Second, did they expect their health plan to offer this solution?

Their answer was a resounding yes and yes. They were encouraged that we were pushing the envelope and without asking, they suggested that other companies on their advisory board would be interested in talking with us. Bingo! They offered to introduce us to other companies on the advisory board and provided me with contact information of every member. I assured them that I would not in any way represent that Safeway was endorsing us, but only that they thought we should talk. I drafted an email for the approval of Safeway. They thanked me for running it past them and made introductions to everyone on the advisory board.

I reached out to all twenty-five companies and asked them those same two questions. The response was overwhelming. Every one of them said yes to both questions. We offered to hold a session to educate them on how incentives were evolving in healthcare. We did not try to sell them anything and wanted them to know the lay of the land and that we were there as a resource if they needed us.

Despite us not trying to offer them any services, of the twenty-five employers, ten asked for proposals, another ten took us up on the offer to hold a conference call to talk more about incentives and the last five said that they would like us to keep in touch and provide them with information periodically. At the end of the conversation, I also asked each of them that if we happen to be working with one of their health plans, could we have that health plan reach out to them and collaborate with us on the opportunity. All twenty-five said absolutely.

I made a phone call I thought I would never make. I called the procurement manager and communicated that while it was an honor to be selected by them, we would have to decline. Prior to IncentOne, I was a mergers and acquisitions lawyer and had a lot of experience negotiating but never before for my own company with my own money. Nonetheless, telling one of the largest insurance companies in the world to effectively "screw off" when you are in early stages is an unnatural act.

We communicated that we believed that we were providing a fair proposal, that our pricing was reasonable and that asking a company like ours to bear the financial burden would not lead to a productive partnership. The procurement lead said to me, "But what if no one uses incentives." I responded with two answers. First, I assumed that they would not go to the trouble of running a six-month RFP process for shits and giggles. Second, I said, that with all due respect, when an individual pays their insurance premium but never uses a doctor, they don't give them the money back. We laughed (or maybe I laughed and he grunted and I thought it sounded like a laugh). We instructed them that we would be happy to be there for them as a resource and continue to dialogue with them about incentives but would respectfully decline.

They were stunned. They asked us if we thought through our decision and its implications. I said that we had. They recommended that we reconsider and suggested a conference call later in the week to discuss. I told him that I appreciated the advice and would do so but it was unlikely we would change our view. As the conversation ended, I added one more thing. I told them if we ended up not doing business together, we would still like to collaborate with them if we happened to come across an employer of theirs that was interested in incentives. While I couldn't see the procurement manager on the other end of the phone, I could hear the steam coming out of his ears. He said, "What are you talking about? Why are you talking to our employers?" I told him that we offered our solutions directly to employers and we come across employers all the time that had them as their health plan. I reminded him that we currently ran some of Safeway's programs. I preceded to list off ten companies that we had relationships with—a few of which were the companies on their advisory board. He said, "You have no right to talk to our employers!" I said, "We don't have a relationship yet and this is why I'd like us to collaborate if the circumstance arises."

He instructed me to be at their offices in Connecticut the next day. I said, with all due respect, you just told me to "go screw" and I don't need to sit in hours of traffic on Route 95 to come to Connecticut to be told "go screw" in person.

I reluctantly agreed. I went to Connecticut and sat in front of twenty of their team members including lawyers, procurement team members, product people, operations people and finance folks. After they communicated their shock about our response and their concern about us talking to employer groups, we gave our view. We communicated that we understood and respected their view but that we would decline. We also instructed them that we already sold directly to employers, that we would like to collaborate with them and that we had discussions with multiple groups who used them as their insurer that had requested proposals from IncentOne. I offered to let them talk to some of these employers. I wanted them to understand that these were not empty claims, but rather that they should talk to their customers who had told us that they could reach out. We wanted this to not only influence the discussions with them, but also to allow them to get a win with its customers if we were not involved. A few days later, after they talked to some of their customers that we'd been in contact with, they agreed to our price.

Easier said than done. You've got to bring all of your creative juices to give yourself the influence and edge to negotiate with strength. You may not realize you already have this strength or won't discover it until you refuse to negotiate from a position of weakness, regardless of the circumstances. Here are a few tips to help you negotiate from the right place:

- **Influence Points**. You often don't need to have leverage to create other influence points. On your own, you may be a small company that no one knows about. What if you tied your business to another influence point? For example, what if you are a customer of Valley Bank and you want to offer your solution to the bank. You might reach out to your relationship manager and express your desire to offer your solution to the bank. Your business with the bank will give you an improved chance with the opportunity.
- **Align to Your Target's Competitors**. Sometimes companies create relationships because of the value. Other times companies take action to prevent or preempt your relationship with one of their competitors. Communicate that you will be offering your solution not only to them, but that you believe that other similar companies (that they happen to compete with) would benefit from your solution.
- **Competitive Process**. Whether it is a vendor or an investor, hold a competitive bid process. When you have narrowed your selections down to few (or one), or if you are left with one selection, this need

not be shared with these parties. Parties vying for your business should understand that they are competing with others.

- **Attitude.** Sometimes your attitude, body language, and tone can be compelling enough to create leverage. Shift your passion for your vision into a natural confidence. Communicate that the success of your business is not a matter of "if" but "when." Regardless of your stage, always negotiate from a position of strength. Pay attention to the principle of least interest even if your interest is greater and always behave like you want a relationship, not that you need a relationship.

- **Never Let Anyone Be the Only Source.** There will be times throughout the process of overseeing your company in which you will only have one source for a solution. This most often comes up with vendors and investors but may also apply to customers and employees. Ideally, you should always have several sources for a solution. In early stages, this is not always possible. When it is not possible, the party that is your only solution should not know that they are your only source. In a perfect world, these relationships would appreciate that this venture is your vision and would never take advantage of the fact that they are the only source. Unfortunately, you must accept that some resources will leverage this knowledge to your disadvantage.

This is hard. In early stages, you want to create relationships with companies that will ride the wave with you. Companies that will see your vision and take a flier on it. Unfortunately, more often than not, companies understandably protect their self-interest. This is not to say that all constituents will do that. If you are fortunate enough to find constituents that share your common vision and are willing to invest in it, so be it. Until that happens, however, you must not expose your vulnerability. While the preferred solution will always be to have a backup plan, you never should communicate that a potential relationship is your single source. Individuals and companies who understand that they are in a competitive environment are likely to perform better and provide better terms.

Take the example of a vendor. With vendors, you are often looking for partners who are willing to take below market or other creative compensation (e.g., equity) in exchange for performance. In these cases, you develop a relationship with these vendors and share information with them. You might have one company bidding to be your manufacturer. You might have one software vendor bidding for your technology business. When your business matures, you will have the ability to mitigate your risk with multiple or backup vendors. You'll have the ability to create contingency plans. Early on, you don't have the capital or management resources for that.

Many vendors who realize they are your single source will use that fact to extract a higher price or to put you in a position in which your negotiating leverage is minimal. We have all heard stories of the contractor working on your house, is 75 percent finished and suddenly communicates that the price is going to be 50 percent higher than expected. You are left with two bad choices—pay the additional 50 percent or fire them—and end up with 75 percent of a house. It's not a coincidence that despite having built hundreds of houses this major price issue didn't arise until the job was 75 percent done. They understand that they are the single source of the solution.

What are some of the tools you can use to minimize this risk? Here are a few tips:

- **Create a Bidding Process.** Conduct a bidding process and communicate to your vendors that you will be considering their bid against other bids. The bidding process can be formal or informal. Communicating that you are accepting proposals from multiple vendors will cause vendors to act accordingly.
- **Be Careful Sharing Information.** When your balloon is full and you build a relationship with constituents like vendors, you tend to share the gory details of your business. While this can let air out of your balloon, this can also be detrimental to the business. When vendors hear a sense of desperation or a risk to your business, or know there is a customer deliverable in two months, some may use this information to alter pricing and terms or use this leverage to create relationships that are not balanced. Vendors should earn your trust by performing. At that future time, you can share more with them.

- **Have Alternatives.** Even when you hire vendors, make them aware that you are constantly looking for ways to improve and always keep alternative vendors on call. It is like having a bench when it comes to employees. This keeps vendors on their toes.

Your job is to act in the best interest of the business. Of course, you would like to strike a vendor relationship that turns into a close one in which you ride the tide together. This is rare, especially since the early vendors who make sacrifices expect to be treated differently as the business grows. Like early employees who make sacrifices, early vendors who work for below-market prices expect preferential treatment.

The same rules apply to employees, customers and investors. When investors sense that they are the only game in town, they have leverage to negotiate more preferential terms. If a candidate knows they are the only one for the job, you may be faced with higher compensation demands. If a customer knows that they are your only prospect, you may be faced with pressure to lower your price or expand your offering to win their business.

This rule is not groundbreaking, but given the frequency with which early stage companies have single sources and minimal backup options, it is a key one to follow. It is never about being dishonest. It is about acting in the best interest of the business. Think of it this way, if you asked a customer, "Are we the only vendor you are considering?" Even if you were, do you think they would tell you?

- **Find Vendors That Think You Matter.** One of the issues you face is dealing directly with vendors. You often don't have the capital to strike normal compensation relationships with vendors. You also can't promise volume or make longer-term commitments because you don't know. Despite these risks, these vendors can be critical to your business success.

How do you give yourself the best chance for success with vendors? I learned the answer from my brother. My brother runs our family's real estate business in which he manages about twenty buildings. Instead of working with the largest elevator companies, insurance brokerages, contracting companies and other vendors, he works with vendors that consider our business meaningful to them. If you provide a vendor with $1 million in business and their revenue is $10 million, you matter. If you provide a vendor with $1 million in business and their revenue is $100 million, you are a rounding error. While working with the largest vendors can add credibility, you may end up being a small fish in a big pond.

Smaller vendors are also more likely to price their services based on the potential of your business as opposed to the business at hand. If a $10 million vendor will win $250,000 of your business now, but your business with them might expand to $1 million, they may see the opportunity and provide the $250,000 for $150,000. Larger vendors usually look only at the business currently in front of them and price accordingly. This doesn't only relate to price. It can also impact the resources committed to your business. When my brother's team calls the elevator vendor, they don't get the young buck out of elevator school. They get the president of the company.

These concepts are not new. They are employed by companies all the time. We all understand "big fish in a small pond." However, when you are a young organization looking for credibility, you often try to align yourself with large, established vendors. Vendors are key to riding the wave of growth and progress. Make sure they wake up thinking about your business.

There is a certain reality to an early stage business. You don't have a lot of dollars. You can't make large commitments. You don't know your volume. You can't promise the future. Even so, you still have to find a way to negotiate favorable relationships with the company. If you keep your perspective aligned to negotiating from a position from strength, and can use some of the techniques described here, you can strike a good deal even if you are offering ice to Eskimos.

SECTION 2:

STAYING FOCUSED AND SANE

Introduction

The daily life of the entrepreneur under the influence of the Four Ps can be challenging and at times overwhelming. With so much on our minds and on our plates, we often lack the brainpower to distinguish the difference between a mind and a plate. When this happens, we develop certain behaviors that seem like they are helping, but are actually making the problem worse. Many of these behaviors are natural reactions. It is natural after losing a deal to ask yourself, "Am I really cut out for this?" It is natural to think about the hundreds of things that you have to do. It is natural to think that sleep and social activities and thoughts and events outside your venture are luxuries you can't afford. It is natural to get distracted by the many things you aren't doing versus the ones you set out to do. It is natural to play with your phone, your iPad, and your email even when you have bigger fish to fry. These perspectives are natural, but they are also debilitating.

As natural as these things may be, these and other closely related perspectives detract from staying focused on the most important issue or the task at hand. In addition, they cause us to expend emotional energy on the state of your life at the least opportune times. There is a time and place for you to focus, for you to get distracted, and for you to evaluate your life.

In this section, you will be asked to change your perspective so that you recognize choices and practice actions that will keep you focused and sane. You'll also learn tips and tools for implementing action at the right time and place.

Chapter 1
One Hundred Hours of Work
And Ten Hours of Time

What We Feel*: There is so much more to do than there is time. Every day, I think about all the things that have to get done and as soon as my mind wanders to all we have to do, it seems like a daunting task.*

Every entrepreneur, at some point, will face some pretty harsh math. You have one hundred hours of work and ten hours of time to get it done. It is an impossible equation, right? Some tasks are big picture, some are tactical, some are immediate and some are longer term. When we started IncentOne, we were at least a year from revenue. For many, this may be multiple years. Regardless, there are many daily items that need to get done and the ratio of tasks to time can be daunting.

It is not surprising then that entrepreneurs come to work, and instead of focusing on the tasks of the day, they worry about what is not getting done, or the big picture items must occur for the business to succeed. This is counterproductive. Focusing on the ninety-nine things that you can't do that day or mentally jumping ahead to task that require multiple days is wasted time and effort.

Your Change in Perspective

Once you have decided on your tasks for the day, stop worrying about other tasks and finish the ones in front of you. In the movie *Apollo 13*, the spacecraft suffers damage and the astronauts move through a series of procedures to prepare the spacecraft for reentry into the Earth's atmosphere.

Given the damage, success is hardly assured. While they are working, Bill Paxton (who plays astronaut Fred Haise Sr.) questions whether Mission Control in Houston is giving the astronauts accurate information. Tom Hanks (who plays captain Jim Lovell) says:

> *"All right, there's a thousand things that have to happen in order. We are on number eight. You're talking about number six hundred and ninety-two… We're not going to go bouncing off the walls for ten minutes, because we're just going to end up back here with the same problems!"*

Work the problem. Focus on the items you have determined require your attention that day. The entrepreneur's path to success is rarely built with "giant leaps for mankind" but steadily won with, determined, daily progress. When we chip away at today's to-do list, we build powerful momentum for our business.

> *During the height of the 2008-2009 financial crisis, my brother and I really battled. I would speak to my Mom and Dad on the phone and my Mom would say, "You guys are brothers and have to figure out a way to work through this." Each time we would talk, she would make that same point. One day I told her that I thought this was a waste of time. Every minute that we spent talking about how we had to fix our relationship was time not spent fixing the business. The day we fixed the business, I told her, would be the day we could fix our relationship.*

> *There was no point of focusing on what could go wrong, all the things we needed to do or about ruining my relationship with my one brother instead of spending every waking minute fixing the business. I put my head down and worked from five in the morning until midnight for nearly two years and got us to a better point. Had I spent my time focusing on the family issues or anything other than moving the business forward, it would have prolonged the struggle. There were times when my mind would wander and think about what had happened between Dan and I. Whenever I would, I turned back to the task at hand. When the business recovered and we sold the business in 2013, Dan and I got back to being brothers. I am happy to say today that we are closer than ever.*

The more time you spend on the ninety items not on your list, the more you stunt the growth of the business. First, you are still not getting the ninety done. Second, you probably are doing a bad job with the ten you need to and actually *can* get done.

> *When I was studying for the bar exam, there were hundreds of hours of material to cover. It's probably the only time in my life when I felt if the testers wanted me to fail, I would fail. Think of it as a test on any class you had, or any textbook you read, or were supposed to read, throughout college. Anything was fair game. It was hard not to spend at least some time thinking about what would happen if you failed. I was confident, but the volume of information the test could leverage, was massive. I got some advice from a friend: "You can spend time studying, or you can spend part of your time studying and part thinking about failing, but if you spend all your time studying you increase your chances of passing."*

When you focus on overall risk and big picture concerns, it can be debilitating. If you focus on your present to-do list, you offer yourself the remarkably satisfying and motivating experience of completing the tasks before you. When so much is out of your control, the chance to finish something each day is priceless. And if you continue to prioritize each day's list, your sense of accomplishment will grow exponentially. After all, each day's work is a piece of the puzzle that will eventually become your "big picture." But if you worry about the big picture first, you'll never assemble its parts and reach your ultimate goal.

Chapter 2
Don't Evaluate Your Life in
The Middle of the Fight

What We Feel: This is much harder than I thought. When things go wrong, it makes my mind wander to why I am doing this. Am I really cut out for this? Am I happy? Is this what I want?

At the end of every boxing match, Jim Lampley, the famous boxing announcer, interviews the winner and asks, "Do you think this is your last fight?" More often than not, the seasoned pugilist who has just spent ten rounds in the ring replies, "I'm seriously considering it." Wouldn't you retire if you just got hit in the face for two hours? But two weeks later, with some rest, TLC, and the threat of another contender closing in, this same fighter is on television assuring the boxing community that his retirement is far in the future.

You absolutely must find time to evaluate your life. Being an entrepreneur can be a stressful and all-encompassing endeavor. Many entrepreneurs have started their venture only to look back and say, "Where did my life go?"

There must be time (often with a glass or two of bourbon) for you to reflect, think about the big picture and evaluate your personal goals. Not having this time to reflect can be damaging. The problem is, entrepreneurs often feel compelled to investigate their personal life only when the shit hits the fan—at the busiest, most inopportune moments in the middle of the business day. This is precisely the time *not* to do it.

When entrepreneurs feel overwhelmed, the gears come to a stop. Running in quicksand becomes walking in quicksand, and then sinking in quicksand. When this happens, for some reason it causes many of us to use this as an opportunity to evaluate our lives. Maybe because we've come to a grinding halt, we think it's time to ask:

What am I doing? I have no life. I never sleep. I don't talk about anything but this business. Everyone thinks I am crazy. I never go out. I haven't been on a date in months, my wife/husband/children are going to forget my name soon, I've forgotten what the outside of my office looks like. My friends have given up on me.

Meanwhile, work piles up like a multiple vehicle car crash and your employees or your cat (if you're working solo) begin to wonder what's going on.

If we gave every entrepreneur truth serum and asked them how often this occurs, the answer would likely be: "at least once a week." Regardless of how often it occurs, it most often occurs "right after getting punched in the face for ten rounds." It almost never occurs when things are going well. Have you ever evaluated your life after you close a deal? I doubt it. If you choose to evaluate your life during the most challenging times or in the middle of your day, it can become debilitating.

First, it consumes significant time and energy. When thoughts about the meaning of life arise, they distract us from the tasks at hand—the tasks that advance the business and make the issues of the day improve. More importantly, it consumes energy that would otherwise be used moving the business forward. These thoughts are not easy ones and they tend to bring up a variety of sensitive subjects and emotions. These feelings easily overwhelm and it's impossible to stay present and attend to your business, while simultaneously evaluating the meaning of life.

Second, these thoughts are often reactive and emotional and result in bad decisions. When the pressure hits you, it is hard to be objective. The grass seems greener, well, everywhere else. If you are venting, it can be harmless. If you are making decisions and acting, it is a problem. You can't evaluate whether to fight, and how to fight the fight, when you are still in the middle of the fight.

Your Change in Perspective

While you shouldn't evaluate the meaning of your life every day, you must put aside time to do it on a regular basis. Otherwise, you fall victim to the momentum of daily activities and obligations without asking yourself, "Am I happy?" For years, I didn't do this. My family had invested in the business. I would never abandon IncentOne without seeing it through. Whether I was happy or unhappy was irrelevant. It was my job to bring it to life and to make sure my family got what they wanted.

But not asking yourself periodically whether you are happy can lead you down a path of doing what you do today because you did it yesterday. There are always changes you can make. Bring in more capital to enhance your team. Change your role. Sell your stake in the company. You always have choices.

Let me clarify: when I say "happy," I don't mean that you are high-fiving all day. The things in life most worth doing are almost always the hardest. Even though it is challenging, there is great fulfillment in building something, and even more in building "your" something. Nonetheless, you must check in with yourself.

To check in with yourself, set aside a time for two hours every other weekend either alone, or with someone you trust who is not involved in the business. You want to reflect when no one is watching. This is a time not to be on stage and to be candid with yourself about where you are.

During this time, ask yourself the following questions:

- **Am I happy?** Even with the challenges, am I enjoying the journey? Do I get fulfillment about the progress we are making? Do I get excited when we win a customer, hire an employee or finish a project?

- **Is the pressure and strain worth the sacrifice I am making?** Be candid with yourself about the sacrifices you are making. They may be personal or financial or the opportunity costs of not doing other things. There is nothing wrong with sacrifice, as long as that sacrifice feels worth it to you.
- **How can I remove myself from the parts of the business I am not good at or I don't like?** Understanding the parts of the business you are not good at or that you don't like are important to growing your business. This is also important for you. These are the elements of your day that are draining you. Identify these parts and use this time to think about how to remove them from your day now or in the future.
- **Do I want to be the builder or the visionary? Do I want to be CEO?** I know your first reaction: "How dare you ask me this question? After all that I have done to get here, now you don't want me to be CEO?" At first, this is an uncomfortable question. Of course, you want to be CEO—you built it. However, being the CEO of an early stage venture is more about building the foundation of a business and managing its daily operations, than it is about your vision. The CEO must do all of the following and more:

- Set the priorities of the company
- Align the organization to those priorities
- Ensure that the company is properly funded
- Inspire people to stick to the vision
- Clearly communicate to the various constituents of the business.

Ask yourself, "Given the parts that you enjoy, and the ones you don't, and the parts that you are good at, and the ones you are not, is there a role that would be fulfilling but different from being the CEO?"

> *A good friend was asked to go into a women's body butter company by one of the investors. He was an experienced sales and marketing executive, with an MBA from the Kellogg School at Northwestern and experience with both B2B and consumer brands. What he found was that the business, which had products that were liked in the marketplace, was being run by two sisters who were masters at body butter and enjoyed creating products. The products were big sellers at*

retailers such as Bath and Body Works and Sephora. However, the sisters knew little about running a business, managing investors, creating distribution, and aligning the resources of the company. The company, despite market acceptance, was on the brink of bankruptcy. The sisters struggled getting the organization to profitability, but boy were they good at body butter.

Once you get over the shock of the question, you might realize there is a role for you that isn't the CEO, but that is more fulfilling. It might allow you to get back to your vision, help the company, and remove you from the pressures of a job—CEO—that you are not sure you want.

This is a subtle perspective shift but one that can have a real impact. Taking the time to check in with yourself is critical. But you can't fight the fight and evaluate your life at the same time. Set a time for yourself every two weeks to check in and take stock of yourself. When the thought creeps into your head in the middle of the day, resist the temptation to address it and wait until your designated time. Put it on your calendar and never miss it.

Chapter 3
Know Where You Need Help

What We Feel: *There are parts of the business that I wish I could avoid. There are other parts of the business that I know I have to do, but I really struggle to do well. Both really weigh me down, but who else is going to do them?*

Understanding what parts of the business you should be working on and what parts you should be passing to others is a critical part of running an early stage company. Entrepreneurs, especially in the beginning, are expected to do everything. There are areas of the business that we could work at endlessly and never get tired. You see this in creative businesses where fashion designers, filmmakers and technologists spend countless hours creating. These parts of the business bring genuine enjoyment, fulfillment and your best ideas. We rarely look at the clock and say, I wish this part of my day would end.

There are other parts of the business that you dislike or even dread. These areas can be as draining and debilitating as others are energizing and enjoyable. I can't tell you how many entrepreneurs say that they would work all night on creating their product or service but would rather stick needles in their eyes than do "accounting." The effort you spend here feels incredibly inefficient and counterproductive. You may be someone that loves to work alone but hates managing people. You may be someone that loves creating a value position but the technology behind it gives you the shakes. Working on these tough spots saps your energy.

Finally, there are parts of the business that need to be done, and while you are capable of the work, you're just not cut out for it. Unfortunately, entrepreneurs often don't realize their deficiencies in this area. If the company needs someone to set priorities, develop a sales plan, create an investment package or determine a sales approach, and you have little experience or capability in these areas, your insistence that you take the lead can set the company back. If the bottom line is seeing results, applying a good "college try" can actually hamper the ability of the business to get the resources it needs.

Both of these activities—the ones you dread and the ones you are no good at—can have two negative lasting effects. First, they drain your energy. Entrepreneurs tend to feel overwhelmed when they are working on these activities—much more than when they are working on areas they love. Second, they prevent important company functions from getting done. If the company needs to set priorities, and needs you to lead that effort, your lack of skill in a particular area not only exhausts you, but hinders the company when the task is not done well. Wouldn't the business operate more efficiently if you steered clear of these activities?

Your Change in Perspective

Knowing what you don't like and what you are not good at is an important step to not only improving your company, but to making your day more rewarding. Your perspective should be to try to minimize the things you don't like and things you are not good at from your day:

- **Things You Don't Like.** It is usually not hard to convince entrepreneurs to remove things they don't like from their day. In the
  beginning, you don't get to make a choice between likes and dis-
  likes—you must do both. You can, however, change this over time.
  Identify tasks or focus points that you'd prefer to outsource or delegate, and create a plan to remove them from your day.

  *Think of a software guru that comes up with a great technology idea. Software
  is her thing but business functions like accounting, managing an office, setting
  up a company and dealing with expenses are not her cup of tea—or where she
  wants to emphasize her time. Knowing this, she might bring in a part-time office
  administrator to deal with these activities. As your business grows, take time to
  protect your energy. If you're happy writing code all night but are exasperated by*

154

spreadsheets, find someone whose cup of tea is accounting. If the tea tastes bad, don't drink it.

Being an entrepreneur can be draining, but working on the parts of the business that you don't enjoy, is often what saps your energy and spirit the most.

- **Things You Are Not Good At.** Your perspective on critical business issues should be "Getting work done well is more important than who does it." Ask yourself:

What aspects of my business am I good at, and what aspects do I struggle with?

Be candid with yourself. Put your ego aside and acknowledge the things that you don't do well. Look at it this way. One of the skills of a leader is to understand your strengths and weaknesses and where to supplement your deficits with other's skills. It is probably relatively easy to be honest about the parts of the business you don't like. Less so in admitting the parts of the business you struggle with.

You may not be able to delegate responsibility for all the tasks outside your wheelhouse, especially in the beginning, but simply acknowledging these weaknesses benefits you and your company in many ways:

- First, if you struggle with an area, you waste valuable time on it and do not produce good results. Someone who has worked with a small business accounting package can set up the finances of your business in a few hours. It might take you much longer—and with much more frustration. If you have never raised money before, you'll discover it's an adventure, but one that thousands of others have already mastered. Instead of spending your limited time struggling, use it to find someone who specializes in your problem area. This saves valuable energy and an unnecessary expense of time.
- Second, when you acknowledge your weaknesses, you send an important message to your team. They see a leader who is candid about his or her strengths and limitations, and demonstrates a willingness to put the business first by reaching out to others for help.

It also suggests to your team that you can look at yourself critically and choose the health of the business over your own ego. Leaders who think that they are good at everything, and stubbornly persist in this perspective despite clear evidence to the contrary, strain their credibility with those around them.

- Finally, investors and other third parties look for leaders who understand that, while they may be talented entrepreneurs, their skills need to be complimented with other assets in order to grow the business appropriately.

Identifying where your skills can be supplemented or complemented can quickly accelerate your company's growth. Once you recognize these areas, you can plan accordingly. Look for a variety of resources whose experience balances yours. Find support from specialists or those with extensive experience in an area you are lacking. Their ease and efficiency will translate into your own effectiveness. Identifying where you need help; being candid with yourself and your constituents is not a weakness, it is a strength. Leaders who recognize their deficiencies and encourage others to do the same, gain respect, solve business issues more efficiently and set the foundation for well-run companies. There's also a good chance your day will be much more enjoyable.

Chapter 4
Rules to Live By

What We Feel: *I can't worry about how I do things. When the business gets going, I'll take care of myself. When we get more resources, I'll think about how to work better. For now, I'm heads down.*

In the chaotic world of entrepreneurship, it is rare that entrepreneurs assess how they work, and how they organize and execute their days. We are often running from fire to fire and don't think about the ways we can be more efficient, more balanced, more rested and more effective. Many entrepreneurs wear this frenetic pace like a badge of honor. In an environment with so many moving parts, you would think that we would be looking for ways to get more organized and structured. Quite the contrary. Entrepreneurs just go and go and go and don't have time to think about how to better manage themselves.

Say to an entrepreneur, "You have to sleep more" and they scoff. Say to an entrepreneur, "You should turn off your phone" and they think you have escaped from an insane asylum. For some reason, entrepreneurs embrace the consistent shunning of their own personal wellbeing and lives. Unfortunately, while this may feel like initiation dues into the club, it ends up making you less efficient and effective.

Your Change in Perspective

With a little attention to your work day, you can vastly improve your performance. Follow these rules and the impact will be obvious.

- **You must sleep.** It is impossible to maximize your time, potential and brainpower unless you sleep. I know what you are saying to yourself, "Who has time to sleep?" Not sleeping is the same as not protecting an asset of the company. If your vision was to make widgets, and you had a killer widget machine, wouldn't you make sure it had fuel and was properly oiled? It is hard to get sleep every day when you are the entrepreneur but you must. Here are a few suggestions.
    - **Eight hours once per week.** One day per week—preferably in the middle of the week—get eight hours of sleep. After the financial crisis of 2008, I was working twenty hours per day, but every Wednesday I went to bed at 10 p.m. and got eight hours. Made a world of difference.
    - **Take daily naps.** Each day close your eyes for thirty minutes. No more than thirty minutes. Any longer and you run the risk of developing "sleep inertia"—that groggy feeling that takes a considerable amount of time to shake off. Power naps not only alleviate sleep deficits, but they boost our brains, including creative problem solving, verbal memory, and perceptual object and statistical learning. Napping improves our mood and feelings of fatigue, is good for our heart, blood pressure, stress levels, and surprisingly, even weight. Where am I going to nap, you ask? Be creative. Under your desk, in your car, in the park, on your lunch break. One entrepreneur said that he would doze off in a bathroom stall when the hours got extra-long. You don't have to go that far, but make a plan for a short break. You'll feel the improvement in everything you do.
    - **Hitting the pillow means sleep.** When you put your head on the pillow at night, don't waste time thinking about problems you can't fix at that moment. When you are lying in bed, there is nothing you can do about your company's issues. Once you decide to sleep, don't think about the business. Find your version of counting sheep. I used to let my mind wander to a college baseball game or to a childhood memory. Regardless of your version of the strategy, make the commitment that once you put your head on the pillow, you are not going to waste time on things you can't impact.

- **Do the hardest task first thing in morning.** Do the most important or difficult task of the day first thing in the morning, when you are most rested and least distracted. Unfortunately, 90 percent of people check their email as soon as they get to work. That turns his or her agenda over to someone else. They do it because it's easy, and feel more effective in a shorter time by answering emails. Focus first on the hardest task of the day. This will allow you to apply your best to the most important jobs. Resist the temptation to do mindless or easy things to gain a brief sense of accomplishment.

- **Silence your technology.** When you are working on something, turn off your email and put your devices across the room with the sound off. Shifting your attention from one task to another, as we do when we're monitoring email while also reading a report and answering text messages, disrupts our concentration and saps our focus. Each time we return to our initial task, we use up valuable cognitive resources reorienting ourselves. Research shows that when we are deeply engrossed in an activity, even minor distractions can have a profound effect. The trouble, of course, is that multitasking is enjoyable. It's fun to indulge your curiosity. Who knows what that next email, tweet or text message holds in store? Finding out provides immediate gratification. In contrast, resisting distraction and staying on-task requires discipline and mental effort. It's up to you to protect your cognitive resources. The more you do to minimize task-switching over the day, the more mental bandwidth you'll have for activities that matter.

- **Never send an email after 10 p.m.** After a long day, our guard is down and our mind is not as sharp. We are careless, make mistakes, and let the pressures of the day impact our decision-making. We also tend to be reactionary and are more likely to get angry or frustrated. If you have something fresh in your head, write your email and stick it in your draft folder. Read it in the morning. Trust me, more often than not, you will say, "I'm glad I didn't send that last night."

Emails to employees and other team members late at night also send a negative message. When we send emails to employees late at night, especially those that require follow-up or effort on their part, it makes them feel as if we don't respect the time they put in or the time they need away from the business. This lack of respect can undermine your culture. Not to mention that constantly being in a work state of mind hinders everyone's performance. Many of the greatest mistakes have been made after 10 p.m. As the leader, we must demonstrate our respect for our team, and their individual lives and efforts, especially for those early team members who are putting in long hours and making their own sacrifices.

- **Don't be at work when you are not at work.** Time is our most valuable asset. We take little time away from work. When you do, don't think about work. When you do something social, or attend an event, or go to a family function, or watch a movie, be present and get engrossed in where you are. It does you no good to go and think about the business. The worst thing you can do is to take time away, go to a non-business function and spend the time thinking about the business. If you are going to take the rare time away from work to enjoy, make sure you are present. If not, don't go.

  Your mind also needs to clear and your brain will appreciate different stimulus. Your mind is working twenty-four hours a day thinking about the business and it needs a break. When you let yourself experience something unrelated to work, it helps settle your mind. It doesn't only need a break to let it rest. It needs a break to think about other things. This will help to unlock the creativity you need to advance your business. When we think about your business all the time, our perspective becomes too limited. We fail to be exposed to solutions that might come from a more balanced existence. Reading the newspaper, discussing current events, talking about fashion, discussing someone else's business or job—all of these introduce new perspectives about the world that not only help free your mind, but might have application to your business. Make time for and be open to unexpected intersections.

Think of yourself as part of the product or service you are delivering. If the diamond in your jewelry wasn't holding, wouldn't you change the setting? If your consulting services were too expensive, wouldn't you change the price? If your wearable device didn't transmit the right data, wouldn't you change the technology? It is no different with you. Especially with the strain you are under and the constant presence of the Four Ps, you need to be better, faster and stronger. These rules will help you build a better product to serve customers, employees, investors and you.

Chapter 5
You Want to Believe

What We Feel*: You have so many issues to solve. You so want to believe that the option in front of you—an employee you may hire, a vendor you may select, an investor you may take money from—fits your needs even though in your heart of hearts you know you are making a bad decision.*

We are under pressure. We have limited time and resources. We want customers. We want money. We want people. We want investors. Nope. We need customers. We need money. We need people. We need investors. Gaining market acceptance is key to our success. Forging relationships with key employees, vendors and investors is critical. When we interact with the market, interview an employee, evaluate a vendor or present to an investor, we want—sorry, need—things to move in a positive direction. We want to believe that the customer, employee, vendor or investor sitting in front of us wants to do business with us or is right for our business.

This "need" clouds our judgment. You will be evaluating a consultant who seems to have a lot of experience and isn't that expensive. He can also start right away. Our first thought is, "Wow, someone who we can afford and who is available?" Do you ask yourself, "If he is good, why is he cheap and why is he not working?" Of course not. We want to believe.

This is a tough balancing act. Many employees who work for entrepreneurial ventures and subject themselves to the hours and pressures of early stage ventures are often young or inexperienced. This does not mean that they are not valuable but simply that they lack certain skills.

The same is true with vendors. In early stages, you don't bring the promise of a long-term relationship or large volume guarantees to vendors. In most cases, the prospect of your business is important enough to them that they will take a chance for the potential. If they are willing to help you, it may be true that they believe in your potential, but it is equally likely that they have extra capacity or gaps in quality that may come out later.

Your Change in Perspective

Entrepreneurs tend to fall into two very different perspectives on this issue. The first—one that is debilitating and one that can be very productive. Entrepreneurs with a flawed perspective let the Four Ps overcome their judgment, and the judgment of others, to ignore the facts in front of them. For example, you interview a prospective employee who has never worked in your industry. You convince yourself that if the individual knows his functional area, you can teach them the industry, even if the industry is nuclear physics. Or you meet with potential investors who have a track record of negotiating contracts that require an exit event in one to two years. You turn a blind eye to this risk, and convince your team that this will force you to be more focused and efficient than your original five-year plan.

This perspective also causes us to underestimate the amount of time it takes to forge relationships with key constituents such as customers and investors. Think of your potential customers. You want to win this customer. You need to win that customer. Don't get me wrong, you can influence and shorten a sales cycle. However, winning customers takes time. At every stage, you must earn the right to advance with customers. Objectively understanding where you are in a sales cycle is critical to tailoring your strategic and tactical approach to winning customers. That starts with understanding where you stand, not where you want to stand with a customer.

The same is true when it comes to investors. You are running out of money and time. You need investment. Not surprisingly, you walk out of an investor meeting assuming the following: *The investor you've just met for the first time, is perfect. The investor is definitely interested and will finalize an investment in thirty days.* Be realistic with yourself. Investments take a long time. Assume six months. If it happens quicker, great. Don't forget, investors are deliberate and see a lot of deals. There is nothing wrong with being excited, but don't let your need or desire (or panic) about the necessity of capital cloud the details of the meeting, terms, or relationship that is actually occurring.

The second group of entrepreneurs have developed the right perspective. They

- Understand the influence of the Four Ps and how it can affect their judgment
- Are honest with themselves about the deficiencies of the employee, customer, vendor or investor
- Acknowledge that they may have to accept these deficiencies
- Establish a variety of communication strategies and tools to address or improve on these deficiencies.

This perspective enables the entrepreneur to acknowledge that the solution in front of them may not be ideal. They ask themselves, "We can't afford the level of employee that we need. This person has some great qualities but some large gaps. Is it worth our time to help them develop?" They understand that there are gaps that must be managed. Instead of leading to frustration, this can lead to a concerted and productive team effort to get the resource to perform.

- **Employees.** When you understand the gaps of a new employee, you can make a concerted effort to train them or build process to expose them to the skills that they need.
- **Vendors.** If you are concerned about a vendor's quality or ability to perform, create a regular process such as a weekly check-in meeting to hold them accountable. Set the tone from the beginning that you expect a weekly written report on progress.
- **Customers.** You may have to take on customers that are not ideal—they don't pay you enough or are not in your target market. However, they provide revenue that you desperately need. Ask these customers if you can use them as a reference. Ask them if they will participate in your product development effort. Ask your customers if they have anyone they would be willing to refer you to.

- **Investors.** When you desperately need capital, it's easy to choose investors who will give you what you most need—money. Without a clear perspective, however, you may be choosing partners who are deeply misaligned with other goals and long-term needs. Establish regular, transparent communication with this investor. Have candid discussions about their goals, your own goals, and design a plan that serves both of your needs.

For entrepreneurs, the early stages of building a business are particularly challenging, simply because you lack resources, established customers, relationships, capital and employees. But in the end, your perspective is everything: you can choose to ignore harmful deficits and continue to "want to believe." To believe that the employee is right. To believe that the vendor will perform. To believe that the investor will fund. To believe that the customer will sign on. Or you can acknowledge this ineffectual perspective and turn the temptation to look the other way, or see what you want to see, into a chance to involve your entire team in better decision-making. You want to believe. The sooner you realize this about yourself, the sooner you can address this natural tendency and turn a frustration into a win.

Chapter 6
You Need a Release

What We Feel: *I've gotten so used to the intensity, the hours and the stress that I hardly notice anymore.*

As entrepreneurs, sometimes the battle becomes a badge of honor. While having the "nothing can stop me" attitude is helpful, it also often causes us to turn a blind eye to what the experience is doing to our body and our mind. Entrepreneurs will say, "Who has time to relax? The only people who can afford to go to yoga at 6 p.m. are people who have never been entrepreneurs." While some may think that this affords you superhero status, it actually is very shortsighted. Think of a runner that runs the 100-meter dash and sprints the whole way. Now ask that same runner to run at the same speed but maintain it for a mile. It is in the DNA of many entrepreneurs to do just that. We take on all challenges, and figure the work and the stress are just part of the deal.

Of course we should work less. Of course we should sleep more. Of course we should spend time having fun. Seems obvious, yet none of this makes sense to the entrepreneur who needs customers or investors, or is worrying about payroll. But if you fail to recognize what this can do to your mental and physical wellbeing, and fail to act on it, it will eventually (or very suddenly) affect you and the organization.

Your Change in Perspective

You need a release—probably more than one. The pressures of being an entrepreneur can be overwhelming. You must have outlets and even guilty pleasure you turn to for a release. This is not contrary to the idea of being an entrepreneur. This is actually a way to be a healthier, happier, more productive and more efficient entrepreneur. These were mine:

- **Working Out.** To me, there is nothing like a good sweat. When you are kicking the shit out of yourself, it's hard to think about your balance sheet. During the most difficult of days of IncentOne, in early 2009, I would arrive at my office at 5 a.m. and jump on the Stairmaster we had in the gym in our office. Every day I would set it to the highest level and sweat my ass off. Sometimes after my day, I would go to the 8:45 p.m. Bikram Yoga class at 83rd and 3rd in Manhattan. Ninety minutes. One hundred and five degrees. It was cathartic. Some of the best workouts I had were during the toughest times because my mind was completely elsewhere. Breaking a sweat every day was a huge release.
- **Reyna and Brendan.** The time I spent with my brother's kids, Reyna and Brendan, was magical. My brother and his wife lived on 52nd Street and Lexington in New York and I would go there Saturdays around 3 p.m. to watch them until about 7 p.m. Seeing their young faces allowed me to take a step back and get lost in their smiles. Seeing them take joy in the basics of life left me with energy to take on the challenges of being an entrepreneur. My brother and sister-in-law thought I was helping them by giving them a few hours to themselves. They were helping me a lot more by allowing me an opportunity to reorient my perspective.
- **Bourbon.** I was never a big drinker. I only drank socially, and I had never found an alcohol that I liked. Of course bourbon is all the rage these days but in 2008 bourbon was nothing more than Jack Daniels. Then, I had a discovery late one night at a friend's bar. You've heard this story already so let's just say I left with a new perspective on bourbon. Even a few sips were calming. Today I am the proud owner of a refined bourbon palate and too much knowledge of brown water. Angel's Envy. Blanton's. Tincup. Larceny.
- **The Twenty-Year Commute.** My Mom and Dad were from the Bronx. When they had me, they moved to Freehold, New Jersey—sixty miles south of New York City where my Dad worked. For twenty years, he boarded the bus in Freehold and rode ninety minutes into New York City to his office on Madison Avenue. Twice a day, each

day, ninety minutes each way, for years. Now that's grit. Now that's dedication. What I was doing paled in comparison. Every time I felt soft, I remembered the sacrifice he made. Staying up late to work on an investor deck always seemed easy when compared to twenty years in a bus on Route 9 headed to New York City.

• **The Greatest Generation and D-Day.** It always bothered me that our generation and today's generation don't realize the courage of our parents' generation. The sacrifices that they made to make the America we know and love, are too often forgotten. This is especially true of the military and of World War Two and D-Day. Soldiers stormed the beaches at Normandy, knowing there was a good chance they would die minutes after they got there. Imagine the courage. Imagine the sacrifice. I'm not even sure we can. If you get the chance, read about it, go to the World War Two museum in New Orleans. To this day, every Memorial Day, I sneak away from whatever barbecue or family event I am at and sit for a few hours at a local Memorial Day service. While fighting to save our business, these stories helped me get back on track when I faltered.

Whether it is bourbon, working out, yoga, meditation, spending time with your family or going to the movies alone, you need your release. Not only will you get the benefit of the release, but also your perspective will change. When we are wrapped up in our own world, it is difficult to see beyond our four walls. When you break a sweat, or think about the sacrifice of others, or see a child smile, your brain takes a break. It stops focusing on all of the things on your plate (and all the things you are not getting to). Give your brain a well-deserved time out and it will really clear your head. This leads to new ideas, new ways of thinking and new, often more creative solutions to problems. Find your release and make it a part of your week.

Chapter 7
Whom Should I Trust?

__What We Feel__: I really think that my vendors and investors have our best interests at heart. It's good to be able to work with and confide in people that want to see our business be successful.

When you start a business, you spend a lot of time alone with your thoughts. Even if you're not a solo operation, there may be very few people that you confide in or talk openly to. You probably have your inner circle. It may start with a circle of one—you—or maybe your small team. To get your business moving, you develop relationships with a select few people who are helping you get ahead. This might be a vendor such as a design firm or manufacturing company who helps you create your product or service. It might be a broker that helps you raise money. It might be an investor that has given you a little capital to get going.

It is not uncommon for entrepreneurs to develop trust with these individuals—even if you barely know them. How many times have you confided your lifelong dreams to a vendor you just hired? Or to an advisor you just met? Or to an investor that is considering an investment. Entrepreneurs have this pent-up need to talk about the dreams and issues of the company—and where all the bodies are buried. Your balloon is full and the air needs somewhere to go.

A company's first vendor or advisor can also often become its psychologist. You have to share your deep dark secrets with someone, right? While this is certainly understandable, it is important to make a distinction between the people that you do business with and those that you trust with your deepest, darkest secrets.

Your Change in Perspective

Trust must be earned. You do not earn someone's trust because you do business with them. Someone does not earn your trust because they do business with you. Think of it like your fraternity. When you join a fraternity, you are told that you should trust all your "brothers" and that they should trust you. It only takes the first time that one "brother" hits on the girlfriend of another "brother" that you realize trust does not materialize because of a name or an affiliation, but from earning it. This is true in your business. You have to earn the trust of others and they have to earn your trust. This applies to everyone—investors, customers, employees, consultants, and vendors:

> *I had a CEO colleague who was manufacturing a product and near the production of the final version, the manufacturer demanded additional dollars to finish the product. The manufacturer felt that additional monies were owed to them and would not deliver the product until they received the money. This put the business in a difficult position so the CEO immediately started sourcing another vendor. She was lucky enough to find one.*

> *Even though the CEO and the president of the new vendor had never met, the CEO shared with the new vendor the details of the current situation, including the fact that the previous vendor had put them in a tough spot. The new vendor told the CEO he understood, and a week later provided a price quote that was in line with the CEO's expectations. The CEO communicated, "If we don't deliver our product for the launch next month, we are screwed." The CEO told the vendor that they would go with them.*

> *Two weeks later, the new vendor's quote grew by almost 70 percent. The CEO was shocked to see a revised quote that the vendor said "was because the devil was in the details and they were not aware of some of the complexities."*

This is particularly important when it comes to investors. Trust doesn't exist because someone invests in your company. You have to earn the trust of your investor. Your investor has to earn your trust. Many investors, especially the most successful ones, view investing with a talented entrepreneur as a win-win. If they enable the business, both the investor and the entrepreneur can win. Some investors, however, view it as a zero-sum game. A dollar that you get is a dollar they don't get. These investors will use their influence to make sure that more of those dollars go to them. The priority should be that when the business thrives, investors and the entrepreneur win. Let's not be naïve. For many investors, the priority is the best interest of the investor followed by what's in the best interest of the business, and then finally, the entrepreneur. Often entrepreneurs treat investors like confidants and share many details that they should keep to themselves—including that their investment proposal is the only game in town. Building trust with an investor is critical but that trust must be earned:

I was introduced to my investor by Jason, the former CEO of a healthcare company. The CEO knew healthcare and also the payment space. Our investor had invested in the CEO's company when he was CEO. In our deal structure, our board allowed for one independent Board member that would be picked by our investor and me. I figured this CEO was the perfect fit since our investor had invested in his company, he had introduced us and he knew the space. I suggested this to our investor. I suggested he knew both of us, knew the space and had no other agenda. He strongly objected. I was surprised.

Prior to closing our deal, I asked our investor for references. The investor gave me as a reference the new CEO of the company of which Jason was formerly CEO. I thought it was strange to have the new CEO as a reference. We had a cordial conversation and I poked and prodded. I got some stock answers and overall a positive reference as you would expect.

Prior to that phone conversation I had never spoken to the CEO. About ten minutes later the phone rang and he was calling again. It was strange because we had concluded but at first I didn't think much of it. He said to me, "I understand you're considering Jason to be on your Board." I was taken aback. Why would he even know I was considering somebody for my Board?

He went on to say that he's been a CEO for a while and always is in the business of trying to help other CEOs. I told him I appreciated that. He then buried Jason. He said that Jason was not trustworthy and was not the type of person that you want on your Board. I thanked him, told him I appreciated his candor and got off the phone. I was blown away. Imagine someone who I've never met before throwing somebody else under the bus. For all he knew, I could've been a reporter for the New York Times.

It told me all I needed to know about my investor. My investor didn't want Jason on the Board and instructed the CEO to coax me to keep Jason off my Board. At that point I should've walked away. A few months later, our investor sued Jason.

I know you are seeking people to confide in. I know you want to be able to share information with the vendors, advisors, consultants and investors that help you grow your business. I know you want to believe that everyone you interact with will share your vision, have your best interests at heart and make the sacrifices it takes to make it happen. Don't let these natural desires cloud your perspective. Regardless of your wants, trust must be earned. Do not trust someone because they write you a check or sign a contract. By the same token, no one should come to the table trusting you. Your perspective must allow you to come to the table with an open mind, but make sure before you confide in someone that they have earned the right. Make sure that people demonstrate the behavior and attitude that warrants your trust. Have they demonstrated it over a period of time? Have they made concessions to help you advance your business? Have they gone out of their way to advance your business? Have they had your back in a sticky situation? Try to be objective and start from the basic premise that they must earn your trust before you start telling them about the petty crimes you committed in college.

SECTION 3:

LIKE IT OR NOT, YOU NEED TO BE CEO

Introduction

When asked whether their goal was to "lead a company," many entrepreneurs will say, "no." They will say that what motivated them was their passion, their niche, their product, their idea. In fact, many may not have thoroughly considered the "company" part of being an entrepreneur. Think of the doctor, the technologist, the jewelry maker, the fashion designer, the consultant, the scientist and the publicist. They see a way for their unique product or service to come to life. They rarely think about offices, finances, capital, organizational structure, team management, priority setting, and the list goes on.

Imagine if an entrepreneur was trying to attract you to come work for their jewelry business. They could pitch you in one of two ways:

> *"We develop pieces for women that combine the world's most exotic gemstones with a personalized approach to styling. Women find our pieces compelling, colorful, playful and unique."*

OR

> *"We hold meetings every Tuesday, set priorities and allocate resources accordingly, and have regular finance review on key company metrics."*

The first sounds a lot sexier than the second. The passion of most entrepreneurs is focused on developing the product or service that they know, love, feel or understand. It's rarely focused on the organizational activities that are required to make a business work. While organizational charts are much less sexy than selecting gemstones, businesses must be led and organized.

If your perspective—like the perspective of many entrepreneurs—doesn't recognize this reality, it will make progress difficult. Even though your passion may be focused on the product or service you deliver, you must lead the company. If you are the technologist, you must lead the company. If you are a fashion designer, you must lead the company. If you are the scientist, you must lead the company. Many companies with great ideas struggle because there is no one leading them.

By the way, even if you don't want the job, it's yours because everyone will be looking to you regardless of your title. Employees, customers, vendors, advisors and investors will all expect you as the entrepreneur to lead. Whether you wanted the job or not, congratulations, you have been promoted to CEO.

Now that you have the job, you must understand the impact you will have if you don't lead, or if you lead with the wrong perspectives. The perspectives in this section are designed to understand how you are perceived, the impact of your actions, the do's and don'ts and how you must act and communicate.

I know—you thought there would be a big party when you became CEO. Just like when you became the entrepreneur, no one handed you a membership card. Same with being CEO. When you are the entrepreneur, even if you don't have the title, you must run the show. This section shows you how.

Chapter 1
A Deliberate, Thoughtful and Unemotional Leader

What We Feel: *I'm constantly worried about not having enough cash or resources. I am overwhelmed all the time and the pressure makes me react to whatever crisis comes across my desk that day. I don't feel like I have the time or emotional energy to think things through. I just react to problems as they arrive.*

There will be plenty of times that you debate with yourself and others, whether you are qualified or even want to be the CEO of the company. Whether you're eager for the position or pushed unwillingly to it, you must be the CEO during the entrepreneurial launch stage of your company. Whether it is just you, a small team or fifty of you, you need to act like the CEO and must do many things, including:

- Set the priorities of the company
- Align the organization to those priorities
- Ensure that the company is properly funded
- Inspire people to stick to the vision
- Clearly communicate with the various constituents of the company.

Being the CEO of an established company is hard enough, but being the CEO of a developing business is the ultimate baptism by fire. In most cases, you must do it all without formal training. It takes most leaders their entire career to develop the skills of a good CEO. Is it fair to expect you to learn all the skills of a CEO when it takes most a lifetime? Of course not. Too bad—you have to learn those skills in a fraction of that time. You're on the accelerated course. You must be the leader.

Many entrepreneurs feel that this formality is only important for larger companies. To the contrary, when you have limited resources, it is incredibly important to make sure you are focusing on the right things, communicating with clarity and making sure everyone is on the same page. And you need to do these things even it is just you.

In addition to the functions you must perform, you must be three things: unemotional, deliberate and thoughtful—all while in the midst of the chaos that comes with entrepreneurial ventures. The ability to keep your head when things around you are going wrong or not making sense is a true skill, but one you must master.

It's unlikely, especially when you're getting started, that you feel "unemotional," "deliberate" and "thoughtful" very often. On the contrary, you're full of vision, passion, energy—traits that make you a dynamic entrepreneur in the first place—but not always a good CEO. Your balloon is too full and being unemotional, thoughtful and deliberate is tough when you're looking for every opportunity to let out a little air. But sometimes you have to hold your breath. Since we are always under the influence of the Four Ps, you must see through the noise and pressure of the moment and make deliberate, thoughtful and unemotional decisions. I know what you're thinking—"I wish I could feel one of those things for even one hour."

I can't say it will be easy, but what's the alternative? You risk making poor decisions and alienating your team, as well as vendors, investors, and clients—and if that weren't enough—having others question your leadership potential and the potential your business can succeed. So how do you shift your perspective?

Your Change in Perspective

There are several things you must do. First, you must take emotion out of the equation. Among other things, emotion causes us to be reactive and on the defensive. When we are emotional, we react immediately and impulsively to the situation at hand, but fail to account for, not only the consequences of our decisions, but the impact on our audience.

Consider this scenario: the vendor working on your technology platform tells you that even though they are 90 percent done and one month from your product launch, it is going to cost you an extra 50 percent to complete it. Your first reaction is to get pissed. Thoughts run through your head: "Why couldn't they have shared this weeks or months ago? Where the hell do they think we can get the money? I can't believe they are trying to take advantage of us." You are tempted to lose it, to send your pal "Tony" to have a "conversation" with them. Or maybe you'll just fire them on the spot. Boy that would feel good—they should know who they are messing with! You may have, in fact, been treated poorly but there are other things to consider before you close the conversation with a knockout punch. Do you have a backup plan? Have you protected your confidential information? Do you have a plan to communicate with your employees or customers? Are there alternatives that can meet your financial goals? You get the point.

In addition, when leaders react emotionally, they send a signal of instability to those inside and outside of the company. Think about how often you reacted to the situation in front of you only to come back a day later and realize the implications of your actions.

> *I was recently at an event at which former US president George W. Bush spoke. He was asked to take us through his thought process when he was told about the attacks of September 11. He was sitting in front of a first grade class when Andy Card, his chief of staff, whispered in his ear, "A second plane hit the World Trade Center. We are under attack." President Bush said the first thing that went through his mind was that he was pissed and wanted to jump out of his chair and get to work. Instead, he sat, waited for what seemed like forever until the class was done, slowly walked out, met with parents as per his schedule and then left with his team. He understood that the most important thing at that moment was to convey a sense of calm.*

Being unemotional is counterintuitive for the entrepreneur. After all, it is likely the passion you have for your idea that fuels your ability to think differently. While removing emotion from the decision-making process is expected in most formal business environments, for entrepreneurs, it is one of the most needed assets, and an operating method we need to tap into every day. We need it to overcome challenges. We need it to keep employees moving ahead. We need it to keep ourselves sane. It is what gets entrepreneurs started in the first place and keeps them going.

Being unemotional is only part of the equation. You also have to be thoughtful and deliberate. For important issues, you must take the time to think through issues. In early stages of entrepreneurship, you often don't have the financial or human resources or the processes to make good decisions. In addition, because you often lack resources, you need to tap into the same creativity that helped you create your vision, and, like your passion, redirect it to support what your evolving business needs. Don't get me wrong. It would be great if the issue with your technology vendor was solved with a courteous "No problem. We were planning for this contingency and have a backup offshore shop doing parallel work." Right. You need to bring a thoughtfulness to your decision-making process to take advantage of your creativity and the creativity of others. It takes some time and talent to get blood from a stone or to make money grow on trees. It's pretty common that you will need to do both.

Finally, you need to be deliberate. Many days for the entrepreneur are just about scrambling. With important issues, you have to slow down, anticipate what's coming, and make decisions instead of reacting to decisions and consequences already made. As hard as it is to change pace—and perspective—go slow when it comes to important decisions. Important decisions are also rarely ones you'll want to make alone. They almost always should include other people, other approval, other opinions, and many other questions. In reality, you're actually answering fifty questions to get to the big one you started with. You have to shift your perspective to not only see that big questions have multiple steps and multiple players, but that you need to give attention to those individual questions and how they get you to the final answer. Slow down the game and take deliberate action.

Not only is deliberation key to making good decisions, it sets the tone for the company. This is true regardless of whether it's a two-person partnership, a solo performance, or a business with a strong organizational chart and an established employee base. When you can take a step back and get the perspective you need, you create a sense of confidence and stability for everyone around you. Everyone is looking to you, and when situations come across your desk, how you act affects every piece of your business, and the perspective of everyone you encounter. This desk, after all, is sitting dead center in a house made of glass.

So how do you change your perspective from how you feel now—reactive, emotional and like you never have time to think—to unemotional, deliberate and thoughtful? First you need to recognize the emotions you are experiencing so that they are not mistaken for justifications or valid reasoning in your decision-making. Some days it may be obvious to you (and everyone else) that you are reacting to emotion and making poor decisions. Other days, your emotions may seem perfectly valid and not "emotional" at all. Taking an honest assessment of your thoughts is critical. Second, you need to understand that these behaviors undermine the day-to-day operations of your company from small details to major decision-making. Would you ever add a feature to your product or service that hurt sales, marketing or retention? Of course not. But that is what you are doing when you act emotionally, or without proper thought or deliberation. It is your appreciation and understanding of these consequences that should help you shift your perspective. Once you understand these consequences, it should be clear why.

What are the impacts?

- **Faith in Your Leadership.** You want to be a true leader. You want to inspire others. You need people to plow ahead in the face of challenges. It's plain and simple. Regardless of your talents and skills, when you react emotionally it makes people doubt whether you are the person that can take the company forward.
- **Impact on Employees.** You need employees to perform. You need employees to move the business forward and to take initiative when they are often underpaid and overworked. It becomes harder

to motivate your team when the person running the show (You) seems unstable, haphazard or reactive.

- **Impacts on Customers and Investors.** Customers and investors can smell instability. When they see emotion they think things like, "How am I going to deal with this person when there is a problem?" and "How is this person going to deal with problems?" Customers and investors will choose to do business with people who work well under fire, and who collaborate professionally even when things aren't going so well.
- **Impacts on Vendors.** Like customers and investors, vendors can sense when you are being emotional and reactive. You never want to be in a position in which a vendor can take advantage of you because they know how to manipulate your tendency to react. Don't let your emotions undermine your ability to negotiate.

Once you realize that the consequences of this perspective are no less damaging than a poor product or poorly delivered service, you will start to police your behavior. Once you become aware of these behaviors, make sure the emotion driving them has somewhere healthy to go. Before the day gets started and decisions get tough, develop your own version of a "deep breath" even if it means keeping a punching bag handy in your office (but close the blinds first, please). You can also take five minutes to write down your feelings, meditate, stretch, do yoga, squeeze a stress ball—you know what's best for you—but find something and have a plan ready in advance. Coping with your emotions is a daily part of the entrepreneurial battle. Sometimes, the day-to-day can get overwhelming, and we discuss coping strategies in more depth in the chapter entitled "You Need a Release." For now, you've got to find a way to manage it every day.

Finally, you need to be accountable. This may be the hardest part, but you can't change your perspective without taking responsibility. Start with having someone hold you accountable. Have an advisor who sees you in action "score" you on a scale of one to ten. Have them keep track of how many times you flew off the handle, yelled or swore. Forget about why—just keep track. (Remember, you always feel these are justified.)

Then hold yourself accountable. Check in biweekly and rescore yourself. Create a fine for yourself—every time you react the wrong way, put five dollars in a jar. You'll find that when your behavior is actually being measured objectively by you and others, you will monitor yourself with more discipline. You'll also be less likely to justify emotional reactions as part of dealing with "the nature of the beast."

Start today by making the commitment to being a more unemotional, deliberate and thoughtful leader. Take stock of your current behavior, reactiveness, and impact on those around you. As you improve your self-awareness and control, the benefits will be obvious. Your passion may have launched your vision into being, but now that passion needs to be redirected in an *unemotional, thoughtful and deliberate way* to support and inspire your maturing business. Someday you will look back fondly and say to yourself, "I can't believe I acted like that."

Chapter 2
Seven Deadly Sins

What We Feel: *With all the chaos, everyone needs to understand that there are going to be things that we say or do that are not appropriate. We can't worry about how everybody acts in every meeting. It is just the nature of the beast and we have bigger fish to fry.*

You think to yourself, "I am building a company, and I am too stressed and busy to worry about other people's feelings all day. So what if I get a little angry with vendors or employees. There's no time to be nice—that can wait until the company is up and running."

Normal and *entrepreneur* rarely share the same sentence. In many entrepreneurial ventures, it is probably a good thing that there is not a human resources department. People are reactive, time bankrupt, sleep deprived and feeling the pressure on a daily basis. In the chaos of your venture, and under the influence of the Four Ps, you often find yourself saying things, doing things and allowing things that would be taboo in a normal environment. If entrepreneurial ventures had, for example, a "curse jar" that required a five-dollar "donation" for every curse, we might be able to solve the national deficit pretty quickly.

Seems harmless enough, right? Many inappropriate things are said or done in the midst of the chaos of an entrepreneurial venture. Our perspective that they are "no big deal" is correct. Anyone with some experience in the entrepreneurial world knows that it's hard to be on your best behavior when you are under the influence of the Four Ps. Does it really matter if we get out of line every once in a while? For the most the part, we can say, "no harm, no foul." Except for the "Seven Deadly Sins" below.

Your Change in Perspective

With so much going on all the time, it is hard to determine what decisions are important and what decisions are just the flavor of the day. There are certain foundational elements of your business that must be established to create order, alignment and discipline. Part of this is setting the behavior guardrails within which you and your team must operate. You must establish a set of ideals and perspectives that are non-negotiable for everyone. There are certain behaviors that have a lasting effect beyond the moment they occur. These "seven deadly sins"—especially when they come from the leader—send a message that can have a lasting effect. With these behaviors, unless you eliminate them completely, they can set poor standards, establish values contrary to the interests of the company, and create a toxic culture that can be hard to clean up. Avoid these Seven Deadly Sins at all costs.

THE SEVEN DEADLY SINS

1. Speaking Negatively about Customers

When you or people in your organization say things like, "Our customers are clueless" or "We can sell that to them," it sends a clear message not only of disrespect, but ignorance about the role customers play in your company's success. If this is part of your dialogue, it is likely your business does not understand the central role that customers play in your success. If your perspective is anything other than creating success for your customer, you are likely to fail. When you think, "Our customers won't care if we take a little shortcut" or "Our customer will not know the difference," you have lost your way. That's not to say that your customer *knows best* or is *always right*. However, if you come to work thinking that you are pulling the wool over their eyes, or not valuing their views, you won't succeed.

If negative talk becomes habitual, you are more likely to think of your customers, not as allies—but scapegoats. After all, it's easier (and faster) to blame the customer for everything that is going wrong than to take a good, hard look at yourself, your product, your service and your people. In the early stages of your business, you will likely have customer issues, especially if you are creating something innovative. Your product or service will not perfectly fit the needs of the customer. Customers will not want to pay for what you perceive to be the value of your product or service. You may not have all the infrastructure to service your customers. These are all common customer issues of young companies.

Organizations must develop products and services that have a clear value—value that customers understand and are willing to pay for. That's hard to do. But if you adopt the negative perspective above, you'll miss a critical opportunity to take stock of your own flaws and make progress. Worse, if you're playing the "blame game," you'll likely miss the aha moment when an unexpected solution suddenly becomes visible. As a result, you may find yourself blaming customers, calling them dumb, or saying they don't "get it." If you give yourself this excuse, you won't take the candid look at your own organization that is necessary to make the changes you need to succeed.

Speaking of customers in a negative light also sends a message to your employees that it is acceptable to blame customers, instead of addressing the issue and troubleshooting a creative solution to problem. Crafting new solutions not only strengthens your team's ability to take responsibility and problem solve, but encourages stronger customer relationships—and your own success.

At some point, you realize that customers are *what stir the drink*. When your customers fail, you fail. We have to continually challenge ourselves to serve our customers with the knowledge that without them, there is no business. If our customer does not understand, or doesn't believe they are getting value from our product or service, we must spend every waking moment changing that. When you exist to serve customers, your perspective pays off in spades.

2. Speaking Negatively about Employees

If you or others in your organization speak negatively about employees, it sends the message that the company does not value people and is only in the business of advancing people when it serves the company's needs. There are times when the skill level of your employees is deficient or part of your team is underperforming. There will also be day-to-day frustrations that come with managing employees. During these interactions, make sure that you speak to and about employees with respect. These individual encounters quickly become a part of your culture and an expression of your brand that reflects on you as a leader and on the reputation of your company. How you speak has a significant effect on employee morale, the efficacy of your leadership, and ultimately, the reputation of you and your company.

There are some common but particularly difficult circumstances that arise from time to time that can throw you off your game if you're not prepared with the necessary perspective.

- **When an employee leaves the company.** When individuals choose to leave, sometimes our concern for the business and the insecurity caused by the gap left to fill, causes us to act inappropriately. Our first reaction is often a negative feeling toward the employee and an assumption that he or she didn't value the organization. We might react with statements like, "They were not that good anyway" or "It was time for them to go" or "We will be better off."

Speaking ill of individuals who leave the organization (e.g., *It's good that "Steve" is leaving. He was not that good anyway*) sends the message that employees are not valued and that the organization lacks respect for those supporting it. This not only has a negative effect on existing employees, and as mentioned above, it can also blind companies to the root causes of that individual's departure. It is easy to blame the individual leaving than ask, "What is it about the organization that would make an employee want to leave?"

One more tip. When employees leave, always ask for an exit interview if they are open to it. You would be surprised what departing employees will communicate when they are leaving.

> *A project manager had been with us for four years. He decided to move to another opportunity. As a project manager, he was in the middle of a variety of cross-functional activities. I asked for an exit interview and he was happy to oblige. He said there was something we should know. He let me know that the technology-outsourcing firm we had been using overseas was run by a relative of our head of technology and he believed there was an inappropriate financial relationship in place.*

- **When an employee is fired.** When an employee is not performing to expectations, it is rare that that individual will agree with you. This can cause hard feelings. Nonetheless, you should treat these individuals with respect. Your view should be that the organization is moving the individual to a situation in which he or she can be more successful.

Regardless of how your employees leave, take the high road. Wish them well and hope that they had a positive experience and that you contributed to their personal and professional goals. There will be some people who work for the company for a day. There will be others who work for years. You want every employee who works for the company to feel that they are better off than they were before. When employees leave, it gives us the opportunity to learn where we fell short and how we can improve as a company. And as you build your brand, you want to be known as an organization that people want to interact with and that treats people with respect. You want ex-employees who think highly of the organization. Employees who leave may come back in the future. Strive for the reputation that your organization is one that employees want to work for, and how you treat individuals when they leave is an important representation of that.

Speaking ill of current or past employees causes mistrust and tension for your existing employees who are probably wondering, "Is this what they'll say about me?" It also prevents you from taking the opportunity to see areas where you can improve your company culture, and build, dialogue, trust—and loyalty—with your employees.

3. Believing There Is No Competition

Everyone has competition. In a complex global economy with increasingly sophisticated technology, competition can occur almost immediately and from any corner of the world. If you or your company believe that you have no competition, or that no one can do what you do, you risk being viewed by vendors, investors and other needed resources, as naïve, inexperienced and ill-equipped to face the realities of doing business in today's world. Instead of strengthening the position of your vision, you risk being perceived as blind, whether by ignorance or ego, or simply the strain of the Four Ps. You become a risk, rather than a risk worth taking. Investors engage leaders who acknowledge, embrace, and strive to overcome the competition. Your ability to see reality must be as strong as your original vision if you want to bring it to life.

Don't run from or ignore competition. Acknowledge it, embrace it and take it head on with your best. Assume you will always have competition. Assume your competitors will be faster, smarter and better funded. Once you accept that this is the status quo, you can focus your energy on discovering how best to use your creativity to beat the competition.

4. Dismissing How Your Team Feels

Everyone understands that entrepreneurial ventures don't succeed, or exist, without hard work and dedication. But that doesn't mean you can ignore the needs and feelings of those struggling alongside you. If you dismiss your employees' state of mind when you communicate or make decisions, you undermine your company's strength, resilience and dedication to the business and its customers. You must respect the dedication it takes to do everything from the simplest daily task to the most complex business transaction. To do that, you have to be committed to knowing intimately how they feel and to demonstrating that knowledge through thoughtful action and encouragement. If you are thinking, *"I don't have time to worry about how people feel,"* your employees are thinking, *"Does our leader really understand the sacrifice we are making?"* That question is usually followed by, *"I wonder if the sacrifice is worth it?"* The effort and perspective of every single person matters. The organization cannot serve customers and its mission and make forward progress if its individual gears aren't well oiled and given proper attention.

5. Yelling, Talking Over People and Cutting People Off

I'd be lying if I said I nailed this one. Many times in meetings I felt that we were wasting time and that I was already past the issue. This caused me to cut people off and say "Got it." It got so common that it became an office joke. Don't do it. Raising your voice is the same. I know what you are saying, "But we just lost our biggest client." Your people want to see you calm, cool and collected, especially when things are going wrong. Do your best to keep good manners even in the midst of chaos. That's where it really counts anyway.

6. Making Exceptions for the CEO

One of the most damaging behaviors of a young company is demonstrating preferential treatment for its leader. When your team believes that your needs come first, or at their expense, or that the rank and file's needs are less important than the needs of the leader, it creates an undercurrent of resentment at all levels of employment. Similarly, when the rules apply to everyone but you, it sends the message that the CEO is above the law, and undermines the faith that you have the team's best interests at heart. On the other hand, when the CEO is the first person on the team to hold themselves accountable, or to be accountable to others, it sends a message that everyone is in this together.

7. Romantic Relationships with Company People

I know, you spend every waking hour on the business and these are the only people you see. I don't care. A great way to screw up a promising business is a personal relationship that goes bad. This includes everyone that works for the company as an employee, as well as all third parties such as customers, vendors, board members, advisors, auditors, lawyers, accountants, distributors, agencies, and vendors. It doesn't matter that someone doesn't report to you. It doesn't matter that they only do a little work for the company. Hopefully this does not warrant explanation:

> *A friend of mine was working for a woman's body butter company. He called me and said, "You went to law school. I have a question." I knew I was in trouble right there. He said he had finally met face to face his European distributor. Prior to that, his team members had interacted with her and her company. It turns out she was attractive and interesting to him. He asked if I thought it would be a problem if he pursued a relationship with her since she didn't work for the company. I said, "Of course it is a problem." He asked why, since they had no contact except their submission of quarterly sales numbers. I told him "What if the two of you had sex, and she turned to you after and said, 'Do you need anything?' and your response was, 'Sure, I could use stronger second quarter numbers.'"*

Blurring the lines between being passionate about a business and passionate about a person can happen in the midst of the entrepreneurial venture. It is one thing for the business to be under the influence of the Four Ps, the last thing you need is your personal relationships feeling pressure, passion, pleasure and pain in the middle of the workday. Never, never, never.

These Seven Deadly Sins aren't just for you, the CEO. They should be an operating agreement for your entire team. This means you must also have zero tolerance for anyone in the organization who exhibits these behaviors—including yourself. If these perspectives and behaviors—Seven Deadly Sins—develop, even for a short time, they become habits that will significantly undermine the strength of your team and the progress of your business for years to come. A strong company culture isn't something you build overnight, but with clear boundaries and a leader willing to model them, you can develop a devoted, effective and supportive team whose strength will match that of the business you're growing together. Our company culture was one of the things that we were proudest of at IncentOne. We had been through so much together that by the time we sold the company, we had a group that was committed and collaborative and always found a way to get things done. It only took us about ten years to get there, but hopefully, after arriving at this chapter, you will start far ahead of where I began.

Chapter 3
You Are Always Onstage

What We Feel: *I don't have the time or the energy to worry about how I am being perceived. No one is paying attention anyway because we are all heads down, 24/7.*

It's ironic. One of the things you worry about as you sit in your apartment, office or workspace is whether the world will even pay attention to what you are doing. Will anyone even notice?

But once someone does take note, you are always onstage. Before reading this, you probably thought you were on the clock a lot. Regardless of how many hours you log at your business, your home office or the local coffee shop, as an entrepreneur you're on the clock twenty-four hours per day, three hundred and sixty-five days per year. This does not mean that you work all those hours (although you probably do anyway). It does mean that you are constantly being watched and judged. Fair or not, you are the face of the organization and there is not a personal entrepreneur and a professional entrepreneur. There's only the entrepreneur and you are always being watched.

When you are the entrepreneur, you never get to leave the stage. It's like a Broadway show that runs all night and never shuts down. People are always watching. Your employees, investors, customers, advisors and vendors are always looking to you. They are looking to see if you are their leader. They are looking to see if they can trust you. They are looking to see if you can take the pressure. They are looking to see if you will make them a success. No time of day is off limits. No topic is off limits.

Slam the phone down once and your stability is questioned. Come late to a meeting and you are disrespectful. Show loyalty to an early employee of the business and you are putting your feelings ahead of the best interests of the company. Some of it is fair. Some of it is not.

Everything you do is on display, and is an evaluation process—especially for investors. You may never actually hear these questions, but it doesn't mean they aren't asking them.

- Do you acknowledge competition?
- Do you acknowledge that the team members that you have today, including you, may not be the team members to run the business down the line?
- Do you dominate the conversation or share the stage with your team members?
- Are you defensive about your gaps?
- Are your communications clear and to the point?
- How do you dress?
- How do you talk to employees?
- Are you on time?
- Do you drink?
- Do you talk over your team members in the presentation?
- Are you close with your family?
- Do you curse?
- Were you late to the meeting?
- Do you seem stressed?
- Are you overwhelmed by the pressure?

Ultimately, investors are asking themselves, "Does she have the leadership qualities we want?" It is not only about the subject matter at hand. For example, write a long, detailed email to explain something and you will think you did a nice job thoroughly explaining an issue. They may agree with your conclusion, but will still question your ability to align the organization with such a "verbose" communication style. You are always onstage.

This is also true with employees. Employees are watching your capabilities, temperament and daily behavior:

- Do you look tired?
- Do you yell?
- Do you slam the phone?
- Do you insult employees?
- Do you say hello when you walk past someone?
- Do you introduce yourself to new employees?
- Are you late to meetings?
- Do you favor certain employees over others?
- Do you welcome feedback and criticism?
- Do you talk negatively about team members, customer or employees?
- Do you insult former employees?
- Do you say one thing in public and another in private?
- Are you trustworthy?
- Did you cheat at cards?
- Do you dress well?
- What time do you get to work?
- What time you leave?
- Do you act as if you know it all or are constantly learning?

When you are busy running the business, you do not spend much time thinking about how you appear to people. You are focused on the tasks at hand. You may be running around with your hair messed up, your shoes untied, and the buttons on your shirt buttoned wrong.

Your Change in Perspective

The first part of this change in perspective is a realization. You must realize that your every word and deed is being monitored by everyone, everywhere. Even the smallest things can make a big difference.

For two years following the collapse of the financial markets and the bankruptcy of many of our customers, we were under a lot of pressure. The work day was twenty hours every day. One day, one of our customers who had committed to extending their contract called to tell me that they now had to terminate it. We had enough bad news and this customer turning from an extension to a termination was not welcome. After I hung up the phone, I slammed my hand on my desk and threw a rubber baseball I kept in my office against the wall. Two years later, after all the dust had settled, our company was out at an event and a long-time employee came over to me. She said she always had confidence that I would see us through. She did say, however, that the only time she felt like we weren't going to make it was the day that I slammed my hand on the desk. We all felt, "If it is getting to you, it must be bad."

In addition to a realization, it is an opportunity. At first, you may feel that with everyone watching, you are bound to screw up. Who wouldn't when you are on the clock day and night. But having an audience also provides you with the chance to influence some very powerful and positive company behaviors. For example, people notice:

- When you are the first to come to work
- When you are the last to leave work
- If you go to the end of the line when with employees to let them go first
- If you admit you don't know things
- If you thank people for their candor (and mean it)
- If you make fun of yourself
- If you display kindness and empathy.

This stage provides you with a forum to have an impact on the culture of your company and the behaviors of others. If you have this perspective, you see your constant stage performance not as a problem but as an opportunity to lead by example.

No one understands better than you that the success of your venture depends on—you. Your passion, dedication and drive are critical. Your ability to lead is equally important. It makes no difference whether or not you will ultimately be the CEO of the company. You may have gotten into this because you are a talented technologist or a skilled marketer. You may have never thought or cared about being a leader. Regardless, at the beginning of a new venture—like it or not—you are the leader. Your actions set the tone. In later stages, when there are more team members, your organization will have a culture that is bigger than you. For now, it's mostly you. If we were to look at a pie chart dividing responsibility for the company's future success, your portion would be about 99 percent. That's a lot of pie, especially when everyone is watching.

You can't escape being onstage, so use it to your advantage and put on a show they'll never forget.

Chapter 4
There's Always a Way

What We Feel: There are so many times when things seem impossible—times when you don't have the resources, money or wherewithal to accomplish the things you need to make the business successful.

When building a company, you don't have the resources—financial or human—to do things the way you would like to. There will be times when your chance of success with a customer, vendor, investor or employee seem slim. Sometimes you lose opportunities simply because you aren't established. There are often real reasons why you can't achieve something. You don't have the money, resources, experience, capital, partners, team members, investors, facilities, capacity, technology—the list goes on.

Your Change in Perspective

Forget all that. As we used to say at IncentOne, "We can find lots of people who can't get it done." One of the core beliefs you need to practice daily should be the faith or confidence that "there is always a way."

Entrepreneurs have access to creativity that can energize a business. Don't be deterred by the fact that there isn't an established path. Most individuals don't have the inclination or wherewithal to color outside the lines. You do. Many great ideas and visions buck the trend. Amazon told us we would never buy a book in a store again. It's your innate ability to see things differently and try different approaches that is one of your greatest skills. These are the same skills that allow you to mastermind creative solutions when it does not seem like there are any.

There is always a way. I don't care how many times you fall down, or how little your bank account has in it. Challenges are only speed bumps along the way. If you are as good as you think you are, you will find a way to achieve results even when it seems impossible. Sometimes it is "all in your head," or in other words, your perspective has more power than you may recognize:

In the fall of 2008 when the financial crisis hit, many of our largest clients collapsed. This caused our revenue to drop quickly. In addition to our revenue getting decimated, our gift card retailers cut off our credit. This one-two punch of lost revenue and dried-up credit left us with a cash crunch virtually overnight. A good amount of our cash went to the rewards individuals had earned for completing behaviors. A cash crunch for us meant individuals that had earned rewards such as gift cards might not get their rewards. For example, a Washington Mutual mortgage processor might have earned several hundred dollars in gift cards for closing mortgages on time.

When the crisis hit, for every $10 of rewards we needed to ship out, we had $2. Prior to the crash, for every $10 in rewards we needed, we had $20. This all occurred in a matter of weeks. Every day gift cards needed to be shipped. Imagine if we were unable to fulfill these rewards, it would have been the death of our business. How do you turn $2 into $10 overnight?

I was in my office one night at midnight thinking about it. I remember seeing marketing programs that sent you free vacations or give you hundreds of dollars for trips to Las Vegas and was wondering if there was a concept that would allow us to get significant value at a low cost. I knew that whatever value we got, it would have to approach the value of gift cards or our customers would never go for it. It couldn't be a discount coupon book. These were individuals who had already earned and picked the gift card of their choice from a well-known retailer (e.g., Barnes & Noble). Only something of equivalent value would work. At 2:30 a.m. one day I came across a company that offered $25 of value that you can use at a network of restaurants at a cost of ten dollars. Their basic premise is that the restaurants in their network need to fill seats in the restaurant that will otherwise go unfilled. Once those seats go unfilled for a meal, the restaurant loses that revenue. For each certificate value at $25, they would charge the customer $10.

I was onto something. I reached them the next day and asked them for their best offer for $1 million in certificates. I knew I would need several millions but started at one million. I communicated that I was making a decision between multiple vendors and needed their best offer. They came back with $5 for $25. Even at $5, this would reduce our cash needs but I needed more. After a few more rounds of negotiation, I told them "no deal" and that if they wanted our business, they had to do better. I thanked them and hung up. I didn't have an alternative but I needed to get those numbers down. They called me back and offered me $25 for $1. I told them fine, but if we went over one million, any amount above that would be calculated at $25 for 50 cents. They agreed.

This reduced each one-million-dollar liability to $40,000 but I still had to convince our customers. Their employees would not get the gift card they selected, but rather an option to select from a national network of restaurants. It seemed to me to be a tough sell. We proposed the following. If an individual was entitled to $25 in gift cards, we would offer them $100 in certificates. While this would increase our cost to $160,000 for a $1 million liability, it gave our customers real value for exchanging their existing gift cards.

Over the next several months we implemented a plan that included everything from training call center agents, changing our website and reaching out to individuals. It worked. This helped us emerge from the financial crisis.

Turning $2 into $10 is not easy. You bring creativity others don't have. When I worked as a lawyer, with billion-dollar deals on the table, no expense was spared. When I was a junior associate, a partner told me I needed to be in London in four hours. When I reminded him it was a six-hour flight, he told me to "figure it out."

Don't let anyone tell you there isn't a way. Don't let the established ideas, and traditional solutions make your perspective static and inflexible. You need to bring your creativity to change results. As an entrepreneur, you have the ability to see things differently than others. You may be required to avoid traditional paths. You may even be required to create a new math that turns $2 into $10.

Chapter 5
Since When Are CEOs
Humble and Learners?

What We Feel: I'm the CEO, so I know more about the business than anyone. For the things I don't know, I will figure them out along the way. I don't have the time to learn new things or the patience to put myself last. I've got to do what I need to do and I need to be aggressive to make it happen quickly.

One of the most important lessons I learned at IncentOne was that it is a blessing to acknowledge when you come across something you don't know, not a curse. When you first start, you think if you don't know something or the company can't do something, it is a flaw. It's quite the contrary. It's critical that you understand, recognize, acknowledge and embrace your flaws and the company's shortcomings. This is counterintuitive. Entrepreneurs are driven, intelligent and confident. Not knowing something seems like a sign of weakness. It's the opposite. The day you understand and acknowledge your weaknesses and embrace the power of learning is the day you make great progress.

Your Change in Perspective

Humility is a trait of strong leaders—the type of leaders employees want to work for and investors want to fund. One of the most important days in the history of IncentOne was when I realized being a CEO was a skill that needed to be developed with the same perseverance, ferocity and willingness to learn that athletes apply to their training. It was no different than ballet or working on your golf game. This is one of those skills that must be genuinely developed. Once you embrace this as an opportunity, it lets air out of your balloon. You won't be wasting time criticizing yourself for a lack of knowledge, and instead will embrace the opportunity to learn and grow.

Take the example of how to get team members aligned to a plan or objective. Let's say your team is skeptical of your perspective on how to release the beta of your product. There are two ways you can handle the same issue. One approach would be to tell them what to do. Another approach would be to introduce the topic and say something like, "I was wrong about how to approach our alpha version and wanted to make sure we got it right this time. My initial gut is that we should launch in the summer, but what do you think?" Express to team members that you would like everyone's feedback on the approach.

Being humble and acknowledging the error of your ways is also a great way to build trust and credibility:

> *We'd been selected as a finalist for an RFP for CIGNA to be their incentive vendor and I was leading the presentation. During a break, one of the CIGNA employees directed me to the restroom and said, "Do you know how to get back? It's hard to make your way around here because all the halls look the same." I said I was fine. After about a half hour of walking around while my team was presenting, I walked in the door. Everyone smiled with that sheepish look of "we told you so." They asked if I was okay and I said, "If the CEO of your vendor can't find his way back from the bathroom, I don't think you should hire us to run your incentive programs." Everyone laughed and we moved on. We wound up winning the RFP. I'm sure that was not the reason why, but I think they knew they were partnering with someone who was real.*

It was embarrassing that I could not find my way back, but not as embarrassing as what happened two years later only a few miles away at Aetna, one of CIGNA's main competitors:

> *We had been selected by Aetna as a finalist for their RFP for incentives. We had been working on this client acquisition for two years and it was down to us and one other company. At the final meeting, there were five members from our team and about twenty-five Aetna participants. As my team set up for the*

meeting, I went to the men's room. When I was done in the bathroom, I washed my hands and then squatted down to stretch. All I heard was a tear in the back of my suit pants. This was not a minor tear. I had torn my pants from the seam behind my derriere to my inseam. It was hard to walk without exposing my backside. The meeting was starting in ten minutes.

I was slated to present for about two hours of the three-hour meeting. I always loved these opportunities to show our wares, but some of our team members were anxious in these environments. Right before I was about to start, as people were settling in for the meeting, I went over to the table (rather shimmied over to the table), and said, "Look at this," and showed them the rip in my pants. They all got a good laugh and it seemed to break the tension.

When you demonstrate humility and embrace learning, you can unlock great things in your team. However, humility has to be balanced. First, it has to be balanced with a sense of confidence. If this humility is not balanced with strength, you can undermine the team's belief in you and in the business. The key is finding the right mix. Second, humility has to be genuine and never used to manipulate. When team members see their leaders genuinely willing to acknowledge mistakes or deficits in a particular area, it inspires them to discover their own confidence to act, take risks, and evaluate their own deficits. This leads to genuine improvement and self-development that will have many positive impacts for your company. But don't forget, it starts with you.

Chapter 6
Set Values That Are Non-Negotiable

What We Feel: *I can barely keep my head above water. The last thing I am thinking about is our company culture. Culture is a luxury we can't afford yet. If it doesn't bring in revenue or cut our burn, should we be focusing on it? Our culture right now has to be to work our asses off.*

Establishing your company culture is difficult when your business is new and going through growing pains. You simply can't spend the time or money you'd like to build a corporate culture and you don't have a human resources department or a chief people officer to own it or help you. You probably can't imagine the day you will hire someone with that title. You do envision, however, the day that your organization lives and breathes the culture that you want. But how far off is that vision?

In an early stage venture, you lack defined parameters for company behavior—including your own behavior. It is like driving on a road without a speed limit, stop lights or lane lines. The amount of tasks that need to get done already creates traffic on your roads. As you hire, you will bring in many different personalities. This adds reckless drivers, speeders, honkers, lane changers and dragsters to the streets. If you don't set some basic parameters for your culture, it will define itself. Given the chaos of early stage ventures, it is rare that a culture that develops on its own will foster positive, collaborative principles. Left to its own devices, or lacking the appropriate attention, you are actually enabling a corporate culture with negative undertones and a tolerance for unacceptable behavior. In other words, you must address the issue because corporate culture will develop on its own regardless of your meager resources and lack of readiness.

Most entrepreneurs adopt the perspective that culture is a luxury rather than a critical foundational element of a strong company. Many entrepreneurs also believe that culture is something to focus on after hitting more important goals like generating revenue and securing investment capital. Makes sense that these things should be higher on the totem pole. Right? Entrepreneurs often also simply assume, that as long as everyone shares the vision of the company, culture will take care of itself.

I got this one wrong at IncentOne. Remember, my experience was at a large New York corporate law firm where it was common to work past midnight. I had an inexperienced view of the impact of culture. Who needed culture? I wasn't thinking about culture—I was focused on building our product, getting customers and obtaining financing. I also fell into the trap of believing that the fact that we were going to change the world by rewarding people for healthy behavior was a vision that was more than enough to keep the team driven and motivated. Culture was synonymous—incorrectly—with my definition of "work ethic."

The values I wanted the company to believe in were clear to me. What I failed to do was to understand that even with all that was on our plate, I needed to formalize, communicate and enforce these values so they were clear and would become second nature to everyone in the company. Simply having everyone understand and believe in the vision is not culture—even though I thought it was.

Your Change in Perspective

Regardless of your stage, you must set core values that are non-negotiable. When your organization lacks guardrails and guidelines, you need to construct boundaries to guide behavior.

In the beginning, keep them simple and to no more than three values. You need to enforce them, and that is difficult to do effectively if you have a long laundry list of values or a series of tactical things that aren't important enough or too difficult to monitor. These are key guardrails for your initial effort, and they will evolve over time.

Some examples of these values might be:

- The only criteria for decisions will be what's in the best interest of the business.
- There is a zero tolerance policy for untrustworthy behavior.
- We will be humble and committed to learning and improving every day.
- There will be no tolerance for a lack of respect.
- We will challenge ourselves to have fun and enjoy the ride.
- We will celebrate wins and successes as much as we stress over losses and failures.
- We will hold each other accountable to our goals, regardless of our position or title.
- We will succeed and fail as a team.
- We will focus on the success of our customers to drive the success of our business.
- We will expect honesty and candor and will challenge each other when we fall short.
- We will do more than customers ask, before they ask.
- We have a duty to each other to give our best effort every day.

Obviously, depending on what you feel is important to your organization, the values can vary widely. Regardless, take the time to think through the things that are most important to you, and set them out clearly and consistently. Put them on the walls. Put a "fine jar" in every room for every time they are violated. Make someone the "culture cop." In the same way that a culture will develop negatively if no values are set, once you put in place some tools to make your values visible, they will quickly become second nature.

One more piece of advice regarding this perspective. Not setting values is one thing. Setting them and not enforcing them is another, and can be worse. This has two elements. First, without a zero tolerance policy, and follow through, you undermine both your values and your leadership. The rank and file lose faith in their leaders not only when rules aren't enforced, but when they are enforced selectively and favor a particular individual. Your enforcement of these values should set an example of the integrity and consistency you expect from your team. Second, make sure that there are no exceptions for you or other senior leaders. In fact, you should be the first one to step up, acknowledge mistakes, and face the consequences. So set your values and enforce them, and you will be on your way to a culture people are proud to be a part of.

Chapter 7
Make Decisions in the Best
Interest of the Business

What We Feel: *Employees want. Customers want. Investors want. Board members want. Family wants. Keeping everyone aligned is hard. Keeping everyone happy is daunting.*

During the initial phase of your entrepreneurial venture, there are many competing priorities. Your employees, vendors, customers, and investors also have different interests, and it is common to have these interests in competition at all stages of the business. With more established businesses, however, existing policies and procedures, managed by a strong team, help to moderate these conflicts as part of company process. You don't have that luxury yet—or the time or the resources—to keep everyone's interests in line all the time.

Your inclination, and certainly mine, is to conclude that it was unnecessary and time-consuming—and probably impossible—to establish an overarching procedure for making decisions. Decisions both big and small were being made left and right under the assumption that whatever got decided was in the company's best interest. It seemed like a reasonable assumption. But you will be surprised, as I was, that if you don't make what seems obvious to you (making decisions based on what's best for the business) clear to all, you may find your team and the other resources you interact with, developing an unhealthy sense of entitlement as your organization grows and your market presence increases.

Don't assume everyone is on the same page. Establish a succinct message from the start and continue to reinforce it with everyone you encounter.

Your Change in Perspective

The only criteria for making decisions is what is in the best interest of the business.

By establishing this principle, you set criteria for decision-making that everyone understands, and is expected to share. This will serve you well in a variety of situations, including employee compensation, vendor negotiations, or internal conflicts—whether it's a disagreement between employees, a necessary disciplinary action, or an employee complaint of unfair treatment.

In your professional interactions, it is important to communicate to others in a brief, candid manner, that the company must balance many competing interests. Employees, investors, vendors, consultants, and Board members all want something different, something specific to them. To unify these often-competing needs and perspectives, emphasize that decisions will be made in the best interest of the business. You may make decisions that seem unfair to a party or seem to favor one party over another. And when there is no established, strongly identified principle, individuals feel their interests are not being met. But when you communicate a standard, you transform a set of assumptions (we all are acting in the best interest of the business) into an official statement, and if it's implemented consistently, others will respect the principle even if they don't agree with the final decision itself. This builds trust over the long term.

Take a technology vendor that is developing your product: one of your employees suggests that the vendor has a spotty performance and that looking for a back-up or replacement vendor would be prudent. You know all the hard work and intellectual capital the vendor has invested in your project—at a below-market price. Ask yourself, "What is in the best interest of the business?" Even though you may be loyal to the vendor, the answer is to have a backup vendor to give you the flexibility to negotiate performance issues with your current vendor, or to make a change if necessary.

If you are true to this principle, it will also help you address negative behavior. A vendor is looking for a long-term contract. An employee wants a guaranteed salary for the future. An investment advisor wants to get your business without bidding on it. Communicating your standard for decision-making, immediately sets an expectation: proposals which favor the bidder at the expense of your business, or that act to the detriment of your business will not be entertained. This saves time and simplifies your interactions by demanding that they find a solution that is mutually beneficial. This does not happen overnight, but if you apply it consistently, it will become standard operating procedure.

Sometimes, there will be decisions that are personally detrimental but in the best interest of the business. In these situations, you still must choose to make decisions in the best interest of the business. Yes, you may take a personal hit, but these situations can be teachable moments for you and your team. When you choose your business over yourself, you reinforce a standard of fairness—rules apply to everyone.

Don't get me wrong. There are circumstances where this is very difficult. Think about employees who have worked tirelessly in the early stages of the business, but are not equipped to be the company's future leaders. In these cases, you must make a tough choice between your responsibility to the business and your loyalty to an employee. It is your job to find a way to align their interests to the best interests of the business. This could take the form of rewarding early-stage employees with options that are maintained even if the employee leaves the company. You may say, "I can't determine who is going to be the management team of the future, but at least if you are not a member of the team, you will be rewarded for your hard work." As an alternative, you can align the employee to a role they desire and at the same time bring in team members that serve to advance the business in a way that the employee could not—as long as you aren't acquiring additional costs for the wrong reasons.

You will not be able to please everyone. You will learn a lot about people and their motivations. Address your standard early and often so that all your resources understand that if they put their needs above your business's best interest, they are not violating some idea you invented yesterday as an excuse or justification. They are violating a fundamental tenet of the business. The goal is to keep the people helping your business rowing in the same direction. We all know what we're supposed to do: stop at a four-way intersection, follow instructions, and don't yell *fire* in the theater. But usually things run a lot smoother when there is a sign posted.

SECTION 4:

STANDING OUT FROM THE CROWD

Introduction

As an entrepreneur, you have to manage the myriad of issues we have been discussing to improve your chances of success. Part of your success is, of course, whether your product or service resonates with buyers and how your idea fits your market. This may seem like a topic for go-to-market strategy not perspective shifts but your success in the marketplace isn't determined solely by the power of your "design" or your ranking among the competition. In fact, for a set of customers to want your product—whether it be from a local flower shop or a technology that can be used throughout the world—of course you have to be distinct from the competition. But competition may not be your biggest threat. Your biggest threat may be clutter. How you decide to overcome this and take your product or service to market, is, in reality, a perspective.

We live in a world of constant sensory overload. Every minute of every day we are inundated with our phones, social media and interactive technologies that make thinking about anything difficult. Consumers and businesses alike have little attention span for anything that does not immediately tickle their fancy.

It is of course critical that you deliver a great product or service. However, there are many great products and services that get lost in the clutter of our daily lives. So while many entrepreneurs focus on the best product or service, it is just as important to think about how you stand out from the crowd.

Think about Dos Equis beer and their "Most Interesting Man in the World" branding campaign. Does that campaign talk about product features such as ingredients, taste, or calories? Or does it create a picture in your mind with what it coveys? Entrepreneurs don't spend nearly enough time thinking about the wide variety of methods to set themselves apart from others.

The entrepreneur's perspective often compels them to make a better mousetrap. What if I told you that you had to sell your product or service on Pluto to aliens? Would you be worried about the latest features for an audience that had never been exposed to a product like yours? So how do you find your Pluto? How do you find the place where you really stand out?

Your perspective must be to find a market, or a way to market, that makes your product or service shine. Where can you be the only game in town? How can you accelerate getting to market? How do you focus on the markets where you can make a name for yourself? The perspectives in this section will help you find your unique place in the world—not in your eyes, but in the eyes of your customers.

Chapter 1
Find Playgrounds Where
No One Is Playing

__What We Feel__: Our idea is so unique that once we get it into the market, our sales will be through the roof. No one has done what we are doing, and it is just a matter of time before everyone finds out. I can't wait to go head-to-head with the market leaders.

It is really, really hard to create a unique product or service. Even when you do create something unique, there's no guarantee you'll gain meaningful visibility. First you have to position it to cut through the clutter. Advertising and information overload is the norm. Whether you're battling to reach consumers inundated with an endless set of choices for virtually each product or service, or corporate buyers overwhelmed by the number of potential solutions they review, it is almost impossible to cut through the noise. Cutting through this clutter, even with something head-turning and new, can be difficult.

Passion for their vision convinces many entrepreneurs that their product or service is so singular and exceptional that it will cut through the clutter on its own. Other entrepreneurs acknowledge the competition but believe that their improvements in the industry—better product, more efficient service, better design innovation—will cut through the noise. Some may believe a clever strategy is enough to out-maneuver the competition—even when the competition comes from some of the largest and well-funded companies. *"We will understand the competition, analyze their marketing and we will just do it better and more creatively. We will take them head on and let our uniqueness shine through!"* There are companies that have successfully faced off with the competition and come out the winner. That said, entrepreneurs need to ask themselves a difficult question, and understand their business well enough to give an honest answer. They may have a unique, newly improved idea, but do they have the differentiation, capital and resources to beat the competition at their own game?

Your Change in Perspective

If the answer is any version of "no," instead of taking on the competition, why not look for a market segment in which your competition is not playing. Don't fight them on their playground—find a playground where they are *not* playing.

> *A good friend's brother named Brian became pals with his personal trainers. After a training session, the trainers mentioned to Brian that they had developed an exercise "app" that helped people track their workouts and other data. They claimed it was better than anything else out there. Brian was intrigued, started using the "app" and fell in love with it. He liked it so much that he wanted to put some money into it and see if he and the trainers could turn it into a business. They felt they could "change the way people worked out." I got a call from my friend. He was concerned that Brian was investing a lot of money into the venture. He knew I was in the healthcare industry and asked me, "Do you think there are solutions like this?" I told him that there were many and had him search "exercise app" on Google. Hundreds of entries came up with different exercise applications.*

> *He asked me to meet with Brian to talk some sense into him. We met in our New Jersey offices. As the meeting started, Brian and the trainers started to walk me through the app. I pulled up the Google search but they still weren't convinced. They thought they had a better mousetrap. In reality, there were hundreds of solutions that were better and were already in market. I asked them to consider, "Let's assume you have the ideal app. That it is absolutely perfect." Then I said, it is unlikely that even if you did, you could stand out from big industry players like Nike, or Under Armor or Reebok who either had or could have a similar tool in everyone's hands in months. I also asked them if they had any relationships that were unique. They said that the CEO of a major vitamin retailer wanted to invest. The vitamin retailer was trying to get into the market for wellness beyond just vitamins. I told them to strike the deal with the retailer.*

The solution got rolled out throughout the country even though it was not as good as other solutions in the market.

Same product. Different go-to-market approach. In fact, as you can see from the example above, one product or service that might be deficient in one market may be differentiating or unique in another market.

The leadership of our technology vendor that helped us launch IncentOne's first product had grown up in the telecom business. They told me that they had been building a service that allowed each individual to have their own personal "800" number that would be the only number anyone would call. An individual could set preferences that would direct it to ring on their home phone, office phone and cell phone at times they set. Imagine that—you only had one number and it rang wherever you wanted. Seemed like a great idea.

But despite a great service and clear value for the consumer, they were having trouble selling it. They were pitching it to the telecom companies. I had two reactions. First, wouldn't telecom companies be the last companies that would want this service? Wouldn't someone using one number instead of many have the potential to hurt their revenue? Second, it seemed to me that the telecom companies—with all of their technological resources, probably already had this technology.

I suggested that they look for a market that didn't live and breathe telecom. Was there a place in which this service could add value to the consumer but wouldn't be measured against or by the leading thinker in the telecom space? After all, even though the technology might not be unique, the service would clearly benefit consumers. Was there a market where companies were looking to provide differentiating services like this to consumers?

After some debate, we thought about the credit card companies. They were constantly spending marketing dollars and offering consumers value added services if they signed up for one of their credit cards. Capital One, American Express, Citibank, Discover, MasterCard and Visa, among others, were spending lots on customer acquisition. Wouldn't a service like this offered to a new credit card holder differentiate an offering? They started offering it to that market and one of the major credit card companies became their biggest customer.

Same product. Different market.

When you bring something to market, focus on the path where your competition is not playing. It's unlikely that you'll develop something truly unique on a regular basis, but it is likely that you will find "an empty playground" or a unique distribution channel where your idea will thrive.

> *When we were selling solutions to corporate America, it made sense for large companies to run all of their incentive programs in one place. But we kept hearing that many of these programs were run locally and there was no real reason to take the time to consolidate the programs and run them through corporate offices. One day I read an article that talked about a large accounting firm that had to pay fines to the Internal Revenue Service (IRS) because they were giving incentives to auditors who completed audits on time but weren't keeping track of them or reporting them as income. The IRS fined them. We immediately started reaching out to people who would be accountable in large companies if this happened to them—payroll managers. We started calling on them and writing articles for* Payroll Magazine. *We attended Payroll trade shows. As soon as we said, if you don't keep track of your incentives, the same can happen to you, they all jumped. The same customers that said they would never take the time to consolidate their programs were first in line to do so.*

Same solution. Different approach.

When the Four Ps are impacting our perspective (especially our passion), we believe that we can create something different that stands out from the crowd on its own merits. This happens all the time. This requires your product or service to be better, faster, stronger. To accomplish this, you will need to spend significant time making your product or service the best out there. You may also need to spend significant capital and marketing funds. These are certainly formulas for success, but ones that require time and resources most entrepreneurs don't have.

Look at competition and success from a different perspective. Take some of the time, effort and resources normally devoted to your product, and direct them to finding the right "playground"—one where you can maneuver and gain visibility that cuts through the noise. Imagine if your effort was not spent on Release #10 of your software or your ninth perfume bottle design, but on the distribution channels that will value Release #5 or bottle design #8, and the niche markets where that value has room to be unique. What is often inferior on one playground is superior on another. The uniqueness of your solution is important. It might be even more important to go to playgrounds where no one else is playing.

Chapter 2
Why Build a Rocket When NASA Has Plenty?

__What We Feel__: Building things from scratch is what startups do. It's what it means to be an entrepreneur. Even so, building it from scratch seems like a daunting task. I wish I had an easier way to get my idea to market than bootstrapping for five years.

The traditional definition of an entrepreneur is someone who builds something from the ground up and "bootstraps it." Entrepreneurs are builders. They have the ability and the desire to take an idea and bring it to life in the form of a product or service that customers want. When most entrepreneurs start, their default mentality is that they will start small and become their own "craftsman." They will make or invent everything they need from scratch. They understand, and even take pride in the fact that they will have to start with limited capital and resources, and that in the beginning they will probably be flying solo. They remain fiercely committed to building from the ground up. Imagine the day we have two employees, ten employees. One hundred employees. Even the term "startup" embodies the notion of building something from the ground up.

But should we always be building from scratch? Most entrepreneurs would instinctively reply, "Hell yes, isn't that the point?" There is no question that the experience of building a company from the ground up is one of the most character-building experiences that you will encounter. Many entrepreneurs take great pride—and rightly so—in building their vision from scratch even though the world we live in makes it harder and harder to come up with something new that cuts through the clutter. If bootstrapping seems like the only option it can prevent entrepreneurs from seeing a second, or third, option that may be better suited for their vision, its

222

scope, and the resources or schedule needed to ensure its success. There are some circumstances where a really good idea won't come to life with a traditional approach.

Entrepreneurs are always up for a difficult challenge, but the smart ones are keenly aware of today's challenges and the radically different landscape afforded by new technology and global competition. Could there be a better way than starting from scratch and building from the ground up? Isn't it less about how you get there, than the fact that you got there? Isn't it more important that your vision comes to life, your customers win, your investors are happy, and you achieve the personal and financial rewards of success?

Your Change in Perspective

As entrepreneurs we often feel like we lack a lot, but we almost always lack three things:

- **Capital:** financial resources to support and drive a growing business.
- **Distribution:** an established network that helps bring a product or service to customers.
- **Resources:** the team members it takes to build a business.

To overcome these gaps, entrepreneurs raise money by convincing investors that their business has merit, forging partnerships to drive distribution, and incrementally bringing on resources. They embark on the traditional startup and building process.

What entrepreneurs do not lack are great ideas. Large companies, on the other hand, have no shortage of capital, resources or distribution.

It is common to open the *Wall Street Journal* and read about companies doing billion-dollar acquisitions, or investing heavily in innovation partnerships. As of January 2016, Apple alone had $215 billion in cash. As of September 15, 2015, the top five cash rich companies held $342 billion in cash (Oracle: $54.37 billion; Cisco: $60.42 billion; Berkshire Hatha-way: $64.25 billion; Google: $67 billion and Microsoft: $96.45 billion)[6]. Companies are putting this money to work to enhance shareholder value through research and development, acquisitions, stock buybacks or paying off debt.

Corporate America, and many international companies, have the precise resources entrepreneurs with big ideas need. Many companies not only have their core employee base and administrative staff, but also can lever-age inexpensive global resources like technology development, call centers and business processes execution. Imagine the conversation shifting from what it is now—whether you can afford one new application developer—to how quickly the business could be mobilized by fifty new hires.

Companies also have distribution. Many large organizations have sales forces with thousands of team members throughout the world. A new inno-vation or product idea can be integrated into the "bag" of the salesperson, and suddenly, the entrepreneur's idea can be offered at scale. Today, you are probably debating whether you can find someone who will sell on a commission-only basis because you can't afford to hire a full-time sales-person. Imagine if you could leverage all of their salespeople?

Bottom line. The two things that entrepreneurs need the most—cash and resources—are something companies throughout the world have in spades. In fact, many of these companies are actively seeking these collab-orations. While they may have resources in excess, they are always on the search for new ideas and innovation. Many companies have even set up "commercialization centers" specifically to encourage and attract entre-preneurs, and to provide the infrastructure to transition innovations into much larger commercial endeavors.

---

[6] Owens, J.C. (2016) "Apple isn't really sitting on $216 billion in cash." MarketWatch.com, www.marketwatch.com/story/apple-isnt-really-sitting-on-216-billion-in-cash-2016-01-26 [Access date 20 April 2016].

Take the Cleveland Clinic for example:

> *The Cleveland Clinic has an organization called Cleveland Clinic Innovations (CCI). Within the Cleveland Clinic world, there are often medical techniques that come to life through the hands on experience of doctors, nurses, support staff and other clinicians. Many of these innovations have some market viability. For example, let's say that a doctor discovers a new technique in the midst of performing surgeries. One path might be for the doctor to take the idea, leave his job as a doctor and create an organization to bring the technique to life. Cleveland Clinic has made it much easier. If CCI sees merit in an idea, they will help provide capital, financing options, partners and other resources to get the technique or product off the ground. This often results in a joint venture with a pharmaceutical company or medical device partner, CCI and the physician or staff member.*

Do we always have to build something from scratch and struggle through the blood, sweat and tears of building a company? Could we have a different perspective? Could we consider the alternative and see if building could be replaced with partnerships with those who have the capital and resources we lack? The opportunity is there. When successful, this type of relationship combines the cash and resources of corporations with the innovation and ideas of entrepreneurs for a mutually beneficial endeavor.

If you decide to take this approach, the focus of your effort changes from company building to positioning your company for this type of partnership. These efforts then focus on the following:

- **Building A Business Plan Geared Toward a Strategic Partnership.** Develop a business plan that outlines the fundamentals of the business, but also clearly defines a "strategic partnership" approach to going to market. The plan should not talk about the business getting investment capital like a traditional startup seeking funding. It should speak of the investment required by the partner to build the business as part of their organization.
- **Differentiating Value.** The focus of the business plan and its overall rationale should be to establish the product's value statement specifically for implementation with a strategic partner, not as

a stand-alone business. This will require a shift from pitching and validating the traditional entrepreneur's solo business venture, to a mentality of co-creation and collaboration. For example, your communication would not focus on "the business will generate revenue of x" but rather "this solution could be integrated into our national sales force and be a strategic 'add on' to our existing product line." You must be able to clearly and concisely show how your idea can bring value when the capital and human resources are applied.

- **Requiring an Investment.** The business plan should include details regarding the investment required by the strategic partner to bring the solution to life. Remember, this is not the investment to grow the business as a stand-alone entity, but rather the investment that must be made by the strategic partner to enable the business as part of its suite of products or services. This plan cannot be general (e.g., the business will need $2 million investment). The more detail your plan contains and the stronger its economic analysis—particularly as an asset to a strategic partner—the more likely that partner is to see its immediate value and act on it.

- **Clarifying Resources Required.** The plan should not only detail the financial resources required, but the human capital involved. The plan should outline the need for a management team, the desired roles of the entrepreneurs, and the other human resources required. Again, remember that you are pitching a strategic partnership with the company that has an existing team. Research their organization to see how their team and your team can form the right mix.

- **Targeting Partners versus Investors.** With a detailed plan in hand, entrepreneurs do not need to spend time chasing investors to build the business, but need to identify and contact their target partners. This starts with an analysis of the industries, segments, and markets that would benefit most from their idea. Once identified, they can target companies actively seeking outside innovation and development, as well as, their advisors (e.g., investment bankers, consultants) that are often charged with finding new innovations. You may also tap into the growing incubator and accelerator network that have relationships with companies actively seeking innovative ideas.

Think of this "strategic partner" approach as just another way to bring your vision to life.

Some entrepreneurs may view this as a "cop out"—that real entrepreneurism requires building from the ground up. Don't think of it this way. This type of partnership is an entrepreneurial venture coming to life—simply through a different path. If entrepreneurs had a quicker way to gain access to capital, distribution and resources to bring their vision to life, wouldn't it make sense to pursue that path as an option?

Think of it this way. You can get from New York to California by car, bus or plane. You choose your form of travel based on time, cost and multiple factors. Some may appreciate the cross-country drive. Some may enjoy the company of others on a bus ride. Others may enjoy the speed of an airline flight. In the end, we end up in California. When you are thinking about how to bring your vision to life, consider whether building is the only way.

This approach is not a magic bullet. Companies will scrutinize your offering and its value to them, and whether a strategic partnership is the right choice for both parties. Choosing this path will require you to hone your approach, your communication, and the details you highlight in order to specifically address the benefits of your idea to a prospective partner. Your strategic partnership doesn't have to, or simply may not involve your entire concept or every product, so be prepared to differentiate the scope of your vision and offering. There will be times when this path makes sense and times it does not. You may like the idea of a partnership, but the terms of the partnership related to ownership, control and financial reward don't satisfy you. Not a magic bullet, but definitely one that should be in your gun.

As an entrepreneur, you will face many difficult questions about what's best for your business. You will also have to find difficult answers for questions about your identity, about what it means to be an entrepreneur. It's easy to lose perspective when we believe there's only one answer or one correct approach to these questions. I can't tell you whether you should bootstrap it or partner up, but I will suggest that your perspective include the flexibility, humility, and creativity to consider many options that will ultimately help you bring your vision to life. Either way there will be hard work involved—it is just that the work is allocated to a different perspective. You wake up every day not thinking about logos and business cards but rather how to package your offering and bring it to the right partner. It will not be for every product or service, but it is an alternative perspective that every entrepreneur should consider. Aligning your vision within a larger partner organization can be a significant identity dilemma for entrepreneurs, but don't let your perspective limit your ultimate goal— bringing your vision to life.

Chapter 3
You Can't Chase Every Customer

__What We Feel__: A customer is a customer. We would go to Saturn if that's what we had to do to close a sale from a paying customer. We can't choose our customers at this point, we have to go after every opportunity and get some revenue coming.

When we become entrepreneurs, we are creating something we believe in. You hear many of us say, "There are so many customers that need our product or service." In fact, sometimes we say, "I don't know of anyone who wouldn't want our product." While this may be partly our excitement talking, or maybe just the influence of a few of the Four Ps, it is also a dangerous path. Don't get me wrong. Your market, product or service may be new or different. It would seem that the opportunity to attack broad markets, and to have no limits on what markets to chase, would be a good problem to have. In one sense it is. At IncentOne, we believed that incentives to drive behavior could be applied almost anywhere. We argued that everything in healthcare came down to getting consumers and providers to act. Diabetes. Heart Disease. Pregnancy. Exercise. Nutrition. Weight Management. The list went on and on. In each and every one of these areas, consumers were not doing the things they needed to be doing to manage their health. And it was costing the health system billions. We said to ourselves, "Is there any condition or element of healthcare that doesn't need incentives?"

As entrepreneurs, we chase revenue wherever we can find it, often without fully considering whether we are winning the customer base we really want or whether we are taking time away from the customers we should be chasing. At IncentOne, one day it was health plans, the next it was employers, the next it was distribution channels. In the beginning, you are willing to talk to anyone about your service because you are looking for positive feedback and validation. I am sure that when I took an Amtrak train to Boston, I tried to sell my health reward solution to the Amtrak employee that ran the concession stand. We have this desire to go after any customer that shows interest—even if the customer is highly unlikely to need or want your solution. "We can go everywhere. We will go anywhere." This is often the revenue strategy of the entrepreneur. Your perspective is, money is money, and we need more money.

It is natural to chase revenue. It is also natural to believe that everyone wants your product or service. But this isn't as harmless as it sounds. There are several problems with this approach. First, you have limited resources and your scarcest resource is time. Every minute you spend on one activity is a minute you don't spend on another. Second, every new type of customer you chase requires you to learn the market, find those customers, create the right marketing message, hire people with market knowledge and develop credibility in that market. Doing that for one type of customer is hard enough. Trying to do it for multiple customer types is impossible.

Third, it is natural that you will encounter resistance from customers, especially if you are doing something new. It will take time to learn how to overcome objections or to help customers understand the value of your offering. If you are not committed to a path, you are likely to turn to another path when you do encounter the resistance as opposed to creatively working through it and learning what you need to about that market segment and how to tailor your approach to the market. Going after every customer opportunity, or market segment, or responding to the inquiry of the day, seems like the fastest path to revenue, but often can be a real distraction from gaining traction in a market.

Your Change in Perspective

Pick a market and go after it. Debate with your team and advisors what that market should be. But once you decide what it is, learn as much as you can about it and be committed to making a name for yourself in it.

Why? When you focus on a single market or customer type, you gain critical benefits:

- **Market Knowledge:** You develop a depth of understanding about a market that can be the difference between gaining traction and getting lost in the shuffle.
- **Reputation:** In a cluttered world, staking a claim and being successful in a specific market builds your reputation. Assume you could have five customers. If you have them in five separate markets, it is hard to build a reputation. If you have them in one market, you can show proof within a known segment. Once you do, you gain a reputation. Once a reputation is established, it is easier to develop a name for yourself. Once you develop a name for yourself, you can bring that reputation to other customer segments.
- **Expertise of Resources:** You can hire or leverage sales, marketing and product resources that have experience in that market.
- **Efficiency:** When you chase multiple markets, you are constantly wasting effort creating and recreating sales and utilizing new marketing messages and tools.
- **Value Propositions:** The value your product or service offers a specific market becomes second nature that everyone in the organization understands.
- **Marketing and Distribution Channels:** These channels are likely linked to specific markets. Each new customer demographic you introduce requires you to manage another set of distinct channels. Focus on one customer identity reduces the number of channels you have handle.
- **Overcoming Objections:** Closer access to customer feedback, objections and purchasing patterns help you align your offering and overcome objections for ongoing success.

Here's a simple example. Let's assume that you are designing jewelry and decide that women whose names start with the letter "B" are your perfect customers. When you do that, you can learn where the "Bs" hang out, where they shop, what they do at night and you can attend the annual "B" association meeting. When you meet someone whose name starts with the letter "C," and they love your jewelry, you have to resist the temptation.

Even though it will feel good to get positive feedback, or even make a sale, if you start to chase customers whose names start with "C," you have now created an inefficiency that is difficult to manage with scarce resources. Soon you are chasing the whole alphabet, aren't good at any of them, and are not really sure why you chase one versus another.

This is a difficult balance to strike. You want to be able to respond to feedback from customers, investors and others. The reality is that if you don't pick a target customer, you will probably do all of your markets poorly.

.

SECTION 5:

COMMUNICATING IN THE CHAOS

Introduction

Wouldn't it be great if at the beginning of your entrepreneurial venture you were handed a "Starter Kit" that included a "Director of Communications" whose job description was:

- To create clear and consistent communications among company constituents (i.e., employees, advisors, customers and investors)
- To create concise messaging to explain the company's products and services to its markets
- To develop regular processes and tools for keeping the organization and its constituents informed about company activities.

How useful would that be? Most entrepreneurs would settle for "manage the noise in the midst of the chaos."

Communicating in the early stages of a company is quite difficult. You need your value proposition to come through to your customers. You need employees to stay informed about the company and aligned to the vision. You need investors to understand how you and your product are different. You need to keep everyone informed and moving in the same direction. All of this must be accomplished without any resources that manage communications or any dollars to execute a communications plan.

Think of all the email, text messages and other communications that fly back and forth throughout the day. Not only is it hard to keep track of it all. It is even more difficult to make sure that the information and messages that are coming through are consistent with the messages you want to portray. While communication may not be at the top of your list, it certainly affects everything you do. You may get a few minutes or an "elevator pitch" with a prospect to offer your products or services. You may be presenting to investors and only get five minutes to tell your story. Companies that communicate well have a much better chance for success.

The perspectives in this section help you be clear, concise and efficient in communicating. We offer perspectives on how to improve your communication so your organization and its constituents stay informed and aligned.

Chapter 1
Think You Are Being
Clear? Probably Not.

What We Feel*: No one understands what I am saying. I explain things over and over again to investors, customers and employees, but they still don't get it. It seems like the more I repeat myself the less they understand.*

It all makes sense to you. You've explained it to your employees so many times. You've had multiple meetings with vendors. It doesn't seem to be clicking. Are they dumb? Were they asleep during the conference call? Didn't your investors read the documents? How can you explain the same thing so many times and they don't get it?

Colin Powell said, "Leaders are almost always great simplifiers, who can cut through argument, debate, and doubt to offer a solution everybody can understand."[7] As a leader, one of your most important jobs is to communicate effectively with the diverse set of constituents that your company engages. Whether you are speaking with a customer, employee, investor or advisor, you must be able to quickly and succinctly convey the element of your business to them. Simple. Comprehensible. Clear.

Yet, there is a consistent disconnect between the entrepreneur's understanding and explanation of an issue, plan or expectation and the interpretation of the customer, employee, investor, advisor or relationship on the other end. While we may think our constituents have a secret club where together they plan new ways to screw with us, in turns out we are the common denominator in this negative repetition. If, as entrepreneurs,

---

[7] Powell, C. (2002) *The Leadership Secrets of Colin Powell* (McGraw-Hill Professional Publishing).

we continue to stubbornly insist that we are the ones communicating clearly, our words eventually will fall on deaf ears. Because, in reality, we are likely the ones not making any sense.

Why does this occur?

- Entrepreneurs live and breathe their business every minute of every day. The rest of the world is selfish enough to be thinking about other things like family, social lives, world politics and their jobs during some portion of the day.
- Entrepreneurs not only live and breathe their business, but they know every detail of every issue. The history of every issue is also meticulously etched in their minds.
- The Entrepreneur's balloon is full and he is looking for a way to let some air out. For some reason it feels good to send a five-paragraph email on why we chose the office space we did.
- Entrepreneurs adopt the perspective, which is normally wrong (and not usually appreciated) that their audience must know all the details of a particular issue to fully comprehend it. When someone asked me how we got the IncentOne logo, it was tempting to reply with the ten-page version but clearly the person asking was only looking for, and only needed, the ten-second version.
- Most of your constituents—advisers, board members, existing or potential investors, employees or consultants—step in and out of your world. You are the only lunatic who thinks about this twenty-four-hours per day. They do not live and breathe your venture like you do. This is especially true if they are operating at below-market compensation or in a limited time capacity with your company. Your mind is two or three steps ahead of even devoted, full-time employees.

Regardless of the cause, our job is not to make it clear for us. Our job is to make it clear for everyone else. We cannot afford to take the attitude that "we have done best we can" or "I don't (can't) believe they don't get it." These conclusions can quickly spell the end of your business. When you say that about prospects, they rarely become customers. When you say that about potential investors, they rarely become investors. At some point, the only thing clear will be the company's lack of direction.

Thinking that about customers is a great plan to have none of them:

> *When we started IncentOne, giving rewards to drive healthy behavior made sense to us. It seemed simple. Reward people for the behaviors that made them healthy and saved the system money. For some reason, it was not resonating. This was not only because in the mid-2000s this was a new concept but because of something we missed. What we didn't realize was that the healthcare industry only thought in terms of your "plan design"—the benefits, co-pays and in-network and out-of-network fees built into your health plan. Everything they did at that time was based on this health plan design. If they wanted to drive a behavior, they would tinker with fees and co-pays. What seemed simple to us was Greek to them. Until we understood that, we could not craft the proper messages. We changed our message to, "Our program complements your plan design for behaviors that are not being driven by your plan design. It is not meant to replace it, but to work hand in hand to supplement it. If that makes sense, then think of it as American Express Rewards for mammograms." Once we did that, their response was different: "Oh, we're not undoing plan design, but for all those things that plan design can't do, or isn't doing well, we would have this program. That's great. We always struggle driving lifestyle factors like nutrition, weight management, and exercise that plan design was never meant to address."*

The only criterion for success is whether the other party understands. If you are failing to achieve this, stop blaming everyone else for being "clueless" and figure out the disconnect. If you find yourself regularly saying, "They just don't get it," interpret this to mean that you are not communicating clearly enough for your audience to understand. It's your job to help them "get it."

The ability to clearly and concisely deliver a message, align a plan, and generate engagement, is key. The implications for your business are significant. When a party understands the essence of something, it leads to deeper discussions on the topic. If an individual cannot grasp the essence of your value story, your product strategy, or your business model, it is unlikely you will get into a meaningful debate on its merits. Think about the left panel of the front page of the *Wall Street Journal*. One paragraph about the top stories. Enough to spark your interest. If you get the core of the story, you read more. Providing the essence of an issue with clarity is the foundation for good communication and will naturally lead to "next steps" with employees, customers, vendors, and investors. If you fail to do this primary groundwork, progress will be harder. Customer sales cycles get longer. Investor deals get harder. Employee motivation falters. Advisors guard their knowledge and time.

Do not underestimate the negative impact poor communication can have if your company earns a reputation for being difficult or complicated to work with. One of the nicest compliments customers gave us at IncentOne was that before they spoke with us, rewards in healthcare seemed complicated and after they spoke with us, it seemed simple.

Even responding to questions with long, complicated answers wears down your constituents. I recently asked an entrepreneur, "What is the price for the product?" The answer was so long and complicated that I stopped listening. If this occurs on a regular basis, interacting with you and your company becomes a chore. Potential investors not only need to be able to grasp the value of your company, but they also need to feel what it would be like working with you as a leader. Will communication be a chore? Will it be helpful and informative or strain their patience and trust? If everything seems like you are talking nuclear physics, they will likely pass. For example, imagine if you asked someone a simple question like, "What is your business model?" and the answer was:

> *"Our business model is still in development and we're thinking through different ways to do it. We have looked at other companies in the space and still don't know what the right model is. Our Board thinks it should be a license model and some of my team members think it should be consulting. I can't decide which way are we going to go. Version 7 of the financial model uses the license model and I'm not sure if that's what we're going to market with for the investor presentation."*

After the entrepreneur is done letting some air out of the balloon, the person who asked the question says, "So what is your business model?"

To avoid that scenario, you could respond:

"License model with a two-year term. We will modify it as we get feedback."

We must cut things to their essence. Clarity comes not from explaining the details, but rather from creating understanding and context for those that don't have the details. This is especially true when you are developing something new in the marketplace. We have thirty seconds to engage a prospect. We have seven minutes in an investor conference to wow an audience. We have thirty minutes to intrigue a customer. In more mature businesses, we can leverage existing understanding, communication processes and relationships. At early stages, we don't have that luxury.

Your Change in Perspective

So how do you make communication simple and clear? Consider these perspectives:

- **One-Paragraph Emails.** Keep your emails to one paragraph— and that paragraph can't be 1,000 words. Most people will not read five- or ten-paragraph emails. Don't risk your audience reading nothing at all.
- **Answer Questions Like You Are a Trial Witness.** Communicate the core point you are trying to make. If you were on the witness stand and a lawyer asked you, "Have you ever taken a drink before driving." You could say, "Occasionally I have, but I know my limit." Or you could say, "I have, but it depends on the type of alcohol. For beers, I can have a few and it doesn't affect me. With wine two glasses is my limit. With liquor, I have a pretty good tolerance so it depends on the drink."

Before this harmless question, you were a witness at a trial. After, you were an alcoholic that has done enough drinking to know how each and every drink affects his driving ability. Get good at nailing the essence of an issue. For example, if someone asks what you will do with a $1 million investment, the answer might be "$500,000 to hire a VP of Sales and a VP of

Technology, $300,000 for product development, $100,000 for operations and $100,000 for miscellaneous." If people want more, they will ask.

- **The One-Pager.** When an issue requires more detail, the communication should not exceed one page. Assume no one is reading more than one page. If you create something greater than a page, pare it down to one page—and not with font selection or size.

  An entrepreneur was asked by a potential investor, "Can you provide me a high-level summary of the business?" She asked me to review it before she sent it. It was four pages of single-spaced content. She asked what I thought and I said, "Not sure because I would never read something that long and neither will your investor."

If you can't communicate something in one page, you aren't bringing clarity to the content.

- **Pretend You Are on Twitter.** Tailor your communications like you do when you Tweet. Distill messages to key phrases. With Twitter, you may start with 200 characters but you pare it down to 140. Eliminate the fluff. Write, "The business requires a million-dollar investment," and not, "Ultimately, within our larger business model which we worked very hard to put together so as to be best adapted for success, we actually found that to really succeed, we will likely be needing further equity in the range of one million dollars or so." Whether it is a larger issue that justifies a one-pager, or a smaller one that deserves one paragraph, think of these as your limits. Chances are, no one is reading more anyway.

Take pride in developing good communication skills. Make a commitment to improving these skills. Anyone can write a five-page paper on a given topic. Good leaders can distill five pages into a single, comprehensible page that everyone will read. Start training your organization and clients to expect the one paragraph and the one-pager. Hopefully they will respond with the same economy.

Albert Einstein said:

> *"The grand aim of all science is to cover the greatest number of empirical facts by logical deduction from the smallest possible number of hypotheses or axioms."*[8] A big idea from a big thinker. He could have said, "Keep it short and sweet."

---

[8] Barnett L. (1950) *The Universe and Dr. Einstein* (Dover Publications).

Chapter 2
What You Say and How You Say It

__What We Feel__: People need to be tough-minded to work in a startup. They can't be so fragile that they are put off by the wrong word here or there. We've all got to have thick skin and not worry so much about how we say things.

Your organization must develop communications skills and avoid key communications mistakes. Think of your organization as a piece of clay. It will take shape based on many factors, especially in an immature market space. Once it takes shape, it will be difficult to reshape the clay. Yet, entrepreneurs often don't realize the messages they are sending. These messages may not have been intended to be sent, or might be intended for a specific situation. Unfortunately, you don't have the resources to manage the impact of these messages and the impressions they create. It's not as if you have a public relations department crafting the messages coming from you and the company. The manner in which you organize the methods, frequency and content of your communications will shape your clay.

As the leader of your organization, you set the tone. Keeping constituents aligned and motivated, especially when you don't have the capital or resources you need, requires a great deal of skill. When people feel vested in the venture (and the adventure), they will sacrifice, spend more time than they should, moonlight after their day job, and be extremely dedicated. In many cases, people will work for free to be part of something inspiring and important. These people need to feel that they are more than employees. They need to feel that they are part of the oxygen that makes the business breathe and that the business is on its way up. It is your job to make them feel that hot air isn't the only thing that rises.

The intensity and length of the normal day leaves little time to make sure that every word and deed is executed or managed properly. In fact, you probably forget most things you said or did by the time the next day arrives. This is to be expected. Most communications throughout the day come and go without much thought. Others, however, set the tone for the organization, and specifically determine how people feel about the vision and their connection to it.

Your Change in Perspective

There are a few communication patterns, often occurring on a daily basis, which impact the "feeling" of the organization. In these interactions, what you say and how you say it makes all the difference:

- **It's We, Not I. It's Ours, Not Mine.** This is your baby. It is your vision. It is your passion. You gave birth to it. You live it and breathe it. You are the only one that burned through your life savings. There is no doubt about your commitment and dedication. Now what about everyone else that you want to be dedicated to the cause? Why will they be committed? Why will they be committed when they are being paid below-market compensation, or only equity, while working crazy hours?

When you use words like "my" or "I," you may not realize the message this sends or the impact it has on people who have invested time and energy in the business and made numerous sacrifices for its success. It is understandable since this is your baby. Entrepreneurs often feel they are entitled to say this is "my" business. For some, it is a source of pride. This seems harmless initially, but it erodes your team's connection to the venture. If you listen to experienced CEOs, they rarely use words like "I" or "my." They understand the impact this has on employees—even those of a larger company. For employees of an entrepreneurial venture, the message reads: "Even though you continue to commit your blood, sweat and tears to the company, it is mine not yours." Imagine if you were part of a team building a house:

The leader comes over to you and says, "Can you go down to the basement and paint the walls?" You go to the basement and it is cold, the room has no lights, it smells odd and you only have a three-inch brush. Nonetheless, you spend the next eight hours painting the basement, three inches at a time. At the end of the day, you emerge and come to the front of the house and the leader is giving an interview with a local television station. The reporter asks, "How did you build this house so quickly?" He says "I've been doing this for a while and have a knack for it."

Enough said. When you are communicating with constituents, always say things like when "we" started the business and "our" plan, "our" team. Speak of resources as a "team" even when you are doing 100 percent of the work. This may seem like a minor point but it will get noticed by everyone you interact with—including your team.

It also gets noticed by investors. When reviewing a fledgling company, investors must evaluate the strength of the leadership and the ability of an entrepreneur to lead. Speaking of things in terms of the team demonstrates a level of maturity and confidence that investors look for. It shows that you are focused on the success of the business, and that you understand that if the business is successful, you will be successful.

- **Instill confidence.** Despite the challenges of your organization, always communicate with confidence. How often do you walk out of a meeting and say to yourself, "If they only knew how screwed up we are"? It is fine to have those conversations with yourself, but not out loud. Even though your balloon is full, resist the temptation to communicate in any way that undermines the confidence of your team, customers or investors. Confidence does not mean that you are not candid, that you don't outline challenges or that you create unrealistic expectations. Confidence is about how you deliver the message.

  I was a senior at Bucknell and three of us—Steve and Fran and I were scheduled to make a major presentation as part of our management class. This was our "final exam." During the presentation we had to convince the board of directors of a large, consumer product brand to switch their advertising business from their current well-known agency, Saatchi and Saatchi, to our new age agency.

The role of the board of directors was played by the business school professors. Our presentation was at 8 a.m. on a Friday morning and would last three hours. At about 9 p.m. the night before, the three of us were preparing and we got a call from a friend. It was a mutual friend's twenty-first birthday party and a group was headed to the Bull Run Inn (the main bar at Bucknell) to celebrate. We said we had an early presentation but were convinced to stop by for one drink. Ten drinks and six hours later it was 3:30 a.m. and we went to sleep. We got up, slapped on our suits and ties and presented for three hours—each of us for one hour. Fran went last. Things were going well despite our lingering blood alcohol content. Fran got to the end of his presentation, and, as we all did in our sections, he took questions. After a few questions, the head of the management department raised his hand and said he had one last question. "As you know, our brand is one of the most trusted brands in the world. Why should we trust it to an upstart agency like yours?" Fran paused and said, "If you want to continue to spin your wheels in a quagmire, go ahead." The room went silent. The presentation ended.

After the room cleared, Steve and I went over to Fran and asked him how he came up with that gem. He said, "I was tired and probably still drunk. I only had fifteen words left and that's what came out. It was just as likely that the fifteen words were, "Are you asking that because you want an answer or to hear yourself talk?"

It wasn't what he said. It was how he said it. Regardless of what is going on, communicate with confidence.

- **Never talk catastrophe.** There will be times you feel that you are on the brink of failure, at your wit's end, too burned out to go at it. You have no money, and you have hit "the last straw" with a vendor, employee, investor or customer. Marathoners talk about "hitting the wall" at mile twenty. Try hitting the wall at mile 1, 2, 3, 4, 5, 6, 7…

Despite this, your communication can never include words like *disaster, catastrophe, quit, falling apart* or any of terms associated with the apocalyptic scenario running through your mind. To you, these may simply be expressions of your current emotion and some air coming out of your balloon. To others, these words are warning bells that may lead them to question their commitment to your vision. It's not uncommon in a moment of frustration to say, "I want to run away and sit on a beach" or "We're not going to make it." These may be true emotions. They may persist or they may be fleeting. In either case, keep them to yourself.

While the catastrophe of the day may be quickly forgotten, the lasting impression of these words will not. These words will stick in the mind of your constituents like a line from a B-movie you'd like to forget. Worse, it will impact their perspective. When your constituents believe you are successfully moving from point A to point B, they view a challenge or a tough day as only a speed bump to overcome. This can often be a rallying cry for an organization. At IncentOne we would say: "We can always find people that *can't* get it done." Overcoming obstacles became a source of pride. However, when doubt sets in, this changes.

It's one thing for your people to work through the doubt that naturally comes with building a business. It is another to hear it from the mouth of their leader. Concerns that come with the territory of entrepreneurship, and that used to fall under the category "the nature of the beast" now become deal breakers—reasons to think twice. As hard as it is, eliminate these words from your public vocabulary, and share them only with your bottle of bourbon—and hope that the bottle doesn't talk back.

- **Avoid Cockiness.** To accomplish many of these lofty goals the job requires, as noted above, confidence. When that confidence shifts to cockiness, you run a great risk. There are times people do business with you because of your business value. There are other times they do business with you because they like you. When you demonstrate cockiness, you make customers and employees think to themselves, "Do I want to do work with this guy?"

  When we started IncentOne, we were committed to being a B2B solution and avoiding the consumer market. We had a lot of pressure to target the consumer market since we had a network of gift cards and the market was giving huge valuations to dot com business-to-consumer companies. We scheduled a meeting with a potential competitor, giftcertificates.com. They told us, in no uncertain terms, would they create the currency for the Internet and that it was a matter of time before companies like ours would be gone. We respectfully disagreed, thanked them for their time, and went our separate ways. Their arrogance always stuck with me. Years later, when the consumer market had collapsed, I was contacted by one of their investment bankers asking if we would consider buying them. I asked if the current management team was the same as if was a few years ago. It was. I declined.

- **Stories Tell the Story.** The evolution of a business with an untested concept is complex. It is difficult for constituents to digest information in a way that keeps people aligned to the vision and motivated to plow through the challenges. Relating your business to well-known stories can accelerate results. In many cases, telling a story can produce more effective results than explaining the issue. First, it clarifies the specific message you are trying to deliver. Second, it gives credibility to the message when independent third parties deal with the same issues. Third, it can create faith in your team when they understand that well-known third parties went through the same thing.

At IncentOne, we were creating an entirely new market in the mid-2000s—rewards for healthy behavior. We had to help employees understand that building a new market is hard, and requires overcoming many obstacles, big and small. We could have said it this way: "To innovate and create a new concept, it takes a lot of time, effort and capital." Most of the time, we just referred to Amazon:

Amazon told the world that no one would ever buy a book in a bookstore. The world scoffed at them. Did they think that Barnes & Noble and Borders and JB Dalton and every local library and bookstore would disappear? They told Wall Street that they would lose billions to ensure that exact scenario. Amazon was founded in 1995. By the end of 2001, they had cumulative annual losses of $2.85 billion since going public in 1997, and after operating as a public company had made a profit in only one quarter ($5.1 million in 2001).

Stories work. Here's another example. You know your company needs to drive some fundamental change. Imagine walking into your company and saying to leadership, "We need to fundamentally revamp our revenue sources and business model. If we don't shift to a model in which 100 percent of our revenues comes from different products in the next five years, we will be out of business." Or try this.

In 1985, Blockbuster opened the doors of its first video rental retail store in Dallas, Texas. By the mid-1990s, Blockbuster was a household name, and at its peak, the company had over 60,000 employees with branches in more than a dozen countries and 9,000 stores. Then came the Internet and Blockbuster's inability to respond to this clear trend. "Imagine a Blockbuster night without Blockbuster, a time when no video store will slap you with a late fee or fine you for failing to rewind. Because in this world, there are no videos, only home computers," the Chicago Sun-Times *wrote back in June 1999. Already, the Internet was being viewed as a potential killer of the video industry. Amazon had just entered the market, expanding from selling cheap books online to cheap DVDs, and a little company called Netflix rolled out a subscription service. It wasn't until 2004, six years after Netflix launched that Blockbuster realized it needed to enter the online DVD rental-by-mail space. By then, Netflix was already turning a profit and Redbox had just launched. Blockbuster was already dead—it just didn't realize it yet. With the rise of Netflix, mail-order DVDs, video-on-demand and streaming services online, the former video giant didn't stand a chance.*

Blockbuster's CEO defiantly declared that Netflix was no threat. His best quote: "I've been frankly confused by this fascination that everybody has with Netflix… Netflix doesn't have or do anything that we can't or don't already do ourselves." Blockbuster filed for bankruptcy in 2010, and was purchased by DISH Network in 2011. On November 6, 2013, Blockbuster tweeted an image of the last rental from the once great video-rental chain. The DVD? Apocalyptic comedy, This Is the End. *The aptly titled rental was made at 11 p.m. on Nov. 9 in Hawaii.*

With all the clutter, it is challenging to deliver messages to the organization that stick. The process of telling and retelling stories will plant seeds, create memorable themes and reinforce important messages for your company culture and your business.

There are many communication styles, but this is a skill that you must develop. Sometimes it requires saying less, or choosing your words carefully, other times a detailed story, a personal anecdote, or simply choosing inclusive language will help you connect people to your business, instill confidence in your leadership and inspire others to dedicate time and energy to your vision.

Chapter 3
I'm Emotional and Intelligent But What The Hell is Emotional Intelligence?

What We Feel*: I don't have the time to figure out how everyone feels about every-thing. I'm not a therapist, or hostage negotiator, or mediation specialist. I've got enough to worry about.*

What is emotional intelligence? Emotional intelligence is the ability to read and understand your own emotions as well as others' emotions in the context of a particular situation. It is the ability to distinguish between different emotions and to respond to them appropriately, so you can make good business decisions.

When I was taking business classes at Bucknell, there were no courses on emotional intelligence. People didn't talk about emotional intelligence in the context of running or building a business. Today, that has changed significantly. There is a clear recognition that, in addition to the nuts and bolts of building a business, it's critical to develop the emotional intelligence that will help you manage your own emotions, your team dynamics, and your interactions with outside resources. The ability to understand and manage your own emotions and the emotions of others are critical to driving a business forward. Today it is common for business schools to have emotional intelligence in their curriculum.

As an entrepreneur under the influence of the Four Ps, your own emotions and the emotions of others, especially those of your team, are constantly being tested. It's not enough to build a product or service and execute sales, manage your marketing and operations. You must also manage the constant human interactions you will have with employees, consultants, vendors, investors, customers and others. The success of these interactions determines how easy and effective—painful or painless—meeting your company's business goals will be.

Entrepreneurs sometimes think that they don't have time for "fluffy stuff"—that emotional intelligence is a nice "extra" to have but certainly not a must have. But emotions have consequences for your business—and they aren't going away. So ask yourself this question: do you want to deal with this issue while it's still manageable, or later when interactions have gotten messy and already affected your business? The fastest way to lose control of your business or the dedication and effectiveness of your team is to ignore the emotions going on around you. You don't need a Magic 8-Ball or team mood rings—simply pay attention to the people you interact with every day. A little emotional intelligence goes a long way.

Your Change in Perspective

The failure to understand the importance that emotional intelligence plays in your effectiveness as a leader, and the success of your business, is a mistake. Similarly, looking for shortcuts like the Magic 8-ball—in which you apply standard answers to different situations—is also a mistake. In the early days of the business, when you don't have the right financial or human resources to put in place normal relationships with employees, vendors, customers, investors and so on, you must be able to drive these constituents under less than ideal conditions. The ability to apply emotional intelligence is a skill that is essential to moving your company forward. You must think of emotional intelligence as a skill set no different from raising money, developing marketing strategy, or learning how to recruit employees. Once you accept its importance and make a commitment to working on this skill, you have to understand that it is not a one size fits all scenario. It's a moving target.

The real trick of emotional intelligence is to be nimble, flexible, and immediately capable of determining what to do in a given situation. This means considering many things simultaneously: first, your own emotions and how the influence of the Four Ps and stress is affecting your judgment, and those around you; second, the emotions and behavior of those across the table from you, and, third, the "table" or situation itself. Are you negotiating a potential deal that you need to happen quickly with partners who are particularly slow and cautious in their investment decisions? If you don't acknowledge the stress (or desperation) you bring to that scenario, you risk misreading their caution and reacting in a way that derails the interaction, and ruins your credibility. It is very hard for others to understand what you are experiencing, and much easier for you to assume that the views of others are "off." Don't expect everyone to understand your situation. In fact, on the contrary, you must make a conscious effort to understand what others are experiencing and how they're affected by your actions, reactions to situations and interaction with them.

It always helped me to think of emotional intelligence as a blender. Blenders provide you with many different buttons to push—chop, blend, dice, puree, liquefy, crush, grind, mix, fluff, whip, beat. As an entrepreneur, you will be making decisions throughout the day. Different ingredients will be added to the mix. Different people. Different situations. Different pressures. Different implications. Different personalities. The key to emotional intelligence is determining which button to press in which situation.

The daily tidal wave of pressure, endless to-do items, and obsessive focus on your vision, can make it difficult to identify and select different buttons in different moments. It's easier to apply the same button all the time— just shove down the "whip" or "blend" button. In the movie *Whiplash*, the psychotic jazz conductor, played by Oscar winner J. K. Simmons, treats everyone the same. By the same I mean, treats them all like shit. He is using the same button on the blender every time. This button will work with some personalities, but not all of them. The ability to discern a specific set of ingredients and apply the appropriate button is the essence of emotional intelligence and a valuable perspective with an immediate effect on your business results.

Don't get me wrong; sometimes it would be great if your blender had buttons that read:

- Whip = Produce a killer sales guy
- Blend = Discover the perfect offshore vendor
- Grate = Convince an investor of your valuation
- Puree = Make problematic employees see the error of their ways
- Chop = Get my biggest customer to pay their bills on time
- Dice = Outline my sales strategy

But remember, emotional intelligence is not about tasks. It is about applying the right approach for a particular individual, in a particular moment. This means reading the person, the scene, and anticipating how it will play out. It's like being a film director, a political strategist, a kindergarten teacher or the quarterback of a football team:

> *You are in the huddle with your team. You have spent enough time in the trenches with these guys to know what makes them tick. You know their emotional makeup and how they react to situations. Some need encouragement, some need to be pushed, and others need to be challenged. "Come on Joe, you can do better than that." "Steve, do you realize your girlfriend is never going to sleep with you again if you keep blocking like that." "John, do you think your Dad would be proud of you now?" "Doug, I guess we got the worst of the Fulton brothers on our squad." "Randy, another catch like that and you'll need your own beat writer."*

What you may not realize is, you have been practicing emotional intelligence your whole life—especially in team activities or family gatherings. There's a reason why your mother spent such a long time making seat assignments for Thanksgiving dinner. She was exercising some finely tuned emotional intelligence. She knew how to manage the cast of characters so that Turkey day would be a lovely family gathering instead of a mafia caliber stand-off. Like holiday dinners, if you understand the people in the room, the things that motivate them and the messages that are being sent, your business interactions will be successful. Get it wrong and your business can turn from *Happy Days* to *The Sopranos* in no time.

> *On the baseball team at Bucknell, we had a pitcher, John, who threw ninety miles per hour and when he was "on," he was very good. John had an eccentric personality and sometimes seemed "off." Having your best pitcher not have "both cleats on the rubber" can be a blessing or a curse. John and I had a great*

relationship. We were playing Villanova and Gary Scott, who later had a long career with the Chicago Cubs, was killing us. Late in the game, John threw three balls and was behind in the count 3–0 to Gary. I called time out and walked over to the mound to calm him down. I asked him what was wrong, and he said, "I can't get this guy out." I said, "Hey listen, it is already 3–0 and there is a good chance you are going to walk him anyway. Why not hit him in the head?" I was totally kidding and was trying to make him laugh and calm down. I went back to my position. John came to the stretch and threw the next pitch right at his head. He then turned to me and gave me the "thumbs up" sign.

Needless to say my emotional intelligence was off that day. Since we are on the baseball diamond:

When I was in high school in central New Jersey, I was heavily recruited to play baseball for a number of prestigious colleges, including Princeton. The coach for Princeton was a grey-haired icon by the name of Tom O'Connell who been there for seventeen years until he retired in 1998. Coach O'Connell had quite a temper. He had recruited me and was disappointed when I decided to go to Bucknell. Coincidentally, Bucknell and Princeton played each other each of the four years I was in school. Before each game, Coach O'Connell and I would have a nice chat and he would remind me of the mistake I had made not going to Princeton. When I was a senior, we played a long game at Bucknell. We had beaten up their pitchers and were leading by more than ten runs late in the game. This infuriated Coach O'Connell. We were in the ninth inning and it was clear that Princeton was going to lose the game. Nonetheless, every time someone on our team would get a hit, he would change pitchers. Not only would he change pitchers, but he would put in a position player to pitch. While this is common in high school, in college, pitchers are specialists and only rarely do they play another position. Each time someone got a hit, he would summon someone from the field to come in and pitch. This would take tons of time and even his team was getting tired of it and was looking forward to the four hour ride back to Princeton. In the ninth inning, I was up. I hit a double and was standing on second base. As expected, he walked out to the mound and pointed to his right fielder to come in and pitch. I was bullshitting with the shortstop and he said that Coach O'Connell did this all the time. When the right fielder started running in from the outfield to take his warm-up pitches, I figured that I knew Coach and half-kiddingly said to him, "Hey Coach, why don't you pitch?" To my surprise, he started sprinting—or the eighty-year-old version of sprinting—from the mound toward me on second base. Had it not been for his shortstop, I would have gotten my ass kicked by an octogenarian—and probably deserved it.

I never said I got it right all the time. Pressing the right buttons at the right time is hard to do when you are under the influence of the Four Ps. Take the time to digest the situation, understand the players, and sense what is going on. We must develop the skills required to better understand, empathize and negotiate with other people. Improving your emotional intelligence is a lifelong endeavor. It requires you to nurture many perspectives including:

- Being aware of your emotions and their effects
- Regulating those emotions
- Understanding your motivations and the motivations of others
- Empathizing with and respecting the feelings and perspectives of others
- Effectively using different communication styles in different situations.

Your perspective needs to embrace the importance of this skill, be committed to developing it, and to determining which buttons to push, when. If you improve your emotional intelligence, you enhance your ability to drive your business forward. It will impact how your team performs, how your culture develops, how you develop trust with company constituents, how you communicate with your team, how well you collaborate and ultimately what kind of culture develops. When emotional intelligence is embraced and applied by the leader, the company's (scarce) resources often experience exponential growth: a "one plus one equals three" effect. Company activities—meetings, communications, process—seem to get easier. Each time you pick the right button on the blender, you will advance the business and your own leadership skills. Each time you pick the wrong one, you will puree your expensive truffles.

SECTION 6:

PEOPLE MAKE YOU CRAZY...
AND SUCCESSFUL

Introduction

It's Thanksgiving dinner. Your uncle is bitching about the cranberry sauce. Your mom doesn't understand why no one can wait until everyone sits down before eating. Your sister doesn't see anything she can eat as a newbie vegetarian. Your aunt just told a story about when she had sex the first time. Your cousin wants to know why carrying around a little marijuana is such a big deal.

People. You hopefully love your family, but you don't get to choose them. We all have crazy family members who sometimes make us wonder how are we related to them. We have to keep in mind that people are different and not a single one of us is perfect. It's all about what imperfections we choose to focus on or ignore. Same in business. As entrepreneurs we have to understand our people. Some will be better than others, and sometimes the better ones will have bigger imperfections. You need to understand how to align the best and the worst with all that needs to get done.

What you learn over time is that once you get to the point that you have a great team of people, you can do great things. But in the beginning, you either don't, or can't, hire the best. You may only attract people that are willing to work for equity or a promise of the future. It is hard in a new venture to attract the best and the brightest. New businesses often must prove themselves before talented folks are willing to come aboard. For those that do come aboard, they often have "gaps" in skills or experience. You may find hardworking and dedicated people, but almost always there will be deficiencies that you must accept. Even if you are taking advantage of advisors, family and friends that are willing to give you some of their time, you often find yourself underwhelmed and not grasping why their level of effort and commitment is not as deep or as thoughtful as yours.

Even with this reality, you must find ways to get the best people you can, and to optimize their performance. Hiring, managing and driving performance is as important as the features of your product or service. Your people may not be ideal, but they will hold your success in their hands.

The perspectives in this section help you make the best of your people. How do you make sure that you make the best of your hires? How do you maximize the performance of the people that you have? How do you keep your team focused, motivated and aligned? Sometimes we forget how hard it is for people to come in and babysit our baby. When they do, use these perspectives to make the most of how you and your team get it done.

Chapter 1
Everyone Sucks

What We Feel*: No one does what they say they are going to do. I know my people are working hard and my advisors are giving me their time, but it would be nice if they could deliver with quality and on time.*

I recently had an entrepreneur tell me, "No one can perform up to my standards." I asked her, "What about Steve Jobs or Arianna Huffington or Martin Luther King or Donna Karan or Jack Welsh? Would they be okay?" I was trying to prove a point but I have no doubt I said the same thing when I started IncentOne.

Entrepreneurs need to understand this feeling, why they feel it, how to manage it and the consequences. It makes a lot of sense. At early stages, you don't have the financial or human resources to put in place "normal" relationships—relationships in which people are paid market salaries and have normal working hours and conditions. This applies to many constituents such as employees, vendors, advisors, board members and consultants. Employees, for example, are often working crazy hours for below-market compensation packages, for equity, or even for free on the side of their current jobs. Vendors are rarely paid full freight and are often asked to make financial concessions for the promise of working with the company in the future. In the early days of IncentOne, we struck a deal with a website development vendor to pay them a small portion of incentive transactions in the future if they agreed to develop our first Internet site for a minimal cost. Advisors or board members may be available only a small portion of their time and may be working for below-market compensation if they are compensated at all. Even individuals who help with raising capital, especially at early stages, may not be paid normal compensation.

Not only do we lack to the capital to pay constituents customary rates, or to pay them at all, we lack the resources to manage them effectively. Combine this with a few other realities: First, no one cares as much about the business as we do. Second, no one has spent as much time thinking about it as we have. Third, these people have lives in which they laugh, relax, sleep, drink for fun and even take things lightly. Finally, what we spend all day thinking about is a blip on their screen. With the exception of full-time employees, these resources dip in and out of your world. When a member of your advisory board wakes up in the middle of the night (like we do), he likely did so because he was worried about his sick daughter or his new boss or his mortgage bill or his golf game. Think of it like a pie. Our pie is 99.999 percent our business. Their pie is life, love, family, business, sports, travel and the rest of their normal lives.

When entrepreneurs interact with these resources, we think they are not committed, are underachieving, or are not doing the business justice. We say, "If they are not going to put their best foot forward, they should not be involved." I recently had an entrepreneur say to me:

> *"It would be easier to get rid of everyone. No one does what they say they are going to do and when they do, their work is bad and late. They don't even read the materials I send them. My Board members are a bunch of old gray hair guys that are supposed to have experience but what do they do for the company? My advisors are a waste—they aren't out making introductions for financing even though they know how much we need money. My employees take the weekend off even though they know how much we have going on. My investment guy schmoozes and isn't building the investment materials."*

And then she said:

> *One of my employees even told me that she wanted to play volleyball and spend time with her boyfriend on the weekend. I just don't think she is dedicated to what we are doing.*

It doesn't just happen with employees:

> *A colleague had contracted with a manufacturer to produce a product. A year earlier she asked the manufacturer to invest time in developing the prototype because if the business took off, they would need hundreds if not thousands of units. She called me and told me that her vendor was being unreasonable. She said that the vendor was not willing to deliver the final product and there were cost overruns that were unacceptable. She was considering legal action. I asked her how long has the vendor been working on this and how much have you paid them? She said over a year and about $10,000. I said, "$10,000 for a year, that's an hourly rate of about $5."*

Translation in entrepreneur "speak":

> *"You selfish bastards. You say you want to help and yet every time we talk none of the company objectives are completed. If you are not dedicated to the company, let me get people that have the dedication this opportunity deserves."*

As entrepreneurs, we lose perspective all the time. In fact, if we had our way, we would ban volleyball for anyone working for an entrepreneurial venture. In our eyes, regardless of their compensation or arrangement, everyone is underperforming. We get frustrated that people won't read voluminous materials and don't spend every waking moment living our perspective. We just believe that everyone sucks!

Your Change in Perspective

The reason we feel that everyone sucks is that we have not taken these factors into account and properly assigned our scarce resources to the tasks for which they are most appropriate. We fail to recognize that given below-market compensation and the other factors noted above, these resources will not be effective and valuable unless we manage them. It's like buying the ingredients for making an elaborate dinner of pumpkin soup with crème fraiche, rack of lamb, braised vegetables and chocolate soufflé, dumping them in the kitchen with the busboy and coming back two hours later and screaming, "I can't believe that you mixed the crème fraiche into the soup."

The sooner we realize this, and understand that it is our responsibility to manage these resources by aligning their skills and time commitment with actions that serve the business, the sooner we will no longer think that everyone sucks. Doing this is critical. After all, we have much more to do than we have time. We have to take advantage of every resource at our disposal—employees, advisors, board members, interns, friends, family or other outside resources that have offered to lend a hand.

The resources in an entrepreneurial venture will only be effective if you understand their situations and allocate an appropriate set of tasks to them. Everyone only sucks if you fail to put them in a position to have a positive impact on the business. Try the following:

- **Understand time commitment and skill set.** Understand each person's time commitment, and his/her specific set of skills and compensation arrangement.
- **Assign tasks appropriate for their commitment, compensation and skill set.** Align their efforts to a finite set of activities that are appropriate to their skill set, time commitment and compensation. To say to an advisor who has a financial background, can you please help us build a financial model versus "help us with the investment process" is a big difference. For the latter, you are likely to come back when your frustrations boil over and say, "I can't believe that it has been two weeks and we don't have any investment leads." However, you might very well be able to get the same resource to build a financial model in two weeks. Pick specific tasks appropriate for their place with the company.
- **Create a Regular Check-in Process.** Create a process to take advantage of their limited time, bandwidth and mindshare. This takes the form of a regular meeting at intervals that are commensurate with their time commitment. For example, for constituents you are paying and that are tied to key deliverables, you might have a weekly meeting to stay on top of product development, marketing plans and the like. For non-paid advisors, a biweekly meeting that

addresses their roles and how they are doing against their areas may suffice.

- **Nurture.** Nurture and appreciate their participation. This involves thanking them, but also clarifying that your job is to best align the company's scare resources with its needs. Communicate that you understand that this is not their day job and that they may not be accurately compensated, but you still need their best effort on behalf of the company. Communicate your appreciation while asking for accountability.

- **Make Accountability Public.** You must create accountability and follow through. Setting standards and expectations in a public forum, encourages a group commitment to progress, empowerment and mutual assessment. Individuals who make a commitment not only to you, but to a group of their peers, are more likely to perform to a higher standard and take responsibility for their work. When commitments are only to you, it is common to hear: "Something came up and I couldn't get to it." However, when that commitment is made to a group, they will find a way to get the job done, especially if progress is also reported and nurtured in a group setting. When you publicly set tasks for your team, make sure that the forum involves their peers, but also a variety of advisors who are also accountable to each other. Committing to tasks in this setting encourages greater integrity and pride in performance.

A colleague needed to move forward on their investment process. One of her advisors was an experienced money raiser and had told her that he would take ownership of the process. The entrepreneur waited for the advisor to act—schedule meetings, talk through the process, set up a data room. None of this happened. When she reached out to the advisor, the advisor would respond, act for a few days and then disappear. When a key deliverable was due for an investor deck, he said he didn't get to it because Duke was in the national championship game. The pattern continued with stops and starts. She asked the advisor to change how they were doing things and to have a weekly investor meeting that she asked the advisor to run. The advisor committed to a weekly meeting during which he would provide an update to the entire team. From that point forward, the advisor was prepared and delivered an on-time, quality product.

Try introducing the following process, which demonstrates that you have taken into account obstacles and limitations but still expect accountability:

> *"First of all, I want to thank each of you for taking time to help the company. Your time is valuable and I want you to know how much it is appreciated. With that in mind, I would like to create a process to make your time as productive for you and the company as possible. I suggest a biweekly meeting for one hour during which we will review what each of you is doing and the specific issues we need to discuss. In the first meeting, we will identify issues that we would like assistance with, and knowing your time commitment, the specific tasks you might assist with. We are open to other suggestions, but hope to make this productive, enjoyable and valuable for you and the company."*

If we don't allocate our scarce resources, our company suffers in several ways. We fail to move forward with the tasks at hand. We create misaligned expectations that lead to frustration with the resources we have. In an ideal world, people would manage themselves and perform without fail. On Earth, our resources need to be managed and we if we do this well, we'll quickly find that the only thing that really sucked was our perspective.

Chapter 2
Hiring Is Game Changing and
A Skill You Must Master

What We Feel*: I get a good feeling from this person. My gut tells me that they would be good to work with. I'd like to get a more seasoned person, but we can't afford it.*

I wish I could still count on one hand the hiring mistakes we made. Your team is the most important asset you have, and yet, for many entrepreneurs with young companies, recruiting is the skill to which we devote the least time and discipline.

This almost makes sense—almost. After all, when you are the entrepreneur, any resource will do. You are overwhelmed. You turn a blind eye to deficiencies that might be obvious. You also worry about money. You think to yourself, "How can we afford to pay that extra $25,000 in salary in our situation?"

In addition to the influence money has on our thinking, hiring and recruiting is just not an area that seems to leap to the top of the pile for the entrepreneurs. Despite the research, tests and tools that sophisticated companies use to evaluate employees, many of us think hiring is nothing more than using a little common sense and trusting your gut. For some reason, hiring is just one of those areas that we don't identify with the need for expertise—just some good "people skills."

Entrepreneurs certainly understand on a general level how important the company's core team is to its success. Nonetheless, the Four Ps and our own lack of perspective regarding hiring and recruiting cause us to shortchange the effort and expertise that should be dedicated to these functions.

Your Change in Perspective

Plain and simple, not making the hiring process a priority is a mistake. Hiring the right person can unlock the value of your business for years. Hiring the wrong person can set it back just as far. This may feel counterintuitive when you are getting started and you are more worried about money than people. But money is not the only consideration, and in fact, your concern for it can distract you from making the necessary calculations you need to succeed. Here are a few tips:

- **Pay More**. I violated this one many times. The difference between someone who makes $125,000 versus $150,000 seems like a fortune when you have little money (or it's your money). The difference in talent and experience can be significant and worth the additional spending. With the right team member, it will unlock more than $25,000 in value. Multiple times during IncentOne I got this wrong. We were anxious to fill key roles. When we saw what we thought was the right candidate, we jumped, but not for the best candidate, but for the candidate that was good, but cheap. I underpaid for executives. This was my money and saving $25,000 per year on a salesperson, CFO, or head of client services seemed important. If I could do it over, I would hire the more expensive leader. Don't get me wrong, spending more is no guarantee of success, but I knew I was passing on better candidates because of cost. When you talk to people that have created multiple successful startups, and ask them their secret, many of them say, "I found a great team and once we did it once, we knew we could do it again and again." Also keep in mind, even though it is $25,000, if for some reason it didn't work out and the person was with you for six months, the difference in cost would only be $12,000.
- **Be Wary of Strategists**. Thinking is easy, executing is hard. You and I could come up with a great business idea, but only few can execute it. As careers advance, fewer people choose to remain in an

execution role and steer toward "strategy" and "strategic thinking." How many people at the age of fifty love getting their hands dirty, building plans, tracking activity and holding people accountable? In a perfect world, you would have separate roles for strategy and execution from the start. Unfortunately, it's precisely in the early stages that you can't afford to have different resources responsible for strategy and execution.

When you hire experienced people, make sure you ask them, "Tell me about your desire to build process and structure, and also execute it." If they answer, "I am willing to get my hands dirty," move on. If they say, "I love building businesses" or "I love watching a team gel," consider them. You need people who "love to" and not ones that are "willing to." I hired many people (especially those from larger companies) who said they were "willing to" get in the trenches but when push came to shove, they expected their teams to get in the trenches. Larger companies often enable leaders to keep their hands clean and let their teams get into the weeds. In a younger company, you need a leader who can design a blueprint and swing a hammer—and is happy doing both.

> *We used to go to a bar on the Upper East Side of Manhattan to watch New York Giants football games. The bar was always packed. The waiters would carry food through the crowd from one end of the bar to another. It would have been much simpler to pass the food behind the bar to get food to patrons. One leader would say, "We should pass the food behind the bar." Another leader would talk to the manager and the wait staff, train them on the process, and reward them when the process worked well.*

That's the leader you need in the early stages of a business.

- **Use Outsiders to Interview**. You are often too anxious to bring on resources to be objective about a candidate. Ask a colleague or advisor who has little to do with your business, but plenty of business knowledge, to interview finalists. Provide them with enough information to understand your needs and then pay attention to their advice. It is much more likely to be objective than your own, especially if you are stuck in the perspective of "No one cares as much as I do" or "I am the only one who can do this work."

- **Your Team Needs a Bench**. Boy this is a tough one. You don't have starters and I am asking you to create a bench. Early stage businesses often have single points of failure. You have a single vendor, customer or employee that is critical to the business. Put another way, what would happen if you lost that vendor, customer or employee? You also need to be able to make changes when things aren't working out. Without a bench, you keep underperforming employees longer and compromise on the non-negotiables (e.g., culture, etc.).

I'll never forget recruiting my last CFO. I was looking for a right hand man. Someone that could be a steward of the business, oversee the financing process and handle the day-to-day finance functions. I knew I was asking for a lot. A consultant I knew recommended Fred. He was formally trained at large companies, had been an operator, had been in entrepreneurial ventures and in venture funded businesses. He also had experience being a CFO of more complicated businesses and was familiar with the investment process. I thought I had hit the jackpot.

I could not have gotten this one more wrong. To say his personality was caustic would be an insult to those who are caustic. While none of this came through in the interview process, I should have known I was making a mistake when he invited me to his house in Connecticut to meet his family. He introduced me to his wife and went to his backyard to play with his kids. I was chatting with his wife and said how I looked forward to getting to know them better. She chimed in and said, "Anything that gets him out of the house." I could tell by the look on her face she wasn't kidding. When your balloon is full and you are desperate to fill roles, you ignore signs. Who says that to your husband's new boss?

It went bad almost immediately. Before Fred joined, we had instituted a program to reward one person from each department each quarter. The entire company would pick one person from each department and the head of the department would have the final say. The superstar in the finance department was a guy named Doug who helped keep the business together during a tough year. By coincidence, about two weeks before Fred joined, Doug got a small and long

272

overdue raise. Doug was a unanimous choice for the finance department. Except for Fred. Despite the fact that Doug was going to be his right hand and would be largely responsible for helping Fred, Fred objected. He said that Doug had just gotten a raise and should not be eligible for the reward.

During the same week this was happening, there was an error made in the finance department. After only two weeks, I did not expect Fred to take responsibility for something that took place just as he joined. What he did after that blew me away. I thought he would say, "We will put in place the process to make sure this never happens again." Wishful thinking. Despite the fact he had been there for less than a month, he threw Doug under the bus.

I should have made a change two weeks after he started. I tried over and over to build a relationship with him. Wasn't happening. I was on the road all the time and when I would come back to the office people would come up to me and complain about Fred. At first, I thought it was a function of a tough-nosed CFO bringing more discipline to the organization. Wishful thinking. Time and time again I spoke to him about his demeanor and approach. Finally, after my last attempt to get us on the same page, I said to him, "Listen, you and I have not seen eye to eye on much, and I mean no disrespect, but if you got picked last on the playground or never slept with the cheerleader in high school, that's not my problem to fix."

I should have made a change right away. Without viable alternatives, making personnel changes seems impossible. To prevent this, as hard as it is, you must nurture relationships with potential employees to create bench strength. You likely don't have the capital to hire a bench, but just like an actor in a play has an understudy, you need to prepare to back up your key resources. If you don't, you will retain the wrong people longer and this will weaken your business. You can't hire a full bench at one time, but make a commitment to recruiting as an ongoing asset management process. When replacements are only a phone call away, you make better people decisions.

- **Don't Hire Teams of People Who Have Worked Together Before.** Critical hires are on your mind all the time. When you have many holes to fill, your hiring process tends to suffer from poor judgment. This takes many forms. It's tempting to hire a team of people who have worked together before. Someone will introduce you to two or three or more individuals that have worked together before. This seems like a huge win. Imagine if you could bring in multiple team members who have worked together and who could bring productivity and synergy to your endeavor quickly.

In theory, that sounds great. Here's the problem. When you hire a team who have worked together before, it is hard to hold one of them accountable, or provide constructive criticism to one of them. You are subject to the whims of that team. Even though you may be addressing an issue with one team member, you have to think about the implications for the entire team. These people know each other enough to have moved as a team to a new company. They are likely "in bed" together. This makes it difficult to hold one team member accountable without ruffling the feathers of the team. When this happens, a normal issue of accountability can threaten the viability of your business. Don't do it.

A recruiter had recommended a firm that could assist us with investment and recruiting. Once they understood our needs, they communicated that they could bring in a team of three people in operations and technology that had worked together before. It seemed like the perfect fit. I hired them as three senior executives of the company. Unfortunately, it became clear that these resources weren't all they were cracked up to be.

I knew I was in trouble when I asked the resource acting as our chief operating officer (COO) about the management meeting structure she intended to put in place. She asked me, "What do you want to talk about at management meetings?" I got scared because an experienced COO would have this nailed but I assumed she was being deferential. It turned out that every management meeting she ran was a random walk. It had none of the structure or process that you'd expect from an experienced COO. Unfortunately, as I held her more accountable, it was clear that the three of them were a fiefdom and were more interested in protecting each other than they were acting in the best interest of the business.

When the chief technology officer (CTO) demonstrated characteristics that would generously be called caustic, I challenged him. It became clear that any challenge to any one of the three was a challenge to all of them. It became increasingly difficult to push through any level of accountability because they were more interested in defending each other than in performance.

When I brought in this team I thought I was killing many birds with one stone. All I was doing was creating a power center that made it difficult to hold a team accountable and build a successful company culture.

The resources that make your company grow and succeed are your people—especially your senior people. Hiring the right people is difficult to do in any business. In an entrepreneurial venture that is under the influence of the Four Ps, it is even more challenging. But if you adopt the right perspective, it will become clear just how critically important hiring is. You'll develop it as a specialized skill, and in doing so, approach building your team with the same purpose and care you devote to other key elements of your business. Every time I failed to prioritize this perspective, the mistake was obvious and far-reaching. But when I approached hiring and recruiting new team members with a deeper understanding of the purpose—and the painful consequences of getting it wrong—we advanced the business and strengthened our company culture. You can't control everything, but this is one skill you can choose to improve and the results will be undeniable.

Chapter 3
Help People with Their Bucket List
And Performance Will Follow

What We Feel: *Our people have to understand that if we are going to bring this to life, we are going to have to work hard and produce results. If we have to motivate our people, we have the wrong people.*

I used to think that the most important thing in building a new business was the right strategy. What I failed to appreciate, and only learned after making many mistakes, was what *Good to Great* nailed, which was "people first, strategy second."[9] My background was one of overachievers. I played baseball in college. I spent three years at one of the most prestigious law firms in New York City. Northwestern Law School, where I got my law degree, was ranked seventh in the country when I graduated and was the worst law school in my firm's candidate class. In the mergers and acquisitions world, it was common to hold conference calls at three in the morning and not to sleep for days. Needless to say, people were expected to drive themselves. When there are billions of dollars at stake and clients are paying hundreds, if not thousands of dollars an hour for lawyers, the need to engage the workforce hardly gets much attention.

Pro athletes, and lawyers at firms like the one I worked at, are self-motivated. They don't need to be aligned, engaged or inspired. I figured everyone was that way. I realized, the hard way, that the real world is not comprised of lawyers at firms who pay them $150,000 starting salaries. The real world is made up of the people who make it go round—the customer service representatives who help you with your credit card, the

---

[9] Collins, J. (2001) *Good to Great: Why Some Companies Make the Leap...And Others Don't* (Harper Business).

construction workers who build your house, the medical administrators in doctors' offices and hospitals, the sanitation workers who clean our streets, the factory workers you make sure your Amazon orders ship and the postal workers who deliver our mail. Remove them from the world and watch society collapse.

I thought that everyone we hired at IncentOne—the customer service reps, the fulfillment personnel who shipped gift cards, the client service representatives and the technology developers, would be self-motivated. If they weren't self-motivated on their own, once they knew that we would change the healthcare system, they would be so inspired that they would hop out of bed at 6 a.m. without an alarm. They wouldn't worry about their mortgage, sick child, struggling marriage, aging relative, medical bills or the cost of their bus pass. It seems silly as I put these words on the page. Boy was I wrong.

How you take care of your people tells you more about your company and you as a leader than anything. Nothing demonstrates cultural values more than how you treat your team. A commitment to your people has many positive effects. It drives their commitment to the vision. It creates ambassadors for your company. When you or your company are criticized, they will defend you. It creates a recruiting department when you don't have one. Customers notice and want to do business with you. Employees will take constructive criticism.

Treat your people like fungible assets that can be replaced at any time and watch the negative effects. When one thing goes bad, ten things will go bad. When an obstacle occurs, they will blame others. When you provide constructive criticism, they will look for a job. When you or your company are criticized, they will pile on.

When I started IncentOne, I could not imagine hiring anyone in "human resources." This screamed "unnecessary cost" to me. I learned the hard way. Every recruiting brochure has the "people are our most important asset." In most cases, it isn't bullshit. It is true.

So the question is, if people are our most important asset, how do you maximize the performance of your people? The perspective of most entrepreneurs is that they expect their people to work hard. Some entrepreneurs expect their people to work constantly. After all, we have a business to build and so much more to do than time. My perspective, like most entrepreneurs, was that we were doing important work, and if someone was getting involved, they knew they were going to work their ass off. That is the default strategy that entrepreneurs use to drive performance. "You signed up for this."

Is this right? The question is, "How do you truly engage your people so that they are not only productive, but deliver at a level which far exceeds your expectations?" And how do you do it so they are fulfilled and excited about what they do with their lives?" I think the answer will surprise you.

Your Change in Perspective

The answer is not what your team does for you and the company. The answer is what the company does for them. Put this perspective in place and you will see performance you have never seen before. Here are two tools that will help you think differently:

- **Find Out What They Want in Life**. Don't ask yourself, "How do I get the most out of our people?" Instead ask, "How do I get our people what they want most in life?"

    Find out what your people want. Not what they want in their business lives but in their personal lives. Not what they want for their professional growth, but what they want in life. Not in a superficial way, but in a way that touches who they really are. Find out what they really want in life. Don't worry about how it relates to your business. That will come.

    Once you discover what is important to them, figure out how to get them what they want. Don't focus on what your people do for the business. It's about what the business does for your people. How do you implement this? Here's what I did at IncentOne. I told everyone the following:

"I want to help you unlock your potential as a person. Not your potential as an employee. Not your potential as an employee of IncentOne. I want to understand what you want in your life. Then it is my job to help you realize that and see if it can align to what IncentOne needs. My belief is if IncentOne helps you realize what you want, then working at IncentOne is a good thing."

At first, everyone was taken aback. Was I serious? I asked for one-on-one meetings with every employee. At that time, we had about one hundred employees. I asked them, "What do you want in life?" Each and every one of them rattled off something related to their work. "I want to learn Excel better." "I want to understand how health plans budget." "I want to learn more about our product." Then I stopped them, and said, "I don't want to know what you want in your IncentOne life. I want to know what you want in your life. Do you want to run a marathon? Do you want to learn a language? Do you want your brothers to get along?"

Everyone started to share. One of our customer service representatives sang opera and wanted to get more lessons. Another wanted to learn how to cook. Another wanted to eat better. Another wanted to learn to drive a stick. Another wanted to help her son get into a specific college. One employee wanted to quit smoking:

Kelly had been smoking recently and wanted to stop. When I asked her why, she said she was stressed about her mom's health. I asked her to come meet with me after work. She told me more about her mom, and she seemed like a terrific person. I said to her, "Do you mind if I ask you something personal?" She said fine. I said, "Your mom seems like a terrific person. You obviously are close and she means the world to you. Do you think she would be proud of you if she knew you smoked?" She started to cry. I said to her, "I'd like to help you stop. Will you agree to that? We will meet each week on it." She agreed. By the time we met the first week, she had already quit.

If they want to learn opera, do an opera event. If someone wants to learn how to cook, hook him or her up with a chef friend to give him or her a cooking lesson. When you come across a client or fellow employee who has a manual transmission car, connect them.

The best way to unlock the potential of employees is to help them achieve what they want in life. When this happened, they began driving forward at work. How could they learn more about the product? Could they sit in on sales meetings and learn about the sales process? The more we showed them that IncentOne was a way to help them in their lives, the more we unlocked their potential. The customer service representative who wanted to sing opera is now one of most respected client services managers running some of our most complex health clients—and boy can she belt out a tune.

SECTION 7:

SURVIVING ON PLANET INVESTOR

Introduction

You'll get a lot of different answers when you ask people, "What is the most important thing in the business?" Proven market acceptance. The best product. Killer marketing. Great people. But at the top of most lists is proper funding for your business. With funding, you get people. With people, you can execute on your vision.

Even for the entrepreneur who has experience raising capital, it is a complex process that takes significant time and effort. For an inexperienced one, it can seem like you are transported to a parallel universe. There will be times you feel like you're in a beauty pageant and if you don't nail the bathing suit, the talent and the Q&A portion of the pageant, you will never close an investment. It also requires you to think through many unresolved issues. What is your three-year plan? What is your pricing model? Which markets will you chase? What are your team needs? It will even make you question yourself, because now you are subject to validation by a third party.

It's like walking into a doctor's office and having a full body scan. Or perhaps more accurately, an enema. Smart investors want to know everything about you and your business. People. Strategy. Marketing. Sales. Business Model. Market Size. Competition. The Team. Customers. Product.

Smart investors also ask tough questions. Why did you design the product this way? Who is your team? How do you price the product? These are things that you have agonized over for months and months. It's like the mailman coming into your home and asking you, "Why do you dress your baby in pink? Why are there toys all over the floor? Should you still be breastfeeding?" How dare a complete stranger question how you handle your business (or your baby) and put a value on your dream. How dare a complete stranger come in and value what is invaluable to me?

Investors come in all shapes and sizes. And they may not be strangers. They can be your family and friends that give you $10,000 to get started. They can be the private equity firm that invests $25 million at a time. Regardless of the type of investor you want or need, the process of raising capital is one that will expose you to a whole new world—and a whole new language: EBITDA. Operating leverage. Participating preferred. Software capitalization. Revenue recognition. Discounted cash flow. Gross margin. Internal return on investment. Initially you're going to feel like an alien visiting another planet (or a tomboy at a beauty pageant). In addition, you are asking someone for their money. While this is not always true (and some of the perspectives in this section hope to change this), you feel like the investor not only holds the money, but all the cards. After all, you need what they have.

Additionally, for many entrepreneurs, raising money feels like a distraction from running the business. When you are building the financial model for your investment process, it feels like you are spending time away from the business. When you attend an investor pitch day, you think you should be building your product. When you walk out of a meeting with an investor who declines, you think, "I should be spending my time on customer acquisition." There will be times during the process that feel like you are wasting time. You think, "This does not produce a customer, a product or a vendor."

It does. True, time spent on fundraising is time not spent on business issues, but capital is essential, and the crux of advancing the business. With capital, you can build a team. Once you have a team, whether it's one key hire or a full team, you now have the ability build to the business. Some think it is the most important thing you do.

In this section, we arm you with the perspectives and skills to take on the process. Like it or not, we all learn that when a business has enough capital, it moves forward faster and more efficiently. Get capital, you grow. Don't get capital, you don't. The right perspective will help you not only manage the process confidently and effectively, but influence the process for your advantage and benefit. With a little help, you'll sweep Planet Investor's beauty pageant—even the swimsuit portion.

Chapter 1
Basic Survival Skills

What We Feel*: I've never raised money before. It feels like a foreign language. I get different advice from different people about how to do it and without any experience, how can I decide the right way to go about it?*

Whether or not you understand the investment process or have raised money before, as the leader of the company, you need to develop skills that increase the likelihood that your company will get funded. In the beginning, it is likely that you're the only one raising money. Acquiring capital might mean asking friends or family for $25,000 or pitching an angel network for $100,000. If you are raising larger sums, it is likely that you will hire an outside party (e.g., broker) who will facilitate the money raising process. In either case, you will be the one who must convince investors of two things—that your business is worth investing in, and that you are worth investing in.

At different points in the book we've discussed the importance of seeking additional guidance and assistance. Raising capital is definitely an area in which outside help can be critical. There are many professionals—brokers, finders, bankers—that do this for a living. That being said, your facilitator's expertise will only go so far. Even if you bring in outside parties to help you with the process, the decision of an investor to invest will depend on your ability to communicate the value of the business, the opportunity the investment offers them, and your capability to effectively put their investment to work. Investors look for differentiated products and business models, but they look just as carefully at whether the people with whom they entrust their capital, have the skills to succeed.

Developing the skills to raise money is key for every entrepreneur. Even if you rely on outside direction, you need to develop some basic skills. The perspectives you develop will increase your knowledge, sophistication, and confidence in a tough but necessary process. Some of the information may be familiar, some I think will surprise you.

Your Change in Perspective

How do you give your company the best chance to raise capital? It is not one perspective, but actually a series of perspectives that improve your chances of success. Some of these perspectives may seem counterintuitive, but following them, you give yourself a better chance, not only to raise money, but to do so on terms you can stomach.

- **Realize You Are Always Onstage.** As we noted earlier, you are always onstage. This is particularly true when it comes to investors. Every single interaction—phone call, email, text message, meeting, interaction with staff—with or in front of an investor, is part of the data they will use to evaluate you as a leader. There is no "off the record" with investors.

  In New York City I had a colleague that had always been involved with a cancer charity. His Mom died way too young from cancer. Long before becoming an entrepreneur, he was dedicated to raising money for the disease. When he started his company, despite his crazy schedule, he kept up his charity work. He became a member of the Board of a local cancer charity. You would think that these are exactly the character traits you would want in a leader. I found out it wasn't so obvious. During a dinner party, one of his investors said to me, "It is great he keeps up with the charity but it takes a lot of his time."

  Disappointing, but the reality is that everything you do, any time of the day or night, is on stage and will be scrutinized.

- **Clear and Concise.** Everyone has heard they need the "elevator pitch"—a pitch that communicates the value of your business in the time it takes to make the trip in an elevator. The need to be clear and concise must permeate everything you do. This applies to every audience, but even more so to investors. You must be able to clearly and concisely explain the value of the business. You also must be able to concisely answer questions. When asked about a business model, your job is not to espouse the theory of business models, history of business models, properties of business models, etc. Simple. Short. To the point. If they want to know more, they will ask. When your balloon is full, and you have been thinking about the business nonstop, you are likely to have two reactions—both of which you must resist. The first reaction is to tell the investor everything about an issue and the second is to believe that the investor needs to know all the details to understand. Imagine an alien landing on Earth and stepping off a spaceship and asking, "What is the profit margin on your software?" Keep it simple.

Investors look at hundreds of investments and will pass if they don't quickly grasp the value of the business:

Clive Davis is a music industry legend known for discovering Whitney Houston and helping artists such as Earth, Wind and Fire, Aretha Franklin, Rod Stewart, Alicia Keys, Barry Manilow, Christina Aguilera, Carlos Santana, Kelly Clarkson, Leona Lewis and Jennifer Hudson. He has listened to thousands of demo tapes. He was asked how he chooses artists from all the clutter. His response was that he chose songs "that made him tap his feet."

Investors need to tap their feet. If a leader cannot clearly communicate the value of the business, investors will pass. In addition, when investors interact with companies and their leaders, they are not only evaluating the merits of the business but also the entrepreneur and his or her team. Investors understand how difficult it is to cut through the clutter of information that exists in the world to launch a new concept or idea. They want a leader that can communicate clearly and effectively. In a cluttered world, even if you have a good business idea, you must be able to succinctly cut through the noise and stand out from the crowd. Think of it this way. There might be an envelope in your mailbox saying that you won $100 million, but there is a 0.01 percent chance that you will open it. Investors want to see how you can rise above the rest and communicate to customers, employees, vendors and other constituents to bring the business to life.

- **Proactively Bring Up, Acknowledge and Address Weaknesses.** Every business has gaps. Every business has competitive risks. This is especially true of early stage businesses. The way you address these gaps, tells a lot about you and the business. There are generally two routes entrepreneurs take when it comes to weaknesses. One approach is to be defensive or downplay the gaps and competitive risks:

"We understand that ABC Company has capital, but their product lacks the quality of ours. Our engineers are some of the most talented and dedicated ones out there and we don't think they will be able to keep up with us."

This approach raises two concerns. First, it demonstrates that you are not objective about your business. Specifically, it shows that your passion and desire cloud your judgment, and your ability to make decisions. Second, it strains your credibility as a leader. As a leader, you must embrace the brutal truth (such as competition and weaknesses) and use your talent to overcome the challenges. When you defend the indefensible, you undermine your ability to lead. Investors are always concerned that entrepreneurs will allow passion to cloud their judgment.

A second, and more effective approach, is to be proactive in acknowledging weaknesses, define the obstacles and consequences, and present an approach for addressing them:

"We believe we are tapping into a lucrative market space. We expect there to be many competitors with capital. Our success will depend on our ability to execute our product strategy. Specifically, if we can deliver our product by the end of the year, and have that product integrated with some of the existing software players we will gain a small but critical lead. From that point, the lead will erode over time and we will need our distribution to expand to stay ahead."

Proactively bring up your deficits and your strategy for strengthening your weak points—before you are asked. This is a pleasant surprise for investors. They are used to leaders defending or minimizing their weaknesses. They will respect leaders who are honest with themselves and willing to put their talent on the line against the challenge at hand. If you acknowledge your weaknesses, and state a plan for dealing with them, it creates trust and credibility with investors.

- **Let the Business Sell Itself.** Don't hard sell your organization. Let your offering sell itself. How do you do that? Use points of validation by third parties—the market, customers, the press, and employees that have proactively joined your team. Investors won't always believe what you say, but they will believe third party validation.
    - **Market.** Has the market shown interest? For example, "The Innovation Group at IBM featured our solution at their annual Innovation Event."
    - **Customers.** Highlight customers. "Four of the largest banks in the country are using our solution."
    - **Key Team Members Who Have Joined.** Mention key team members. Talented people joining your team is a point of validation. "Our head of technology used to lead the SAAS technology group at ABC Company."
    - **Well-known Press.** Highlight press that you have received from meaningful publications. If the press is the five page *Johnstown Gazette* in a town of 1,000 people, skip it. Highlighting small press can actually undermine your credibility because investors may view that sample as "the best you have."

These techniques help you present key evidence of your viability with the validation of independent third parties. This is more powerful and credible than your personal assurance or effort to convince potential investors that your solution is "great." Let the third parties of your world sell your business. Then it sells itself.

- **Messaging Guidelines to Build Credibility.** These guidelines help you establish credibility with investors:
  - **Offer investors the opportunity to talk to third parties.** As we just mentioned above, third party validation is a useful tool to present to investors—especially if you offer before they ask. But you can also encourage investors to talk directly to customers, vendors, and employees and validate your success first hand. Companies who shy away from offering references or offer them begrudgingly are viewed with skepticism. Companies that offer them before they are asked are viewed as confident and capable of leveraging legitimate with true third party proof points.
  - **Avoid superlatives.** Savvy investors aren't swayed by the use of superlatives to pitch or vet a business. They have heard hundreds of entrepreneurs tell them they have "the most" revolutionary, "the strongest" new technology or "the best" user experience. When they hear these words, they may assume either that you have true belief in your idea, or that your passion clouds your judgment and the ability to face reality and respond accordingly. If the business is "the greatest" discovery yet, let them find that out without saying it.
  - **Avoid talking about deals that aren't done yet.** When you mention deals that aren't finalized, investors say to themselves, "If they are mentioning things that aren't done yet, they don't have much done." Remember, most savvy investors are skeptical.
  - **Avoid attaching human characteristics to businesses.** Businesses don't have emotions. When you attach human emotions to businesses, it strains your credibility. In your job, do business solutions come across your desk where you say "I love that"? You might "love" a person, a dress, a book or a dog, you don't "love" accounting software.

You want investors to invest or pass based on the merit of your business, not on how you approach the process. By using these techniques, you avoid creating doubt in the mind of investors and let the business sell itself.

- **The train is leaving the station—whether they're on it or not.** Act as if it is a matter of time that your solution will be a success. Portray that your offering will succeed regardless of whether this investor is smart enough to get on board.

  In the early days of IncentOne, we garnered a lot of interest. We, like other entrepreneurial ventures, thought we had a good idea. What entrepreneur doesn't? In the few trade shows we attended, we did no promotion and attracted enormous interest. On the last day of one of these events, the head of our marketing firm walked the trade show floor with me. We had a productive day and at the end I asked him, "We are this nonentity in a sea of established players and there seems to be a ton of interest in us—why?" He said, "Michael, when you talk about IncentOne, it comes across that the train is going to arrive at the station and it is only a matter of whether others will be smart enough to jump on board. It seems like IncentOne is going places by the way you communicate."

  This is not to suggest that you should be arrogant. You believe in what you are doing. It was enough for you to leave your job, burn your savings, and sacrifice a normal life. Now is not the time to be modest.

- **Never Act Like You Need Money.** There will be times when you go into an investor meeting running out of money or when this investor is your only prospect. You may not even be able to afford the cab ride over. It doesn't matter. When you walk into any meeting or take a call with an investor, never act like you "need" money. This shows an air of desperation and causes the investor to think, "If this is such a good idea, why are they out of money?" And, "If this individual is such a good leader, how could he let the business become underfunded?" I don't care if you don't have a dollar to your name, never act like you need money. You "want" money to take advantage of the market opportunity.

- **Do Not Let Them See the Strain.** It is hard to turn off the pressure and strain of being an entrepreneur. You must, however, turn it off when you meet with investors. When investors see this strain, it creates doubt about your ability to plow ahead. While you think the day you get capital will make things easier, investors understand that while things get better in many ways (e.g., hiring staff), it also gets more complex. They want a leader who has staying power and when they see the strain on your face, it creates doubt.

- **Never Negotiate from a Position of Weakness.** Negotiating first and foremost is about leverage. Unfortunately, in the early stages of a venture, you have little leverage. You often are underfunded, unknown, working on an unproven business model and subject to legitimate criticisms. Creating leverage when you have none requires creativity. Some examples:
  - Communicate a set timetable by which you expect to close an investment. You, not them, are setting the timeline for investment.
  - Set a plan for a larger investment amount and state that you will take a lesser investment if the valuation does not meet your expectations. This shows belief in your vision and that there are multiple paths to get there. You, not them, are setting the criteria you want in an investor. When you do that, make sure you have a plan for the lower investment amount. The first thing they will say is, "Great, can we see the financial model for that plan?"
  - State your criteria for an investor. "We are looking for an investor who has experience in the space, invests from $5 to $10 million, focuses on SAAS companies, takes a minority interest and has an investment time frame of three to five years." When they sense you are interviewing them (which is part of what you should be doing), they sense the confidence of a leader who knows how to handle the business's needs and is going places.
  - Investors should never know that they are your most viable investor prospect. They need to understand if they want your business, they need to act to take advantage of it. Think you are being deceptive? Think of it this way. Do you think that if you asked your investor, "Are we the only investment in this space you are considering?" And if you were, they would say, "Yes you are." Please.

Creating leverage when you have little is a real skill. You may be saying to yourself, "It's a good thing they don't know how dysfunctional we are." They know. They have Thanksgiving with their families too.

- **Addressing the Future CEO.** One of the most difficult issues that entrepreneurs face is what their role will be in the future. After all, you are the one that put all the time, money, blood, sweat, and tears in the business. How dare they question your role. Wrong answer. Investors are looking for leaders that know what a company needs and are candid about their desires, strengths and weaknesses. There is a simple, standard answer that you must communicate, and, more importantly, believe:

"The future leadership of the company is critical to our success. Today, I act as the leader of the company. I have never been a CEO before, and when we get to the point to discuss leadership, I would welcome the opportunity to discuss what role would be appropriate for me and what is in the best interest of the business."

This is a tough one and this by no means suggests that you won't be running the show. However, investors have seen many businesses come and go, and can smell CEO qualities a mile away. An individual who states that they will be CEO even if they are not qualified to do so undermines his or her credibility. This not only causes investors to doubt the strength of the business but also the judgment of the leader. Talk about this topic openly and communicate that the criteria for the decision will be whatever is the best interest of the business. Your transparency will help diffuse a potential deal breaker for an investor.

- **Ask for Enough Money.** One of the telltale signs of inexperienced leadership is not knowing how much money your business needs to succeed. This is almost always true with new businesses, especially those that are based on new and unproven models. This is one of the big mistakes we made at IncentOne. We thought the market was ready for rewards for healthy behavior in 2004. We underestimated how much time and money it would take to get the health industry to buy in. Investors want leaders who understand what it takes, ask for what they need, and know how to fight to get it. So when investors hear you ask for an amount that clearly under-estimates your needs, they think that the opportunity may not be as significant as you suggested or that you don't understand what it takes to bring the solution to market. After all, if the opportunity is big, wouldn't you want to go big and own it?

I know what you are thinking. If I ask for so much money before we are proven, our valuation will be too low and we will have to give away too much of the company. There is a way to manage this. Ask for more, and have a plan for less. If you are raising $3 million, you could offer the $3 million in stages—$1 million now and $2 million in one year. You communicate that your plan calls for a $3 million investment, and that you are willing to take as little as $1 million if the valuation does not meet your expectations for the larger raise. You must, however, do a few things:

- **Have a Plan for the Lower Amount.** Not a plan scratched on a napkin. Financial models, use of proceeds. The whole thing.
- **Communicate That You Understand This Is Not Ideal.** Actively communicate that you understand that this is not the ideal amount for the business, but that you will take less if valuations are not to your liking. This shows that you know your business needs substantial capital, that you understand what it takes, that the opportunity is worth it and, at the same time, that you are confident in your market opportunity either way.

Ask for the dollars it takes to get the job done. We have all made this mistake. We try to protect our equity. There are many deal structures that can solve this issue, but when you raise too little, you never get to take a deep breath and execute your plan.

- **Avoid Deal Fatigue**. Many people say things like, "With your business, getting investors should be easy" or "You should be able to close an investment in a month." Anyone who says that has never raised money. Raising money is hard and takes time. Investor meetings. Due diligence. Revising financial models. Meeting your team. On-site visits. Interviews with customer references. Valuation discussions. Letters of intent. Legal documents. Then the lawyers. Have you experienced anything that involved lawyers that was described as "quick and easy." Trust me, from an ex-lawyer, it's a unicorn.

Accept that it is a six-month process. Okay, get up off the floor. It is what it is. I know, you need money tomorrow and this creates a great amount of stress. Don't let your need for money cause you to believe that it takes less. If you do, not only will you have the stress of running your business and raising money, but you will add the frustration of your investment not closing when you think it should. You have to avoid what they call "deal fatigue"—the fatigue that comes with how long it takes to get investments done. It is a marathon, not a sprint.

Whatever stage you are at, there are many details in the investment process that you are not as far along as you think. When you think you are 90 percent done, you are 50 percent done. Your desire for money or excitement at closing a deal does not change the reality. If you believe your investment negotiations will be completed in a finite number of days—and you're wrong or simply unrealistic—that miscalculation, especially if regularly repeated, will wear on you. Assume six months. If you do better, great. Don't think you are closer to the end than you are. Go through the process. Don't get too up or down. Keep plugging along. There will be plenty of time to celebrate when it is done.

- **Make Investors Put Skin in the Game**. The normal investment process includes signing a letter of intent when the investor has decided to invest. While the letter of intent sets valuation and the terms of the investment, it does not commit the investor to invest. The investor can pull out without liability. However, the letter of intent normally includes provisions that severely limit you in the form of an "exclusivity" period of anywhere from sixty to 180 days during which you cannot negotiate with any other investor. Sounds like a bad deal. You are tied up and they have no obligation to close. Your leverage is completely gone.

  To overcome this, have the investor put some skin in the game with the following deal structure. Have them make a meaningful portion of their investment, say 20 percent, as a loan to the company on the date of signing the letter of intent. This is done through a simple loan agreement that will make them the senior creditor of the company. The loan agreement includes a provision that states "that if the investment closes, the loan converts into equity at the valuation stated in the letter of intent." If the investment does not close, the loan stays in place and the investor is the senior creditor of the company.

This accomplishes many things. First, the investor puts some skin in the game. When you have some of their money, they are more likely to close the full investment and negotiate fairly. Second, even though you will be subject to an exclusivity provision, you are doing so when they have already given you some money. Next, they are motivated to move quickly since you have their money. Finally, it provides the investor with security because they are the senior creditor of the company—senior to any other loans or other equity investments that might come. If the investment does not close, this protects them.

If you have never raised money before, doing so is an art. It requires various approaches to messaging, process and communication that compel an investor to say, "I want to invest in that company and that leader." The perspectives in this section may not be comfortable, but they will change the investment process from one that controls you to one that you control. While business fundamentals are usually what dictate whether investors invest, your presentation and demeanor can have an equal or greater impact. You must present your business and team as the right opportunity and deliver your message with clarity, confidence and creativity. Following these perspectives does just that, and allows you to put your best foot forward even when you feel like you are going backwards. Closing an investment is never easy. Develop and enhance these skills to improve your chances of securing an investor who is both willing and worthy of your business.

Chapter 2
Build a Process and
Increase Your Odds

What We Feel*: Raising money takes so much time and effort, and it seems like we are scrambling for every meeting and follow-up. Every investor seems to want something different and more than the previous investor.*

Raising capital in the midst of running a business is challenging. Often it is the most important thing that you do and the one for which you are the least equipped. In the beginning, you may also lack third-party brokers, finders or investment bankers helping you with the process. Both the substance and the process can be challenging.

For many new ventures, the investment process is a constant scramble to put together new PowerPoint presentations, documents and financial information for every investor meeting that comes your way. It may seem as though each investor is asking for something unique or different than the last one, but preparing one-off packages and reinventing the wheel for every new meeting is incredibly time consuming and inefficient.

Your Change in Perspective

While the process may differ slightly from investor to investor, in actuality, the process is generally the same each time:

- Initial contact.
- Sign Non-Disclosure Agreement.

- Request for basic materials (Executive Summary, Financial Model, Presentations).
- Follow-up questions.
- Follow-up calls or meetings for deeper dives.
- Meeting key team members.

The order of this process may vary, but the process and necessary materials are the same. If you are a smaller business, you will not need all of these components but can select the ones that make sense for you.

The goal is to develop a process and a set of materials that you build once and use over and over regardless of the investor. While it will take some time up front, once complete, you will be able to spend your time on the substance of the meeting instead of rushing to deliver new material after every investor meeting. The advance preparation is well worth it. For example, when an investor says, "I've got a few questions about your pricing model and your development costs," the normal result is you scrambling to create some reports, rushing to pull together different opinions, and wasting a lot of valuable time. Wouldn't it be great to say, "We've got a set of frequently asked questions that provide answers to your question and to other inquiries usually addressed to us regarding most of our key business features. We'd be happy to pass that data along"? Obviously, this investment process is designed for more significant investments.

Create an inclusive structure that addresses the majority of standard investment opportunities.

- **Process:** while the process may vary slightly, your goal here is to control the process versus the process controlling you. After initial contact is made, drive the following process:
  - Distribute and sign Mutual NDA.
  - Distribute Executive Summary, Deal Structure Document and Presentation 1.
  - Investor reviews materials and asks for follow up (e.g., request for more information or follow-up call or meeting).
  - Distribute the FAQ document and Presentation 2. If a call or meeting is requested, distribute Agenda 1.

This will not cover the entire investment process, but it will stream-line most of it.

- **Documents:** create each of the following documents:
    - ○ **Mutual Non-Disclosure Agreement:** Standard mutual non-disclosure agreement. A form can easily be downloaded from the Internet.
    - ○ **One-Page Executive Summary:** One page with the key highlights of the business.
    - ○ **Key Messages—One-Pager:** For internal use only, these are the key messages you are looking to communicate to an investor. No more than five key messages and no more than one page.
    - ○ **FAQ Document:** Document organized by major topics that outlines answers to the common questions generally asked by investors.
    - ○ **One-Page Deal Description:** Description of the terms of the financing you are proposing and the use of proceeds.
    - ○ **List of References:** A list of customers, advisors, and other significant resources with names, relationship to the company, and current contact information.
    - ○ **Financial Model:** Financial model (usually in Excel) with a minimum projection of three years, monthly projections for year 1, and quarterly projections for years 2 and 3.

- **Two Key Presentations:**
    - 12-slide PowerPoint presentation (Presentation 1). This is the primary presentation you distribute when first interacting with a potential investor. It should be written in a font no smaller than 14-point.
    - 21-slide PowerPoint presentation (Presentation 2). This expands on Presentation 1 and adds details on the various areas of the company. It should be written in a font no smaller than 14-point.

The slides and the content for these two presentations are as follows:

Slide	Description	Pres 1	Pres 2
1. Cover Slide	• Logo, presenters and date	X	X
2. Company Overview	• Overview of company • What you do • Highlight key wins, customers, successes • Key points in history (founding date, key events, investments to date)	X	X
3. Elevator Pitch Slide	• Elevator pitch	X	X
4. Market Opportunity	• Size and importance of the market • Market problem and current solutions	X	X
5. Your Solution	• Product/service overview	X	X
6. Competitive Advantage/ Unique Value Proposition	• Why your product or service is unique	X	X
7. Team 8. (if weak move down)	• Current team with backgrounds and roles • Include board, advisors and other assets	X	X
9. Market Traction (call "customers" if you have them)	• Key customers • Other evidence of market traction	X	X
10. Business Model	• How you price your product or service • How you make money • Key revenue streams	X	X
11. Competition	• Competitors	X	X
12. Financial Projections	• Financial projections – summary • Financial metrics with investment (e.g., EBITDA, date of positive cash flow)	X	X

13. Sales Strategy	• Strategy for selling your product/service		X
14. Pipeline	• Pipeline of current sales opportunities		X
15. Product Strategy	• Strategy for differentiating your product/service		X
16. Client Management	• How you manage clients?		X
17. Marketing	• How you market your product/ service?		X
18. Technology	• What technologies power your solution?		
19. Operations	• What operations support your product/service?		X
20. Finance	• How is financial management being handled?		X
21. Raise Details/ Use of Proceeds	• Structure of investment • Use of proceeds		X
22. Closing Slide	• Contact info	X	X

- **Key Messages—One-Pager.** The investment process can be new to you or your team members. Create a document that lays out the top five messages that you want to investors to understand. For example:
  - ○ Differentiated business model
  - ○ Key customers that are using your solution
  - ○ High operating profit
  - ○ Break even in eighteen months
  - ○ Brand recognition with key industry players

  Investors are dipping in and out of your world and if you can get you and your team aligned around core messages, it increases your chances of getting them to stop and listen.

- **FAQ Document:** The objective of this document is to anticipate questions investors are likely to ask when they want more detail about the business. Investor questions vary slightly but for the most part they all want to understand the same things. This FAQ document tracks the same twenty areas provided in Presentation 2. It is a Question and Answer format with the top five questions in each area. When an interested investor says, "We will have follow-up questions" wouldn't it be great to say "We have a document that addresses a lot of these questions for you." For example, in the area of "Team" the five questions might be:

1. Who are current members of the team, the Board and key advisors and what are their roles and backgrounds?
2. What is the current organizational chart and reporting structure?
3. What key team members do you need to add and in what order?
4. What do you see your role in the company going forward?
5. What are the compensation arrangements with current team members?

You would develop a table that would have each functional area, with the questions and answers in one chart:

	1. Who are current members of the team, the Board and key advisors and what are their roles and backgrounds?
	2. What is the current organizational chart and reporting structure?
Team	3. What key team members do you need to add and in what order?
	4. What do you see your role in the company going forward?
	5. What are the compensation arrangements with current team members?

Create this for each of the areas outlined in Presentation 2. If you find a question is being asked repeatedly but is not included in this document, add it to the document. This document should address 90 percent of the questions and limit ad hoc work for you and your team.

- **Standard Agendas.** For interested investors, there will be follow-up meetings and calls. These meetings look for details on each functional area of the company included in Presentation 2. Create standard agendas that track the tools you have created. For example, a standard agenda for Follow-up Meeting 1 (Agenda 1) would track the slides in Presentation 2 and set out a three-and-a-half-hour meeting structure:

Area	Presenter	Duration (mins.)	Topics
1. Company Overview	CEO	10	• History • Highlights • Funding to Date
2. Elevator Pitch Slide	CEO	10	• Elevator Pitch
3. Market Opportunity	CEO	10	• Market Size • Market Penetration
4. Your Solution	CEO/VP Product	10	• Solution Overview
5. Competitive Advantage/ Unique Value Proposition	CEO	15	• Differentiator
6. Team	CEO	10	• Key Team Members • Bios/Backgrounds • Organizational Chart
7. Market Traction	CEO	10	• Customers • Market Acceptance
8. Business Model	CEO/CFO	10	• Pricing Model • Pricing Assumptions
9. Competition	CEO	10	• Competitors
10. Financial Projections	CFO	10	• Income Statement • Balance Sheet • Cash Flow Statement

11. Sales Strategy	VP of Sales	10	• Go to Market Strategy
12. Pipeline	VP of Sales	15	• Pipeline Overview • Significant Deal Highlights • Sales Team
13. Product Strategy	VP of Product or IT	10	• Product Overview
14. Client Management	VP of Client Relations	10	• Client Strategy • Client Satisfaction • Client Team
15. Marketing	VP of Marketing	10	• Marketing Strategy • Marketing Plan/ Tactics
16. Technology	VP of IT	10	• Technology Overview • Team Overview
17. Operations	VP of Operations	10	• Operations Overview • Team Overview
18. Finance	CFO	10	• Finance Overview • Team Overview
19. Raise Details/Use of Proceeds	CEO/CFO	10	• Raise Terms • Summary Use of Proceeds
20. Closing Slide	CEO	10	• Next Steps • Contact Info
TOTAL		210	

When a follow-up meeting is requested, communicate that you have a standard agenda and materials for the meeting that you would be happy to send out. You may not have all of the roles noted under "Presenter." Adjust accordingly. You may also find that in specific areas there are additional follow-up meetings that request specific detail. These often include:

- Team
- Pipeline
- Pricing Model
- Financial Model

You can deal with these topics as they arise or develop short documents or presentations that address these areas with more details in the same process (i.e., standard agenda that ties to the presentation/materials).

- **Presentation Guidelines:** Follow a few rules when presenting to investors:
    - Multiple team members need to present. You want to show your investors the breadth of your team.
    - High-level first, then detail. Investors tune out when they ask an initial question and get a ten minute answer. Short and sweet at first. If they want more detail, they will ask. For example, an investor asks, "Who is your most successful customer?" You should respond, "ABC Company who has realized a three to one return on investment." They will ask, "Can you tell me more about their program and how your solution helped them save money?"
    - Listen. Let investors finish questions before you answer. Don't jump in to answer or interrupt.
- **Training:** with a standard process, you can train your team on the documents, the process and the key messages you want to deliver. Hold training sessions with team members and rehearse their specific parts. With the Key Messages document as your guide, develop and train on messages that you want to reinforce in each area of the business.
- **Data Room:** Create a "data room." Using an online document management tool (e.g., Box, Dropbox) that are often free or low cost. The data room includes the major documents of the company and additional items needed for investment. It is also organized around the functional areas in Presentation 2. For example, in the area of "Customers" it might include:
    - Customer contracts
    - Customer pricing documents
    - Customer profiles

A data room allows you to create one universe of documents that can be accessed by anyone with credentials. When you create new documents or tools, you add them to the data room. This data room may be created for the investment process but then can be leveraged by the company for all of its daily activities.

The hard part of the investment process is not only proving your model. It is the additional work required while you are running the business. By having standard tools that you create once, and a standard process that leverages these tools, you minimize the ad hoc work you have to do and can focus on the important job of communicating your value to investors.

One final thought. The way you manage your investment process is also an indication of how you manage your business. A structured and organized process, with set tools, meetings and agendas, and clear messages, shows the type of discipline that investors value. When an investment process seems ad hoc, with days going by between asks and a scramble to put materials together, investors notice the lack of structure and discipline of the business. Don't forget investors are always watching.

Chapter 3
Get an Independent Advisor

What We Feel*: Our broker really seems to understand the issues we are facing and helps me understand the process. Even though I don't know him that well, it's comforting to have someone that I can confide in and trust through the investment process.*

When you're under stress and lack the money you need, you often don't realize everything that is occurring with your investment process. Typically, companies raising any significant money will hire a third party, often called a broker, who has experience raising capital and has relationships with funding sources such as angels, venture capital and private equity firms, family foundations and companies with investment funds. When you hire these individuals, you are hiring them for both their experience and their relationships. Working with an individual who brings both of these skills can be invaluable. Usually these individuals can be retained for a success fee (i.e., a piece of the amount raised) only or for a small retainer plus a success fee. These resources will leverage existing relationships and bring investment parties to the table to consider your company.

Through the investment process, you will work closely with your broker. Brokers often become a confidant. Ideally, you would be able to be completely transparent with this individual about your own thoughts, the company, and the company's valuation. You would discuss the state of the business. You would confide in them how worn out you are. You would share that the business is running on fumes. You would share your thoughts on valuation. You will work side by side with this individual and it would be great to be able to confide in them, especially during the long investment process.

Your Change in Perspective

There is a catch. Even though you hire the broker to work for you, the broker's relationship with the investment sources they bring to the table can be more important to the broker than the broker's relationship with you. Your broker can bring investors to the table because they have worked together—sometimes over multiple years on multiple deals. It's simple math. To the broker, these investors represent multiple past and present deals and you represent one deal. As a result, despite being hired by you, the broker's loyalty is often more to investors than to you.

Unfortunately, if your broker has a loyalty to potential investors, your information may be inappropriately shared with these investors. Imagine an investor being told, "The company is running on fumes and will settle for a lower valuation" or "John is worn out and will likely reduce his demands if you push."

A similar situation may arise if you choose to hire executives who have relationships with investment firms. To an entrepreneur, this seems like a terrific solution. Imagine if you could kill two birds with one stone—bring in a seasoned executive and capital in one fell swoop. However, like the broker, if an executive brings investors to the table, the relationship between the executive and the investment firm is a long-standing one. Don't get me wrong, sometimes this can work. It can, however, put you in an uncomfortable position of having an executive and investor that are more aligned with each other then they are with you or the success of the business.

How do you deal with this? When you are ready to raise capital, develop a relationship with an advisor who can guide you, but does not bring potential investors or executives to the table. You want this individual to be devoid of the conflicts of interest faced by the broker or the executive. This individual should be able to give you sound, impartial advice. In addition, when brokers and executives bring investors to the table, they will understand there is an independent party evaluating and providing guidance to you. Tell this person your desired valuation. Cry to this person. Tell this person how worn out you are. Confide in this person. When they have no motivation to use a specific investor or pursue a path, you will have a trusted advisor to steer you in the right direction, and a safe place to blow off steam. Or let some air out of that balloon.

A Perspective on Perspective

Perspective is not a solution to a single problem. Rather it is the energy that brings new life to a challenge, new solutions to a roadblock and new ideas to a quagmire. Perspective is the oxygen that fuels your ability to thrive while facing the personal and business challenges of being an entrepreneur.

The foundational perspectives you've just read encompass you, your company, your resources and how you approach these elements under the influence of the Four Ps. But perspective does not end here.

Perspective is not simply a solution to these common entrepreneurial challenges. Perspective is a skill that must be developed, nurtured and brought to each and every situation you encounter. Think of it as a tool in your toolkit that you put on the table when you enter a meeting. Not a hammer, but a Swiss Army knife or Leatherman with multiple blades, scissors, pliers, a screwdriver—one tool that offers you unlimited strategies for problem solving with no other obstacle than your own creativity and vision.

This is the power of perspective. When you're receptive to a new point of view and flexible enough to shift your thinking, you have an enormous advantage in the entrepreneurial landscape as new obstacles and old ways of seeing things threaten to halt your progress. It can help you make immediate changes for your business, and it can change the way you see the world for years to come.

Never underestimate the power of perspective. I haven't forgotten the perspective shift I made at twelve years old. It continues to have a profound effect on everything I do.

When I was twelve years old, I was on a US All Star soccer team that travelled to Germany for an international tournament. For the year prior to departure, the parents and communities raised money to fund the team's trip and to allow many of the families to go as well. As you can imagine, as young athletes we were excited to see a new place and even more excited to take on the competition.

I was co-captain of the team along with John, a rival of mine from the town that we both grew up in—Freehold, New Jersey. John's father was our coach. Not only were John and I rivals, but his father—our coach—was always telling my Dad that John was a better athlete than I was and would push my Dad to get into it with him. My Dad never did. Regardless, while John and I were childhood rivals back in the states, we were the two co-captains of this US soccer team.

The team's accommodations in Germany were cool. While the parents stayed in hotels nearby, we stayed in Army barracks with many of the other teams. We got to play soccer and G.I. Joe at the same time. On the night before the first game, we did what you do when you hang out with German boys—we drank beer. Granted, probably not the best time to discover your alcohol tolerance. We did not drink much but for most of us it was our first experience with beer.

In the middle of the night, I woke up and couldn't breathe. I would find out later I was a little allergic to certain beers. I went over to the coaches' tent and told our coach what was happening. Coach suggested that I go stay in the hotel with my parent and get a good night's sleep. I did.

I showed up the next day and my co-captain John pulled me aside and told me that we were having a team meeting in one of the tents. It was odd because normally if there were going to be a team meeting, his Dad would pull John and me aside, explain to us what was going to happen in the meeting and then call the meeting. I didn't think much of it. I walked into this meeting of twelve-year-olds and got ambushed. John said that the team had decided that because I didn't stay in the tents with them, I shouldn't play that day.

I was shocked. There were many friends of mine on the team. Imagine twelve-year-olds coming up with something like this. To this day, we never found out the source, but no doubt it was an adult and not a group of twelve-year-olds that hatched this idea. After some battling, I was allowed to play and we had a successful two-week trip.

On the flight home, my father came up to me in my seat and told me to come take a walk with him to the back of the plane. He said, "I want you to make a decision." I thought he was talking about whether to order the fish or chicken for dinner. Instead, he said something that would change my perspective on almost everything I did and have done in my life.

He said, "If you want to be the best player and the leader, this is the type of thing that is going to happen. People will be jealous, take shots at you and treat you unfairly. There is nothing wrong at all if you don't want to be the leader and just one of the guys. But if you do decide that you want to be the leader, you have to accept that this is the deal and deal with it without complaint." Then he said, "And I want your decision by the time we land in New York." Did I realize that I was having one of the most important conversations of my life in the flight attendant's galley? Of course not.

We were sleepy when we landed in JFK and made our way to the baggage carousels. As we grabbed our last bag, my Dad said, "What did you decide?" It was clear we were not going home until I made a decision. I said. "Okay, I want to be the leader."

While I didn't realize it at the time, from that point forward I had a new perspective. In everything I did—sports, school, business—I always had the view that "All's fair in love and war" and looked at challenges, as my Dad so wisely said, "as just part of the deal." It has shaped my perspective on almost every aspect of my life.

While there are many skills that you will hone over time in your quest to be a better entrepreneur, nothing will be as fundamental or profound as developing the ability to recognize and change perspective.

* * *

Today, we talk of "emotional intelligence" as a skill that must be identified, developed and mastered to be an effective leader, businessperson or contributor. Emotional intelligence has also become part of the curriculum at undergraduate and graduate business schools and is frequently written about in well-respected business journals. I would propose that perspective deserves the same attention when we look at not only entrepreneurial opportunities and challenges but the challenges that businesses of all sizes and stages face. As you learned from my experience, and probably your own, perspective has a powerful and significant effect on our outcomes and will be the ultimate difference between success and failure.

It's hard to ignore that kind of influence. The right perspective—or even simply a different perspective—can change a path from deterioration to progress, from atrophy to strength, from concern to trust—from spinning your wheels to wild success. So it is my hope that the perspectives we have provided will help you on a daily basis and become part of your entrepreneur's toolbox and vocabulary. I also hope that these perspectives become a conversation starter with other "lonely" entrepreneurs.

Perhaps most importantly, I hope that you see the role they can play in your personal and business success. You have an incredible opportunity (without a single other tool or advantage) to bring your vision to life through the power of your own perspective.

Conclusion
The Lonely Entrepreneur

It's not what I do, it's who I am

Do you really believe that being an entrepreneur is not a job, it is an identity? Is being an entrepreneur just about "now" or is it part of your journey to live a more fulfilling life? There is no wrong answer. But my guess is that you can't imagine returning to the "old self" that existed before you became an entrepreneur. I'd also bet that you have five—or one hundred—ideas swirling around your brain and a few hidden in deep storage waiting for your copyright application to be processed.

For me, creating *The Lonely Entrepreneur* was the next step in my journey as an entrepreneur. After selling my health rewards business, my plan was to simply start a small consulting firm around health rewards. With the reputation we built, that would have been easy. Then I stumbled upon *The Lonely Entrepreneur* and the feeling shook me awake and reminded me that I *am* an entrepreneur. New ideas are a part of me—like oxygen. And while *The Lonely Entrepreneur* is of course about entrepreneurs, it is also my latest idea. And like you, I feel the *pressure* to bring it to life, the *passion* to help other entrepreneurs, and the *pleasure* of seeing real progress, or hearing an entrepreneur say to me, "*The Lonely Entrepreneur* helped me change my perspective and make progress in my business." I also feel the *pain* of getting something off the ground again—the feeling that we are not getting solutions and support to entrepreneurs as quickly as we should. Now, however, I know what to do with those thoughts and perspectives.

The Lonely Entrepreneur is the next road in what I hope to be a long journey. The entrepreneurial spirit fills the air of my days. This oxygen makes me excited to get going in the morning, but it is also bittersweet. As I am finishing this book, I have spent days and nights in the hospital breathing very different air, standing vigil with my father as he may be nearing the end of his life. So I will leave you with two thoughts:

First, even with all of the emotion I feel each day, the entrepreneur in me can't stop. I see the breathing tubes that don't fit perfectly in his big Jewish nose and how a simple clamp could be developed that would help patients (of every ethnicity and religion) everywhere. I see how the hand washing cleansers could be data-wired to track use and prevent infections. I see how the right voice recognition technology could save overburdened nurses hours in tracking and reporting all the patient information that must be recorded or communicated to doctors. And still in the midst of all this, while so many things run through my brain, through my heart and my soul as I watch my Dad, the entrepreneurial identity is still, even now, a living, breathing thing inside me that will not shut down. I just wish I could invent a magic pill to help an eighty-one-year-old live forever.

My second thought is this: my Dad is living a great life. But he has one regret. He has a deep belief in one idea that he never did anything about. Imagine looking back on your life and regretting the idea you never pursued. I would do anything to give him that chance. As entrepreneurs, we owe it to each other to never, never, never let that happen. We can't let the nagging voice of our insecurity taunt us—"Am I really cut out for this?" "Can I really make this happen?" It isn't a choice, it's who we are. We must find a way to be better entrepreneurs so that we never look back and say to ourselves, "I wish I had." Mark Twain said, "Twenty years from now, you will be more disappointed by the things that you didn't do than by the ones you did do."

Let's make a promise to each other. We must make a conscious effort to become better entrepreneurs so that the ideas, thoughts and visions that seethe through our veins come to life. That doesn't mean that we must execute on every crazy idea we have. In fact, part of being a good entrepreneur is knowing which ideas are the right ones to pursue and when. But we must embrace our identity—and this means committing to a lifelong journey to bring ideas to life and to be the arbiters of our own visions.

It is not likely that my father will have that chance. But you and I can do something about it right now. If you are an entrepreneur, do not allow the ideas you have today, and the ones you will find tomorrow, to sit idle inside you. Become a stronger entrepreneur, develop empowering perspectives and give your ideas a life of their own. Give your visions all the oxygen they need, not just to breathe, but to thrive and flourish as they should.

I hope that **The Lonely Entrepreneur** has put one more hour in your day, one more arrow in your quiver, or one more tool in your toolbox. But perhaps more importantly, I hope it has started you on a lifelong quest to be the best entrepreneur you can be, to be the innovator and leader you want to be. The right perspective lives with you wherever you go and gives you the freedom to create, to be an entrepreneur in the twenty-first century, to follow dreams, and to embrace the unexpected and unknown. Don't forget that the future is up to you: the difference between success and failure is *your* perspective. And, remember this remarkable insight. "Change the way you see things, and the things you see will change." Your oxygen may depend on it.

I'll leave you where we started—The Cold Shower (no, not that kind). There were so many days I ended my workout with that brutal water hitting my face. It was hard to see what those days really meant, what they really were. In the end, they are just one point in the path of my lifelong journey. I feel lucky—to have been shocked by the cold—because after five minutes, there is no doubt about who I am. I am an entrepreneur.

Acknowledgements

Ideas are just ideas until someone brings them to life. *The Lonely Entrepreneur* was just an idea until many people made it happen. There are too many to thank but tireless efforts of a few that spent their precious time reading pages, challenging ideas, making improvements and, most importantly, thinking about how we could help the entrepreneur and those that support them. To Laura—for your countless reviews and ideas and attention to detail that has made *The Lonely Entrepreneur* much better. And for your friendship and support. And to Jennilyn and Victoria, or as they are known, "J" and "V". To V—the future exists because of your sacrifice and passion when you already had many day jobs. It is a blessing to be part of your future. To J—not only for the countless overnights and expert editing and thinking but for the inspiration you are for your strength and unbridled determination. I would take your spirit against any army.

I would be remiss if I didn't let those that made the vision of IncentOne come to life under intense pressure know how much your dedication and commitment means to me. I hope every time you walk down the street and see a health reward program, you smile. To Randy—only you and I know what it was like at 400 Patterson Plank Road and listening to NPR. I will forever be indebted. To Felipe—none of this would have been possible without you. To Doug—for your loyalty and sacrifice when the shit was hitting the fan. I will never be able to repay you. To Carol, for your loving support and energy through this all—thanks "sis."

To all those at IncentOne over the years who worked so tirelessly to bring a vision to life—it has been my honor to witness your dedication and commitment. You know who you are—and a part of each of you is in *The Lonely Entrepreneur.*

And to the entrepreneur, it is your spirit that inspires—and don't we all crave a life of inspiration. If we all seek a fulfilling life, we need your commitment to one thing—don't ever stop.